LUFTWAFFE LOSSES OVER NORTHUMBERLAND AND DURHAM
1939 – 1945

Broken Eagles 2

Other books by the author

Wartime Teesside
Luftwaffe Over the North
Failed to Return
No. 640 (Halifax) Squadron
Broken Eagles (Luftwaffe Losses Over Yorkshire 1939 -1945)

LUFTWAFFE LOSSES OVER NORTHUMBERLAND AND DURHAM
1939 – 1945

Broken Eagles 2

Bill Norman

Leo Cooper

First published in Great Britain in 2002 by Leo Cooper
an imprint of Pen & Sword Books Limited
47 Church Street, Barnsley, South Yorkshire S70 2AS

*For up-to-date information on other titles produced under the Pen & Sword imprint,
please telephone or write to:*
    Pen & Sword Books Limited
    FREEPOST
    47 Church Street
    Barnsley
    South Yorkshire
    S70 2BR

    Telephone (24 hours): 01226 734555

ISBN 0-85052-913-1

British Library Cataloguing in Publication Data

Printed by CPI UK

CONTENTS

Acknowledgements

The help given by the following in the preparation of this book is gratefully acknowledged:

Michael Allen DFC★, ex-141 Squadron; Don Aris, 141 Squadron historian; Ulf Balke – whose book *Der Luftkrieg in Europa* was particularly valuable for KG2 operations over northern England and who provided invaluable help with first-hand accounts from former Luftwaffe crews; Günter Bartnik, ex-8./KG2; Squadron Leader George Bennions DFC RAF (retd); Günther Bischoff, Germany; Landon Bolton, Colne; Kevin Brady, Peterlee; Squadron Leader Lewis Brandon DSO DFC★ RAF (retd); Melvyn Brown and Steve Hall, Padbury; Heinrich Buhr, ex-KG2; Ron Butler, ex-15 Air Sea Rescue MCU; Matt Campbell, Boulmer; Chief Constable, Northumbria Police; Peter Clark, Wooperton; Jim Corbett, Fenham, Newcastle upon Tyne; Rudolf Dawson, Hartlepool; Mrs Margaret Douglas, Holy Island; Jonathan Falconer, Sutton Publishing Ltd; Bill Fulton, North East Air Museum; Chris Goss; Ernie Hardy, for research at the PRO; Julian Harrop, Regional Resource Centre, Beamish Museum; Peter Hepplewhite, Tyne & Wear Archives; Hans Hilpert, ex-Stab./KG26; Hartmut Holzapfel, ex-KG2; Nellie Hope, Amble; Peter Kirk, Allestree; Tim Kitching, Normanton; Friedrich-Wilhelm Koch, ex-3./KG4; Frank Lanning, DFC RAF (Retd), ex-141 (Defiant) Squadron; Tom Lee, Crowborough; Frau Stefanie Machalett, Germany; George Mather, Whitley Bay; Major A.J. McCluskey, RAMC; Stuart McMillan, Skelton, who drew the Staffel crests; Michael Meyer, Germany; Heinz Möllenbrok ex-3./KG2, who provided invaluable help with introductions to former KG2 crews; Claus Nattermann; the Editor, *Newcastle Chronicle & Journal*; the Editor, *The Northern Echo*; Stefan Reeckmann, Germany; Alex Revell; Kathleen Rutherford, Spittal; Willi Schludecker, ex-KG2; 604 Squadron Association; Ernst-Adolf Schneider, *Gemeinschaft Deutscher Seenotrettungsdienst*; Hans-Joachim and Jörg Schaber, Germany; Jim Shepherd, Amble; Wing Commander E.A. Shipman, AFC RAF(retd), ex-41 Squadron; Chief Librarian, South Shields Library; Jimmie Stanton, Boulmer; A. Stoker, Morpeth; Brian Stringer of *The Princess Royal Restoration Association*, Hartlepool; the Editor, *Sunderland Echo*; Heinrich Suschake, ex-4./KG2; Derek Walton, Seahouses; Frau H. Walz, Germany; Ken Watkins, Dorking; Alan White, Houghton-le-Spring; Frau E. Wiemer, Germany; Rolf Zöphel, ex-KG2.

I also wish to acknowledge the use made of Kevin Brady's *Sunderland's Blitz* (The People's History, 1999), Miss Amy Flagg's *History of Bomb Damage in South Shields*, (an undated manuscript in South Shields Library) and Roy Ripley's and Brian Pears' *North East Diary, 1939-1945* (an undated manuscript in Darlington Central Library). These sources provided the basis of the air raid details given in the introduction to each of the separate sections. The three volumes of the monumental *The Blitz, then and now*, edited by W.G. Ramsay have also proved extremely useful.

The many people who kindly loaned photographs are acknowledged in the following pages; ownership of copyright has been credited in all cases where it is known.

German Air Force terms
used in the text

Luftwaffe organization

Staffel:

The Luftwaffe *Staffel* consisted of nine aircraft and was roughly equivalent to an RAF squadron. *Staffeln* (the plural) were numbered from 1 to 9.

Gruppe:

Three *Staffeln* made a *Gruppe*, the basic flying unit of the Luftwaffe. *Gruppen* (the plural) were numbered in Roman numerals from I to III. The full complement of a *Gruppe*, including the *Stab* flight (see below), was thirty aircraft.

Stab:

Each *Gruppe* had a *Stab* (headquarters' flight) of three aircraft.

Geschwader:

Three *Gruppen* made a *Geschwader*, which had its own *Stab* flight of four aircraft. Thus a *Geschwader* at full strength had ninety-four aircraft and was roughly equivalent to an RAF Wing. The role of a *Geschwader* was indicated by a prefix. The prefixes used in this book are given below.

(F)	*Aufklärungsgruppe* (long range reconnaissance)
JG	*Jagdgeschwader* (fighter wing)
KG	*Kampfgeschwader* (bomber wing)
KGr.	*Kampfgruppe* (bomber group)
Ku.Fl.Gr.	*Küstenfliegergruppe* (maritime cooperation group)
NJG	*Nachtjagdgeschwader* (night fighter wing)
ZG	*Zerstörergeschwader* (destroyer wing [long-range twin-engine fighter])

Unit notation: In view of the foregoing, the notation II./KG2, for example, refers to the second *Gruppe* of *Kampfgeschwader 2*. The more specific 4.II/KG2 refers to the fourth *Staffel* of KG2. Because *Staffeln* 4-6 made up *Gruppe II*, the notation 4.II/KG2 was usually abbreviated to 4./KG2

Luftwaffe ranks[1]
(with RAF equivalents)

Flieger (Flgr.)	Aircraftman 2nd Class (AC2)
Gefreiter (Gefr.)	Aircraftman 1st Class (AC1)
Obergefreiter (Obgfr.)	Leading Aircraftman (LAC)
Hauptgefreiter (Hptgfr.)	No RAF equivalent
Unteroffizier (Uffz.)	Corporal (Cpl)
Unterfeldwebel (Unfw.)	No RAF equivalent
Feldwebel (Fw.)	Sergeant (Sgt)
Oberfeldwebel (Obfw.)	Flight Sergeant (F/Sgt)
Stabsfeldwebel (Stfw.)	Warrant Officer (W/O)
Oberfähnrich zur See (Ofhr.)	Senior Midshipman (naval rank); officer cadet
Leutnant (Lt.)	Pilot Officer (P/O)
Oberleutnant (Oblt.)	Flying Officer (F/O)
Hauptmann (Hptm.)	Flight Lieutenant (F/Lt)
Major (Maj.)	Squadron Leader (S/Ldr)
Oberstleutnant (Oberstlt.)	Wing Commander (W/Cdr)
Regierungsrat (Reg. Rat)	Squadron Leader (S/Ldr). *Regierungsrat* was not a Luftwaffe rank but a rank in the German Weather Service. The holder was a meteorologist who flew with the *Wekusta* weather reconnaissance units. Such people wore Luftwaffe uniforms but had their own system of ranks and insignia.

Other Luftwaffe terms used in text

Luftflotte:	Air fleet
Oberbefehlshaber der Luftwaffe:	Commander in Chief of the Luftwaffe. Often abbreviated to Ob.d. L
Gruppenkommandeur:	Group commander
Seenotflugkommando:	Air-sea rescue unit
Seenotrettungsdienst:	Air-sea rescue service
Staffelkapitän:	Staffel commander
Werk nummer (w/nr.):	Manufacturer's aircraft serial number (e.g. 2086). Different from an aircraft's *Geschwader* and *Staffel* code (e.g. 7A+KH), which was prominently displayed on the fuselage.

---

1 From Alfred Price, *The Luftwaffe Data Book*, Greenhill Books, 1997

RAF terms used in text

AI:	Airborne interceptor radar (on-board radar).
Bogey:	Unidentified aircraft.
Freelancing:	Operating independently; not under ground control.
GCI:	Ground Control Interception (airborne interception controlled by a ground station).
Serial number:	Number allocated to the aircraft by the manufacturer (e.g. K8889). Different from an aircraft's squadron code (e.g. HU-T), which was prominently displayed on the fuselage.
Vector:	Compass bearing transmitted by ground stations to guide an aircraft towards the interception of another.

Introduction

Many books have been written about the air war over this country during 1939-1945. Generally speaking, they have tended to concentrate on events in the south of England, and have usually focused on the aerial conflicts that characterized the campaign now known to history as the Battle of Britain. Of course, the scale of aerial warfare over the southern counties in 1940 holds an important place in the history of this country and it is right that its significance is recognized. However, an over-concentration on wartime events in the south of England – almost to the exclusion of other areas of the country – might well give rise to the belief, albeit unintended, that little of note happened elsewhere in the United Kingdom during those troubled times. One of the aims of this book and its immediate predecessor is to endeavour to redress the balance a little.

Broken Eagles 2 (Luftwaffe Losses Over Northumberland and Durham) is the second in a two-volume work that records all of the known Luftwaffe losses over the three north-eastern counties of England during the Second World War. The first volume, entitled *Broken Eagles (Luftwaffe losses Over Yorkshire, 1939-1945)*, was published under the Leo Cooper imprint of Pen & Sword Books, in 2001 and dealt with the losses of seventy-two German aircraft and their crews over Yorkshire and its coastline during the period of hostilities. This current volume records incidents over the two counties further north. At least sixty-four German aircraft crashed in the counties of County Durham and Northumberland or off their respective coastlines during the 1939-1945 conflict and 256

German aircrew became casualties of war: twenty-nine per cent of those were captured, the rest were either killed or listed as 'missing in action'. Like its predecessor, this book records the losses of both aircraft and personnel and gives details of the circumstances under which such losses occurred.

Both books have their origin partly in the warmth of response by the people of Teesside to the discovery and subsequent burial of a German flier whose body was found entombed in the buried wreckage of his aircraft in 1997, fifty-five years after it had crashed at South Bank. The full circumstances relating to this incident have been given in the first volume and to relate them again here would be an unnecessary extravagance.

My subsequent researches also owe something to observations made in March 2000 by a former Luftwaffe airgunner who has since become my friend. Heinrich Buhr participated in many bombing raids over northern England, usually in aircraft flown by another friend of mine, Willi Schludecker. At an arranged meeting at Shoreham in March 2000, I introduced them to the ex-Beaufighter pilot who had damaged their aircraft so badly one night in July 1942 that the resultant crash put Willi Schludecker in hospital for six months.

No doubt in the hours prior to the meeting, the ex-Beaufighter pilot, Peter McMillan, and his guests felt more than a little trepidation. However, if that were the case, doubts were quickly dispelled when the former foes met at Shoreham airport and Heinrich Buhr stepped forward, extended his hand towards his wartime assailant and broke the ice with the booming words, 'Hello. We are the Hun – and you are a bloody lousy shot!' The laughter that followed heralded the beginning of a friendly and most enjoyable three days, during which the former foes found that they had much in common.

It was during one of many conversations over the three days of that meeting that the old airgunner pointed out that men who had challenged each other to deadly duels over England during the Second World War had been the pawns of politicians. 'We were adversaries,' he said, 'but we were never enemies.' It was a striking statement to make, and it was made to the man who might easily have killed the speaker in their encounter off the east coast of England some sixty years earlier. It was certainly a sentiment in stark contrast to the stereotypical views that many people tend to have of their opponents in times of war and for me it was another stimulus to curiosity. In the late 1990s, the people of Teesside displayed a most impressive generosity of spirit towards a former enemy. Following Heinrich Buhr's statement, I found myself wondering whether the same generosity of spirit was in evidence during the air war over the north of England and I was more than a little surprised to subsequently find that it was.

I recently received a letter from a fellow in Sheffield who had just read the first volume of *Broken Eagles*. In his letter he wrote that, 'Whilst reading the book, I felt an awful sadness wrapping itself around me; sadness for the waste of so many young German airmen sent to their deaths over the North Sea.' The same could be said of young men of all nationalities at any time and in any place for that is the nature of war; it thrives on the waste it creates.

The men who fought each other in the skies over northern England some sixty years ago faced death and destruction on an almost daily basis. They were all brave men, irrespective of their nationality. Many books have been written about aspects of the air war over these islands during the period 1939-1945. Usually, they have been written from the perspective of men who bravely defended these islands more than half a century ago. This book, perhaps, is a little different. For, like its predecessor, it attempts to give insights into what happened to men from the other side who were destined to meet their match in northern skies. I hope that it succeeds in its purpose.

Both books in this two-volume work group the Luftwaffe's losses into specific chronological periods, each one of which is preceded by an introduction that sets the contexts in which those losses occurred. Readers of both volumes will realize that the books contain introductory sections which are broadly similar in content but which have been modified in appropriate places to accommodate differences in the local detail. This apparent duplication is quite deliberate. The rationale for doing this is simple. There will be some readers who wish to read both volumes; there will be others who will wish to read only about their own geographical area. The aircraft losses recorded in both books took place in the same broad context. Thus the apparent duplication is justified by the need to ensure that readers of either volume will be fully aware of what that context was.

Bill Norman
Guisborough, 2002

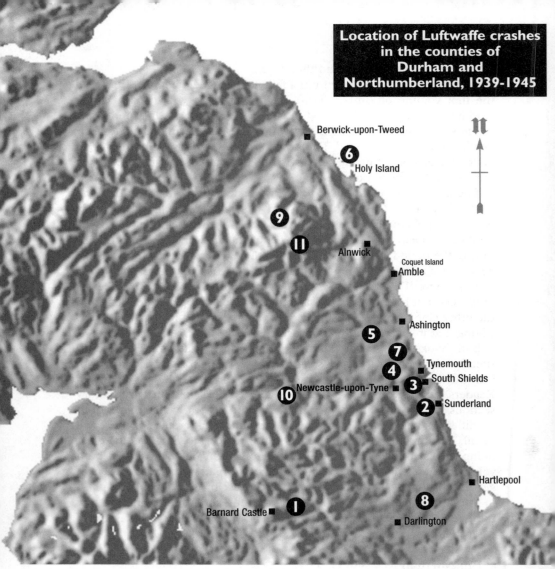

Location of Luftwaffe crashes in the counties of Durham and Northumberland, 1939-1945

KEY

1.	Me110D	15.08.40	*Streatlam*
2.	He111P	05.09.40	*Sunderland*
3.	He111P-4	16.02.41	*South Shields*
4.	He111H-5	06.05.41	*Newcastle-on-Tyne*
5.	He111H-5	07.05.41	*Morpeth*
6.	Ju88A-5	07.05.41	*Holy Island*
7.	Ju88A-4	01.09.41	*Bedlington Station*
8.	Do217E-4	11.03.43	*Great Stainton*
9.	Do217E-4	25.03.43	*Madan Law, Cheviot*
10.	Do217E-4	25.03.43	*Twice Brewed*
11.	Ju88A-14	25.03.43	*Linhope*

1

DAYS OF CONFIDENCE
(1939-1940)

Although the Luftwaffe was the most powerful air force in Europe when war between Germany and England was declared in September 1939, it lacked aircraft suitable for long-range strategic bombing operations. The main purpose of the German Air Force was to serve in a tactical role in support of the Army and, therefore, the Luftwaffe was equipped only for wars of short duration and limited objectives.

The Wehrmacht's operational philosophy for swift success in attack demanded the application of maximum force at the decisive point of the battle (the concept of blitzkrieg). To serve that end, the Luftwaffe's operational strategy was aimed at the rapid destruction of enemy forces on the ground and the paralysing of the remnants of those forces long enough for the German Army to occupy the invaded country. To ensure the success of its own campaigns, the Luftwaffe's blitzkrieg strategy consisted of two phases. The first of these required available air power to be concentrated in a series of surprise assaults on the enemy's air force to ensure the rapid destruction of the opponent's aircraft, as well as his aircraft-producing plants and ground installations. In the second phase, assuming the success of the first, the Luftwaffe was free to concentrate all of its available striking power in direct support of the German ground forces. To be effective, the strategy required that campaigns would be short and sharp and would result in the annihilation of the enemy's air power. That was the case with regard to invasions of Poland, Norway, the Low Countries and France – but the Battle of Britain changed the pattern and the Luftwaffe became embroiled in a war for which it was not really prepared.

There were four Air Fleets (*Luftflotten*) in Germany on the eve of the Second World War and each had responsibility for air operations in its own designated quarter of the country.[1] The most powerful of these Air Fleets were *Luftflotte 1* and *Luftflotte 4*, both of which had been reinforced for the impending invasion of Poland, and which were located in the northern and southern quarters of eastern Germany respectively. The western half of Germany was controlled by *Luftflotte 3* (in the south) and *Luftflotte 2* (in the north). The western edge of the operational area of *Luftflotte 3* bordered on Belgium and France and thus its operational functions westwards were restricted until those countries were invaded in May 1940 and the Phoney War ended. *Luftflotte 2* bordered on Holland to the west but the German coastline (and its access to the North Sea) marked its northern boundary. Thus, during the first year of the war, operations against the east coast of Britain in general, and the north-east coast in particular, were usually carried out by aircraft of *Luftflotte 2*.

Britain declared hostilities against Germany on 3 September 1939 but the Royal Air Force was initially reluctant to commence the shooting war, partly because of its somewhat limited military capability but also because it was reluctant to engage in operations that might endanger foreign civilians. This initial reluctance was mirrored by the German Air Force, though not always for the same reasons. There is the possibility that the deferment of the Luftwaffe's commencement of operations against these islands was partly political, with German leaders hoping that the speedy demise of earlier victims of Nazi expansion would persuade an isolated Britain to agree terms without a fight. However, there were also sound military reasons for delay. In fact, until Germany had open access to countries on its western borders, any air campaign that it might hope to wage against Britain would necessarily be severely limited. Thus after Poland, German aircrews were rested and squadrons were re-equipped in preparation for campaigns against Norway, France and the Low Countries in April-May of 1940. Until those objectives had been achieved, relative quiet prevailed during the period that became known as the Phoney War.

Until the Luftwaffe was ready to test itself against the Royal Air Force, much of its time was spent on aerial reconnaissance (mainly seeking units of the Royal Navy's Home Fleet) and anti-shipping activities aimed at disrupting Britain's maritime trade. Consequently, the Luftwaffe was a regular visitor to the north of England almost from the outset after the Heinkel 111 bombers of *Kampfgeschwader 26* (KG26) and floatplanes of the *Küstenfliegergruppen* (naval cooperation units) targeted the sea lanes off the coast of Northumberland and County Durham.

The east coast shipping convoys, sailing between the Firth of Forth and the Thames, commenced in the first week of September 1939 and were a regular feature of British maritime activity until the cessation of hostilities six years later. Disruption of this traffic was an early priority of the Germans and, in addition to bombing and strafing attacks on ships by aircraft, the mining of the shipping lanes was in evidence from the outset. The estuaries of all of the North's major rivers used by maritime traffic were also targeted and the destruction of vessels by mines was destined to become a depressing feature of the war along the north-east coast. In the closing months of 1939, much of this work was undertaken by U-boats and German minelaying destroyers – four of which laid 240 mines off the Tyne on the night of 12-13 December of that year[2] – but as the months passed, the task was increasingly undertaken by aircraft.

North Sea convoy.

Such operations yielded much success but they were not without cost, as the following pages will show. The coastal activities that characterized the period of the Phoney War in the north continued for the rest of 1940 but in the summer of that year the Luftwaffe quickened its activities, shifted the emphasis of its strategy and began to move against targets on the British mainland.

Following Germany's successful invasions of Denmark and Norway (9 April) and France and the Low Countries (10 May), the Luftwaffe's operational bases in the west were moved much closer to Britain. By June, *Luftflotte 2* had established bases in Holland, Belgium and a small part of northern France at the Channel coast, and *Luftflotte 3* had relocated as far west as France's Channel coast. In addition, a new Air Fleet, *Luftflotte 5*, had been established in Denmark and Norway. As a result of these advances, most areas of Britain came within range of the Luftwaffe's bombers.

The month of June brought a number of incursions over Northumberland and County Durham. West Hartlepool's 'baptism of fire' occurred on the night of 19-20 June 1940, when bombs that were probably intended for the ICI plant at Billingham fell in the area of Musgrove Street. The resulting explosions demolished properties, inflicted casualties and claimed the life of ARP Warden John Punton (aged fifty-four), the first Civil Defence worker to be killed by enemy action during the Second World War. Other bombs fell in the Stockton-Billingham area, where ICI's chemical works seem to have been the target. Two nights later, Tynemouth, South Shields and Sunderland

Borough received the first of many visits from the Luftwaffe but these initial forays were light and the damage inconsequential. On 2 July 1940, the first bombs fell on Newcastle, when a solitary Junkers 88 of 7./KG4 carried out an early evening assault that had Vickers-Armstrong's Elswick factory as its objective, although reports at the time (and since) claimed otherwise (see pages 48-49). Minutes later, another aircraft of the same unit aimed four high explosives at an oil storage facility at Jarrow: the bombs missed and exploded in a nearby residential district. The final casualty list registered thirteen people killed and 123 injured: they were the first sizeable war casualties to be inflicted in the counties of Durham and Northumberland.

Generally speaking, such attacks were carried out by single raiders or by small numbers of aircraft seemingly more intent on testing defences rather than inflicting large-scale destruction. However, ICI's chemical plant at Billingham, on the north bank of the Tees, was singled out for particular attention on the night of 19-20 June 1940, and was raided by an estimated twenty aircraft, believed to have been Heinkel 111s of KG4. In spite of the sizeable number of aircraft taking part, the damage inflicted was small-scale and inconsequential, largely because bombs fell on open ground in and around the works.

After the British Government rejected Hitler's offer of terms in mid-July 1940, the Luftwaffe was ordered to eliminate the RAF as a fighting force and to attack shipping and ports to prevent supplies reaching these shores. Although, as mentioned earlier, there had been anti-shipping activities as well as scattered attacks on mainland Britain prior to this date, from mid-July aggressive air activity was increased – mainly in the south of England, where the stage was being set for the Battle of Britain.

In the north, the situation remained relatively quiet, although the threats to coastal shipping continued and the sounding of air raid alerts remained a regular feature of daily life. Between July and October, such warnings sounded almost every day and every night along the north-east coast; sometimes they sounded several times in a day and several times in a night. This was partly due to the fact that enemy aircraft, intent on other purposes or aiming for other destinations, were regularly flying by offshore and thus they constantly threatened the possibility of turning towards land and attacking coastal areas. Thus warnings were often sounded because an attack was a possibility rather than clearly intended. These constant alerts proved to be highly disruptive to civilian and industrial populations alike because no-one knew quite what to expect. Consequently, although there were many false alarms, the more cautious members of the population developed the practice of staying in shelters overnight, irrespective of whether raids were threatened or not.

Throughout July, minelaying aircraft regularly operated off the

Heinkel 115 attacking a trawler. [The War Weekly, January 1940]

northern coast and occasionally crossed it. The coastal strips of Northumberland and Durham were subjected to, what amounted to, nuisance bombing on at least five occasions. Sometimes the night bombers were seduced by false lighting on decoy sites and unloaded their deadly cargoes on open country and did little harm. Such was the case on the night of 12-13 July 1940, when ICI Billingham was once again the objective. However, the bombers were duped and large numbers of high explosives and incendiaries fell near the Greenabella decoy site and shifted little more than earth. Sometimes, however, bombing was more accurate, as it was on the night of 28-29 July, when twenty-five high explosives fell across Newcastle and caused considerable damage but, mercifully, few casualties.

In August 1940, the German Air Force increased the intensity of the campaign in the south when enemy bombers embarked upon a series of heavy daylight raids aimed at shipping and RAF Fighter Command. In the north, things remained much quieter. Sunderland's first air raid casualties occurred around midday on 9 August 1940, when a Heinkel 111 bomber of 7./KG26 scattered fourteen bombs across the town, damaging industrial and commercial properties and killing four workers in Laing's shipyard. However, in spite of the personal tragedies caused by such incidents, that raid was typical of those experienced earlier by north-eastern counties: small-scale, limited in impact and carried out by one or two aircraft at most.

In fact, there was no bombing of the northern counties in any strength until 15 August 1940, when sixty-three Heinkel 111 bombers of KG26 and their fighter escort of twenty-one Messerschmitt 110s of *Zerstörergeschwader 76* (ZG76) launched an abortive daylight attack against northern aerodromes. The fighter escorts proved to be no match for the single-engined Spitfires and Hurricanes that rose to meet them from bases at Drem, Acklington, Usworth and Catterick and the raiders were routed at great cost. In the confusion that followed the interceptions, some 300 bombs were strewn across the north of County Durham, with the areas around Seaham Harbour and Easington Colliery being particularly affected. The raid cost the Luftwaffe eighteen aircraft. The price was too high and the toll exacted by the Royal Air Force ensured that the German Air Force would never again attack the north of England in strength during daylight hours.

Britain's daytime fighter defences were highly effective, particularly when used in conjunction with radar plotting and Fighter Control. The former robbed the Luftwaffe of the elements of surprise that had served it so well in its continental campaigns; the latter enabled fighters to be directed to within sight of their targets without having to waste time and fuel on fruitless patrols. These factors, together with the Luftwaffe's lack of an effective long-range fighter to escort bombers over northern England in daylight, meant that future raids over the mainland would be limited to the hours of darkness, unless cloudy conditions in daytime offered protection.

The strength of Britain's daytime fighter defence system also ensured that the Luftwaffe was eventually forced to abandon its large-scale daytime assault on RAF Fighter Command and its ground installations on the wider front (principally in the south) in favour of large-scale attacks against industrial targets at night. The protection provided by darkness, coupled with the general ineffectiveness of Britain's night time defences, allowed large-scale raids to be launched against urban targets further afield, both in the Midlands and along the western coast as far north as Liverpool. Anti-shipping sorties, however, continued to be carried out both day and night and bombs continued to fall at various times on targets as far apart as Hartlepool and Berwick-on-Tweed – but rarely in quantity and never involving significant numbers of aircraft.

Although Britain's daytime fighter defences were well developed and highly capable almost from the outset, the country's night-fighter defences were in their experimental infancy and generally ineffective. A rudimentary night-fighter force of twin-engined Blenheim aircraft equipped with early airborne-interception radar devices was in the process of being established by 1940 but until developmental problems could be solved and operational equipment refined, Spitfires and Hurricanes were pressed into service as night fighters. The latter arrangement did enjoy occasional success but the system was far from satisfactory because the night robbed the defenders of their vision or, at least, severely impaired it, and interception was a game of chance.

In his highly readable memoir, *Night Flyer*, Lewis Brandon has described other difficulties that airborne defenders had to cope with in the early days of the war. For example, few aircrews had experience of night flying and even fewer had experience of night fighting. Furthermore, air-to-ground communications were short-range and indistinct, cockpit instruments were poor for blind flying, not many airfields had runways and all landing grounds had poor lighting for take-off and landing. There were few aids to interception in the air and there was an absence of homing devices to bring fighters safely back to base.[3] Returning safely to base and landing in the dark was a major task and the accident rate was high. But in spite of all of these obstacles, the anti-aircraft guns, barrage balloons and single-engined day fighters miscast in a night fighter role – '...and using the methods of daylight interception with searchlights substituting for the sun...'[4] did enjoy occasional success but, generally speaking, the night bombers came and went virtually as they pleased. The Spitfires and Hurricanes were subsequently joined by the Defiant but the use of ill-equipped day fighters for such a difficult and specialized task was a stopgap measure at best. More often than not, aircraft were sent off into the night to seek raiders without knowing where to look, and with their crews often being more preoccupied with not getting lost.

Notwithstanding the fact that German bombers engaged in night raids over Britain could come and go virtually as they pleased, the lack of training in night bombing, coupled with difficulties in navigating over the sea and at night, meant that Luftwaffe crews did not always find their target, particularly if it was relatively small and inland from the coast. It was a problem that RAF crews operating at night over Germany also had to wrestle with, but while Bomber Command continued to place reliance on astral navigation and dead reckoning (and crews often got lost as a result), the Luftwaffe developed a system of directional navigation beams to guide their bombers to their targets. This *Knickebein* system enabled suitably equipped aircraft to fly along a radio beam that was transmitted from a continental station and projected over the intended target. A second station in a different location transmitted a further beam and this intersected with the first over the designated objective to indicate the point where bombs were to be dropped.

When the use of *Knickebein* over England was first detected in June 1940 it caused considerable alarm but by the following September

British countermeasures had been developed to render detected beams unworkable. Initially, such countermeasures involved jamming the beam signal but this practice was soon replaced by the more subtle masking of the signal. British ground receiver stations intercepted the signals and then rebroadcast modified versions to distort beams to induce raiders to bomb in areas where they would inflict less damage. This masking of the beams was known as meaconing. A similar system was used to confuse Luftwaffe crews who were returning home after bombing raids and were using radio signals transmitted by direction-finding beacons located on the continent. Meacon stations in Britain intercepted the beacon signals and reradiated them to give a false bearing. It was then hoped that the resultant confusion would cause returning aircraft to lose their way and run out of fuel before reaching their home base. There were seventeen meacon stations dotted around Britain, including one at Horse Close Farm, Marske, some six miles south of the river Tees.

The realization that their beams were being interfered with prompted the Germans to introduce two rather more sophisticated alternatives towards the end of 1940. The first of these was *X-Gerät*, which used three secondary intersecting beams; the second was *Y-Gerät*, which used only the single navigational beam but which allowed the progress of the bomber to be monitored by its ground station at all times. These refined versions were allocated to two Luftwaffe units that were gradually assuming the role of target illuminators. *X-Gerät* was assigned only to the Heinkel 111s of *Kampfgruppe 100* (KGr.100), while *Y-Gerät* was taken by Heinkel 111s of III./KG26. Both of these units, together with II./*Kampfgeschwader 55* (II./KG55), which relied purely on accurate navigation, formed the Luftwaffe's emerging Pathfinder force.[5] By early 1941, the British had developed countermeasures for both beam systems but revised versions were reintroduced by the Luftwaffe in 1942.

In spite of the aids to navigation introduced by the Luftwaffe in 1940, the effects of weather, navigation difficulties and British countermeasures often meant that in the winter of 1940-41 large-scale destructive bombing attacks against England could only be effective against big inland targets – namely large cities, such as London and Birmingham – or centres on the coast, both of which could be found quite easily.

Notes

1 Price, Alfred: *The Luftwaffe Data Book*. Greenhill Books (1997) fully explains the movements of *Luftflotten*, as well as offering much other useful information relating to Luftwaffe organization and operational units, 1939-45.
2 Ripley, Roy (with Brian Pears): *North East Diary, 1939-1945* unpublished mss Darlington Central Library
3 Brandon, Lewis: *Night Flyer*, William Kimber (1969) Chapter 1
4 MacMillan, Norman: *The Royal Air Force in the World War*, Vol.iv 1940-1945, Harrap(1950) Chapter 1
5 Jones, R.V: *Most Secret War*. Hamish Hamilton (1978) tells the fascinating story of the detection of the beams; Wakefield, Ken: *Pfadfinder, Luftwaffe Pathfinder Operations over Britain 1940-1944*. Tempus (1999) fully explains the operations of III./KG26 and KGr.100.

Losses
November 1939 - November 1940
1939

17 October 1939 (north-east of Berwick-upon-Tweed?)

Aircraft:	Dornier 18	8L+DK	w/nr. 809	Ku.Fl.Gr 2./ 606
Crew:	Fw. ? Grabbet	pilot	pow	
	Oblt. z. See. Siegfried Seloga	observer	pow	
	Unfw. Hilmar Grimm	wireless op	pow	
	Uffz. ? Seydel	mechanic	+	

[Strictly speaking, this loss should not be included in this volume because the aircraft crashed outside of the Northumberland – Durham area. However, it has been included because the German fell to an Acklington-based squadron after being intercepted off the Northumberland coast.]

This aircraft (8L+DK) was one of two Dornier, Do18 seaplanes that left their base at Sylt, North Germany, early in the morning of 17 October to carry out a joint general reconnaissance operation as far as the Firth of Forth. The other aircraft was 8L+AK, commanded by *Staffelkapitän Hauptmann* Wodarg, and both aircraft crossed the North Sea within sight of each other. When they were near the Isle of May, in the Firth of Forth, they were engaged by fairly accurate anti-aircraft fire from the destroyer HMS *Juno* and consequently shifted course southwards. Very shortly after that, Grabbet's machine was attacked by three Gladiator biplane fighters.

Küstenfliegergruppe 606

The Gladiators, of B Flight, 607 Squadron, had been scrambled from Acklington at 12.40 hours with orders to intercept enemy seaplanes operating off the Northumberland coast. Fifty minutes later, the trio, consisting of Flight Lieutenant John Sample, Flying Officer Dudley Craig, and Pilot Officer W.H.C. Whitty, were fifty miles east of Blyth and flying in V formation at 8,000 feet on a heading of 270° when they sighted 8L+DK. It was 6,000 feet below the fighters and flying south at an estimated 150mph.

Seemingly unaware that another Dornier 18 was in the vicinity, Sample gave his full attention to 8L+DK. He ordered a No.1 Attack and his section formed into line astern as they swooped down to approach their quarry from the rear. When the Dornier crew sighted their would-be assailants, the fighters were 1,000 feet above the seaplane and two miles north of it and the German dived steeply to fifty feet above sea level, presumably to protect his underside from attack from below. It was

GLADIATOR

while the Gladiators were focussed on Grabbet's machine that Wodarg, in 8L+AK, managed to slip away.

During the first foray with the fighters, Grabbet dropped his machine even lower and, according to his attackers, was at times no more than ten feet above the water as the engagement progressed. The combat was destined to last twelve minutes, during which time the return fire from the Dornier would be almost continuous.

Sample attacked first, opening fire at 500 yards and closing to 200 yards before breaking away to allow Craig and Whitty to make similar approaches. The enemy made a fight of it, with the German pilot manoeuvring at every chance to allow his rear gunner the opportunity to open fire clear of the tail unit. But the Gladiators' bullets found their mark, unlike those of their opponent, and at the end of the first assault, the Dornier's engines were emitting a continuous stream of thin white smoke or vapour.

As Whitty (No.3) broke away at the end of the first attacks, Sample was already lining up for his second run, which was followed in turn by attacks by his two companions. On the second attack, each pilot opened fire from 300 yards, closing to 200 yards, and held their bursts longer than in the first assault. The enemy gunner replied with tracer but the only shots that got near passed over the top starboard main plane of each attacking Gladiator. At the end of his second attack, Sample's ammunition was exhausted but Craig and Whitty had enough for a third pass before they, too, were forced to curtail their endeavours.

When the Gladiators broke off and turned for home, only the Dornier's wireless operator, *Unterfeldwebel* Hilmar Grimm, remained uninjured. At the start of the battle he had thrown himself to the floor of the wireless cabin and had been protected by the engines above him. Of the rest, Seydel had been killed, Seloga had been shot through the leg and the cheek, and one arm of Grabbet had been so badly wounded that it subsequently had to be amputated. However, although the Dornier was close to the water, it was still in the air, but it was now flying a north-easterly course, which would take it back towards HMS *Juno*.

If it was Grabbet's intention to fly back home, he was soon disappointed. His aircraft was so badly damaged that he was eventually forced to make an emergency landing – a task that he accomplished only with the help of his wireless operator. With the plane safely down on the water, Hilmar Grimm then transmitted an SOS that was picked up by

Wodarg, in 8L+AK – and by HMS *Juno*. Wodarg subsequently landed alongside 8L+DK with the intention of rescuing its crew. However, it was soon realized that it was impossible to do so, partly because the stricken Dornier's dinghy had been holed – thus adding to the difficulty of transfer – and because one member of the crew was already dead and two others were too badly wounded to help themselves. An additional complication was that HMS *Juno* again appeared on the scene and opened up once more with fairly accurate gunfire. Thus Wodarg, realizing that his comrades would at least be rescued, felt that he had no option but to take off and leave his friends to their fate.[1]

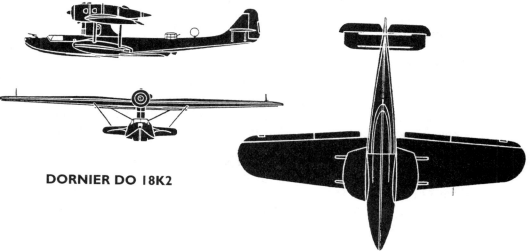

DORNIER DO 18K2

The precise location of the crash site of 8L+DK is currently a matter of conjecture. 607 Squadron's Operations Record Book for 17 October 1939 records that '...although the aircraft was not immediately destroyed, it was subsequently found by a trawler about 50-60 miles from the coast and four of the crew rescued and taken prisoner'. Kenneth G. Wynn[2] claims that the Dornier was critically damaged by the fighters and crashed into the sea some fifty miles off the English coast, while *Blitz, then and now*, vol.1[3] claims that it was shot down 'forty miles east of Berwick'. However, the Luftwaffe Quartermastergeneral's Loss Returns for this date records that Seloga and his crew were lost to '... flak from an enemy destroyer and crashed 40kms off the English coast on a bearing of 76° from Berwick'. The cause of the crash attributed by that source is incorrect, but the current writer has assumed that the location is probably based on Hilmar Grimm's SOS transmission and is likely to be right. If that is the case, the crash position is about twenty-six miles north-east of Berwick-upon-Tweed.

Wynn claims that the crew were later rescued by a trawler; the *Sunderland Echo* (28 September 1971) claims that the German crew was picked up by destroyer HMS *Juno*. The Quartermastergeneral's record tends to favour – but does not prove – the *Juno* option. Perhaps 607 Squadron's Gladiators did damage 8L+DK sufficiently to make it vulnerable to other attacks and to provide an opportunity which was seized upon by *Juno* – but then, of course, there is the trawler to consider.

With the presence of other enemy aircraft in 607 Squadron's operational area, a second section of B Flight, consisting of Flying Officer Bazin, Flying Officer Pumphrey and Flying Officer Thompson, was ordered up at 13.30 hours. The trio subsequently sighted, and engaged, four Heinkel He115s twenty-five miles east of Blyth but with no observable result.

29 November 1939 (east of Amble)

On the morning of 29 November 1939, Squadron Leader Harry Broadhurst, 111 Squadron, Acklington, claimed a Heinkel 111 bomber, which land-based observers saw crash into the sea five miles east of Amble. The bomber was 111 Squadron's first victory of the Second World War.

Shortly before 08.25 hours on 29 November 1939, Broadhurst (in Hurricane N2340) was flying north up the Northumberland coast at 3,500 feet when the Heinkel emerged from behind a cloud bank. The bomber was flying eastwards at an altitude of 4,000 feet. At 08.25 hours and eight miles east of Alnwick, Broadhurst turned to intercept, ducking into cloud for about thirty seconds in order to mask his approach. On emerging, he saw that the bomber was immediately above him and so he pulled up in a climbing turn to position the Hurricane under the tail of the enemy aircraft. He must have practised stealth, or the bomber crew was lax, for the German took no action until the Hurricane had closed to 500 yards. Then the raider dived for cloud 1,500 feet below while the ventral gunner, located in the gondola on the bomber's underbelly, opened up on the pursuing fighter.

Broadhurst held his own fire until he had positioned himself 400 yards dead astern of his quarry. At that point the bomber's top gun came into play, its tracer bullets streaking over the Hurricane's cockpit cover but failing to find their mark. That defensive response ceased with the first burst from the Hurricane's eight Browning machine guns. As the bomber and its pursuer raced out to sea, Broadhurst noticed that the cloud ceiling was getting lower and this gave him a little more time to take aim. Then he closed to 150 yards, firing continuously. The fusillade of machine-gun fire struck home to deadly effect. Almost immediately, the raider turned on its side and dived vertically into cloud, its downward plunge marked by a trail of billowing smoke. Broadhurst tried to follow and was still in cloud when he fired his last remaining rounds in the raider's direction without being able to witness the result. Then almost simultaneously, he broke into clear air to find himself diving headlong towards the sea, which seemed to be desperately close. Only by pulling up violently was he able to avert disaster.

Broadhurst did not see his victim crash into the water but on returning to the top of the clouds, he found that their ceiling was only 1,000 feet above sea level. Thus he considered that the Heinkel pilot would have had considerable difficulty recovering from his dive, particularly as the cloud base was so low. Broadhurst suspected that the Heinkel had crashed into the sea and so he submitted his claim for one Heinkel destroyed. His claim was substantiated later by land-based observers.

The writer could not find a record of this loss in the Luftwaffe Loss Returns for the period around the date in question and thus cannot provide details of unit and crew. *Blitz, then and now* vol.1 claims that the bomber belonged to *Stab*/KG26 but the published history of KG26 by Rudi Schmidt[4] records no loss by KG26 for this date.

30 January 1940 (east of Coquet Island)

Aircraft:	Heinkel 111H-2	1H+KM	w/nr. ?	4./KG26
Crew:	Fw. Helmut Höfer	pilot	missing	
	Uffz. Richard Feist	observer	+	
	Obgfr. Albert Hain	wireless op	missing	
	Gefr. Werner Korsinsky	mechanic	missing	

This aircraft was on a sortie to the Firth of Forth when it was intercepted and shot down some ten miles east of Coquet Island by Flight Lieutenant Caesar Hull (L1849) and Sergeant Frank Carey (L1728) in Hurricanes of 43 Squadron, Acklington.

veſtigium leonis

Kampfgeschwader 26
(Löwengeschwader)

On a day of grey clouds and a white crested sea, Caesar Hull was ' at readiness' for convoy patrol duties and was standing alongside his aircraft when Flight Lieutenant Peter Townsend landed at the end of his own convoy patrol and signalled Hull aloft. Hull took off immediately. Seemingly, a raid had been plotted off North Berwick; it was travelling south at 180-200mph and attacks on coastal shipping were likely. Hull was alone when he lifted off at 12.40 hours but another Hurricane was soon hard on his heels. Prior to Hull's departure, his No.2, Sergeant Frank Carey, was air-testing his own Hurricane, which had a suspected faulty magneto. When Carey saw his flight commander flying directly out to sea, he suspected possible action and, choosing to ignore the possibility of magneto failure, set off in pursuit. At about 12.50 hours they found two Heinkel 111s five miles east of Coquet Island and apparently preparing to attack fishing boats. In the ensuing chase, one of the enemy aircraft escaped but the other was less fortunate.

Selecting the latter as their target, Hull ordered Carey to carry out a No.1 attack whilst he (Hull) climbed above the Heinkel and away to the raider's starboard side in order to head off its escape to seaward before commencing his own attack. As Hull lined up his Hurricane for a beam attack, Carey approached the raider from astern and at a rather flat angle. He began shooting from 400 yards, using zero to fifteen degrees deflection, then ceasing as Hull made his own approach before shooting again to cover Hull's breakaway. When Hull came diving in for his first beam attack, he commenced firing at 300 yards and broke away with ten yards to spare. In fact, he held the dive for so long that Carey thought his leader's intention was to ram the bomber.

After that first assault, the Heinkel's starboard engine appeared to be damaged for the attackers noticed that white vapour was pouring from it. Vapour was also observed from a point underneath the fuselage and this at times clouded Carey's windscreen – but not enough to prevent him from seeing and aiming. However, although the bomber might have been damaged in the first foray, it took six synchronized assaults by both fighters to finish it off. On each occasion Hull came in from the beam to astern while Carey came in from the rear. During the first two attacks, return fire from the raider's dorsal rear gun position was directed alternately at each fighter but after the second onslaught there was no response at all from that quarter. Following the fourth attack, the bomber's undercarriage was partially lowered and after the final burst the enemy aircraft turned slowly to starboard and spiralled gently down towards the sea with its engines still running. As it did so, the Hurricanes ceased firing and climbed above their victim to watch as the Heinkel glided to its inevitable demise. The Heinkel broke up on impact with the sea and sank in minutes. There were no survivors and Hull and Carey were of the opinion that the German crew were all dead by the time the third attack had been completed.

Beedle, in his history of 43 Squadron,[5] claims that the Germans were picked up by one of the vessels they had been attacking, but he would appear to have been mistaken. The Luftwaffe Loss Returns show one dead and three missing in this incident. Schmidt, in his history of KG26,[6] lists the crew as missing, and Hector Bolitho[7] quotes a letter (dated 31 January 1940) from Flying Officer J.W.C. Simpson of 43 Squadron stating that there were no survivors. This is also confirmed by Peter Townsend[8] who recalled that when Hull landed he was excited but shaken '...for he had killed four men with a single blow'.

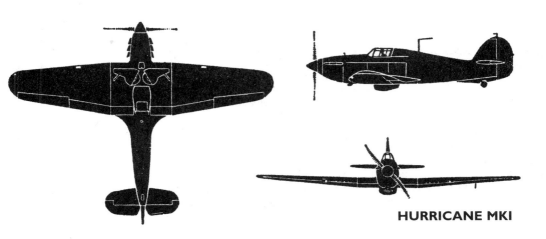

HURRICANE MKI

3 February 1940 (Druridge Bay)

On the morning of 3 February 1940, Heinkel bombers of at least four *Staffeln* of KG26 were engaged in anti-shipping operations along the coastline of north-eastern England, where shipping was bombed off the Farne Islands and along the more southerly stretches of the north-east coast. The Admiralty War Diary for the day claims that as many as twenty-three enemy aircraft may have taken part in these raids. It is believed that the attacks claimed at least two vessels: the *Alexandria*, of unknown nationality, which sank east of the Farne Islands, and the Norwegian steamer *Tempo* (629GRT), which caught fire and sank off St Abbs Head at 55°59′00"N/01°35′00"E.[9] The *Tempo* went down with the loss of four crew fifteen minutes after being bombed by three aircraft. Several other vessels were damaged, including the Greek steamer *Nicolau Zografia*.

The raiders were engaged by destroyers, escort vessels and the anti-aircraft cruiser HMS *Cairo* (Pennant No.D87) but it was the Hurricane fighters of the Northumberland-based 43 Squadron that had tangible success. Berlin Radio subsequently acknowledged the loss of three Heinkel 111s. One of those was forced down just north of Whitby (see *Broken Eagles:Yorkshire*)[10], another came down in the sea about one mile south-east of Coquet Island (just north of Druridge Bay) and a third ditched fifteen miles east of Tynemouth. The Admiralty was of the opinion that two other enemy aircraft may have been lost; one off the Farne Islands and one whose radio distress signals were intercepted from far out in the North Sea. However, examination of the Luftwaffe Loss

Returns for the day reveal the Royal Navy to have been too optimistic: no other loss is registered but the Returns do show that a fourth Heinkel suffered forty per cent damage and was forced to crash-land on its return to base.

Aircraft: Heinkel 111H-3	1H+HL	w/nr. ?	3./KG26
Crew: Uffz. Walter Remischke	pilot	+	
Lt. Luther von Brüning	observer	+	
Fw. Herbert Panzlaff	wireless op	+	
Fw. Herbert Peterson	mechanic	missing	

Blitz, then and now. Vol. 1[11] claims that this aircraft, which came down in Druridge Bay, was shot down by Flying Officer John Simpson, 43 Squadron, Acklington.

The morning of 3 February was misty and damp, with occasional showers and with low cloud down to 900 feet. When news of the threat to convoys reached 43 Squadron, Acklington, Hurricane fighters of Flight Lieutenant Peter Townsend's section were the first to be ordered off (at 09.10 hours), initially with orders to patrol South Shields although they were later redirected to Whitby. Five minutes later, Flying Officer John Simpson (L1727) led Flying Officer J.D. 'Eddie' Edmonds (L1955) and Sergeant John Arbuthnot (L1742) away from Acklington to patrol the Northumberland coast from the Farne Islands to Coquet Island.

At about 09.30 hours Simpson's section sighted two enemy aircraft attacking shipping five miles south-east of the Farne Islands and singled out one of them. John Simpson later recalled the day in a letter to his friend Hector Bolitho:

We found a small convoy after about half an hour and we were circling it when I saw three splashes in the water, to one side of the centre ship. It was a small ship, with a sail and one funnel... A fishing boat, I suppose. I realised that the splashes were from bombs and I looked up and saw an immense aircraft just below the clouds.

It was the first Heinkel that I had ever seen and I just hoped that it wasn't one of ours. The Heinkels look quite like Ansons from underneath. Several times we have had Ansons for Heinkels and have only just realised in time. Much to the alarm of Coastal Command pilots. But I was certain this time. It looked dark and ugly and I pulled up the nose of my Hurricane and pressed the tit. I hit him fair and square in the wings and the fuselage. One of his engines stopped and bits of metal flew off. He then disappeared into some wisps of cloud... We circled for a few seconds and my No.2 (' Eddie' Edmonds) said he could see the crippled Heinkel in a gap in the clouds and he fired.

The Hun was now flying low towards the English coast. I caught

28

up and finished all my ammunition on him. He was burning so well when he disappeared into the mist above the sea. My ammunition tanks were empty so I called up Eddie and we set course for base. [12]

Interestingly, Simpson later admitted to his friend Bolitho that, because the He111 had not been seen to crash, he (Simpson) had not been absolutely sure that it had been destroyed, although his section claimed it as such. However, later in the day, the claim was confirmed by a telephone call from Air Vice Marshal R. E. ' Birdie' Saul, who was then in command of 13 Group, Fighter Command. This confirmation creates something of a puzzle.

Blitz, then and now. Vol.1 reports that He111, 1H+HL crashed in Druridge Bay, near Amble, at 09.30 hours on 3 February and goes on to state that Simpson and his section were responsible for shooting it down. On the other hand, the Squadron Operations Record Book for 3 February 1940 seems to challenge this by stating that 'It is thought that this (Simpson's Heinkel) was the aircraft picked up fifty miles from the Farne Islands in the afternoon...' (although currently there is no evidence to confirm any incident in that area, although one Heinkel was forced to ditch fifteen miles off the Tyne). Certainly the time of Simpson's combat is a close enough match to the loss of 1H+HL – if the time of the crash is correct. However, on the same morning, another claim was also made in respect of a German bomber that allegedly crashed in Druridge Bay.

Three Gladiators of Yellow Section of 152 Squadron, Acklington, were scrambled at 10.40 hours. They were east of Druridge Bay at about 11.15 hours when they sighted a Heinkel 111 flying a north-easterly course over the Bay at an altitude of 300 feet. Squadron Leader Shute (Yellow 1) made the first attack (a quarter attack gradually coming round into a No.1 attack) from 250 yards range and expended 2,150 rounds in the process. Sergeant F.E. Shepperd (Yellow 2) followed that with a similar manoeuvre and a continuous burst of 500 rounds. When he had finished, the Heinkel's undercarriage was being lowered and considerable volumes of black smoke were enveloping the enemy machine. By that time, Shute was already following up with another assault from astern with a sustained burst of machine-gun fire that he maintained until breaking off fifty yards from his target. On this second run he was accompanied by Pilot Officer Falkson (Yellow 3), who took up position as No.3 echelon and opened fire at the same time as Shute. Falkson aimed at the Heinkel's fuselage behind the top rear gunner and saw his tracers striking home. The return fire, which had been experienced from the bomber's upper and lower turrets prior to the fighters' assaults, ceased immediately after this dual attack.

The enemy machine was still emitting black smoke and losing speed as it descended into cloud with one wing down and with its undercarriage lowered. The Squadron's Operations Record Book (ORB) records the incident and points out that the Heinkel appeared to be in difficulties when it was seen to change course towards the south. The entry in the ORB does not record that the Heinkel was seen to crash, but an entry on 6 February 1940 includes a confirmation from 13 Fighter Group that the enemy machine that crashed in Druridge Bay was the machine attacked by Yellow Section. There is some two hours time difference between the claims made by 43 and 152 Squadrons, but unless two Heinkels crashed in Druridge Bay that day at least one of the claims would appear to be invalid. As mentioned earlier, the Luftwaffe Loss Returns record only three Heinkels lost (and one of those crash-landed near Whitby, Yorks.), with a fourth crash-landing on its return to base. The latter is recorded as having had forty hits in the right engine – which would seem to match the observation in 43 Squadron's Operations Record Book.

Until the time of the Druridge Bay crash is established there will be doubts about who was responsible. Fortunately, there is no such difficulty with regard to the second Heinkel to be shot down by a northern-based squadron that day.

Aircraft:	Heinkel 111	1H+GK	w/nr. ?	2./KG26
Crew:	Obfw. Fritz Wiemer	pilot	pow	
	Fw. Franz Schnee	observer	pow	
	Uffz. Alfred Dittrich	wireless op	pow	
	Uffz. Willi Wolff	mechanic	+	
	Uffz. Karl-Ernst Thiede	gunner	+	

This aircraft was in the vicinity of merchant shipping off the Northumberland coast when it was shot down at 11.15 hours fifteen miles east of Tynemouth by Sergeant Frank Carey (L1726) and Sergeant Ottewill (L1849), of Yellow Section, A Flight, 43 Squadron, Acklington.

The Heinkel had taken off from its base at Lübeck-Blankensee three hours earlier and had been forced by poor visibility to cross the North Sea at an altitude of 300 feet before making landfall near Middlesbrough and commencing its patrol northwards.[13] The aircraft was in the vicinity of shipping off the Tyne when it was spotted by the Hurricanes.

Carey and Ottewill had been scrambled at 10.10 hours and were on patrol fifteen miles east of Tynemouth when Carey noticed shell bursts from an Allied merchantman. On investigation, a Heinkel 111 was sighted some 300 feet above the sea and some two miles east of the vessel. It was caught after a short chase and Ottewill was detailed to head off the bomber and prevent it making for cloud some 800 feet higher, while Carey launched his first assault with a No.1 attack. In fact, the German immediately tried to climb to safety as soon as the fighters were spotted and when Ottewill realized the intention he immediately joined in the fray. The fighters moved in together from behind and from above in an assault which, according to the Germans, '...seemed to come

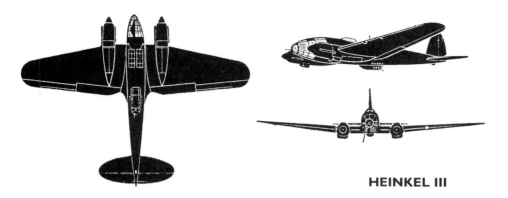

HEINKEL III

almost simultaneously from both sides...'

Ottewill opened fire at 400 yards and held it until he had closed to 150 yards, during which time he saw numerous pieces falling off the fuselage of the Heinkel as his bullets struck home. Then the bomber, with its starboard engine stalled and its undercarriage lowered, began to turn. Ottewill's final burst put the bomber's port engine out of commission. By then, both fighters had exhausted their ammunition but the damage had been done; with both engines out of action, the German pilot had no option but to ditch. Watched by Carey and Ottewill, the Heinkel touched down some fifteen miles off Tynemouth and remained afloat long enough for most of its crew to evacuate with safety but not long enough for them to release their rubber dinghy. The bomber sank in just over a minute, casting its crew into the sea and forcing each of them to rely on the buoyancy of his lifebelt.

Ottewill's combat report states that the five members of the bomber's crew were then rescued by trawler. In fact, only four of the crew were picked up by the Swansea-registered trawler *Harlech Castle* (number SA42), skippered by Thomas Trendall. According to the trawlermen, the fifth German (Thiede) seemed to be dead in the water as the trawler went alongside and his body disappeared before it could be retrieved. However, it seems that he did not die from injuries. His comrades claimed that Thiede was unwounded but his buoyancy aid had been punctured and thus it seems likely that he had drowned before help arrived. Of the rest, one crewman was unhurt, two were wounded and the fourth (believed to have been Wolff) died of wounds before the trawler reached the Humber. Thiede's body was later recovered from the sea (though not by *Harlech Castle*, the crew of which never saw the unfortunate airman again) and was subsequently buried at Scarthro Road Cemetery, Grimsby. However, such was the strength of local feeling against German airmen because of repeated attacks on trawlers that it was considered inadvisable to bury Thiede with Service Honours.

Subsequent searches of the Germans revealed that they were not carrying personal papers and it was believed that they had probably discarded such in the interests of security before being taken on board *Harlech Castle*. However, one notable exception was found in the pocket of a flying jacket. The find consisted of a Signals Table giving details of wireless frequencies, recognition signals and the call signs of the entire KG26. In addition, there were details of the call signs and radio frequencies used by aircraft of 1/(F)122, the unit which was carrying out reconnaissance for the Heinkels.

Hector Bolitho,[14] quoting John Simpson, mistakenly claims that it was Hull and Carey who were responsible for the shooting down of Heinkel 1H+GK and goes on to say that:

> The crew of that aircraft had stood on top of the fuselage when their plane had landed on the sea. Simpson said afterwards: 'It was so like Caesar... He dived on them, but without firing, just to beat them up. They all jumped into the water and he was delighted. He kept on saying: "It was wizard."'

Fritz Wiemer, pilot of He 111 1H+GK of 2./KG26 that was shot down off the Tyne, 3 February 1940.
[Frau. E. Wiemer via Stephan Reekmann]

However, 43 Squadron's Operations Record Book clearly shows that Carey and Ottewill were the victorious pair and that Hull, although on patrol with two others at almost the same time as Carey and Ottewill, did not shoot down an aircraft on that sortie. Of course, it is entirely possible that Hull came across the ditched crew during the course of his own patrol and decided to have some sport – but the fact that the Heinkel was said to have sunk in little over a minute makes that unlikely.

EYEWITNESS

The Harlech Castle incident
3 February 1940

Thomas Trendall, the skipper of the trawler *Harlech Castle* that rescued the crew of Heinkel 1H+GK, subsequently related the following account of the incident to writer Leo Walmesley.[15] Additional material from the *Bridlington Chronicle*, (9 February 1940) has been added in parentheses.

There's chaps in this port, especially them who've been messed about with these Jerry planes and seen their mates killed and wounded, who say that if they came across the crew of one of 'em that had been shot down and were in the sea, they'd just leave 'em to drown. You can't blame 'em in a way, for it isn't war, shooting and bombing unarmed ships...It's just murder, but the Missus is right what she says – that when it comes to it, there's no fisherman can leave another chap to drown, no matter what his nation is or what he's done. It's against his nature.

As it happened, on this particular trip I'd been having an argument with the Mate, Jack Riley, about this very thing. We'd both seen other ships attacked and he knew all the chaps from here who'd been killed, and Jack said he'd be damned if he'd ever alter his ship's course to pick up a Jerry airman. He'd be lucky to get off with just drowning, which would be quick enough in winter time, a damned sight quicker and less painful than dying of a bullet through your stomach, or being burnt alive with an incendiary bomb. I said to him, 'Jack, if it ever came to it you'd be like everyone else, and you'd save the devil', and I tell you he laughed at me...

It was about ten of the morning of 3rd February, and we were off the Tyne, with a south-east gale blowing with a very heavy sea and squalls of snow. You wouldn't have thought that the devils would have been out in weather like that, but they were, and so were some of our Spitfires (sic). We'd heard bombing and machine-gun-fire, but we'd seen nothing, and I'd just gone below to find a chart when some-one shouted there was a plane bearing straight down on us. Before I got up to the bridge I heard another shout, 'It's down in the sea!' and sure enough there it was on our starboard beam, a big black plane with iron crosses on it, and almost at the same time I saw one of our Spitfires (sic) circling round above us. Well, I don't know how they managed it at the time, but four of the Jerries were already out of the cabin of the plane, standing on the wreckage waving to us to go to their help. I said to Jack Riley, who was standing close beside me, 'Now, what about it, Jack...are you letting them drown?' and he said, quick as lightning, 'Nay, we've got to save them, skipper,' and I said, 'Yes, they're some poor mothers' sons...'.

I put the ship to starboard, went slow ahead, came right round and went slow astern. By that time the plane had sunk and we saw four men swimming and another floating with his face down and he looked as though he was dead. The others had their flying kit and lifebelts on. If they hadn't they couldn't have escaped drowning for there was a heavy sea running. All our own lads had turned out for the rescue and I noticed one of them had only his dungarees on and bare feet, and I remember that, like the Mate, he'd always said that he'd never pick up a German from the sea, and there he was as lively as any of us when it came to hauling the first of those airmen aboard. We'd thrown lifelines and they were hanging on as best they could, but shouted at us to be quick. (We threw ropes to them then we fixed up tackle and having passed the ropes under the men's armpits while they were in the water we hoisted them from the sea one at a time) They were all big men, and it wasn't too easy for their clothes were waterlogged. But we managed it in time, all but the one who'd been floating face downwards. He must have been dead to start with. Anyway, we saw no more of him.

They were chilled to the bones through immersion in water but my men took them below, removed their wet clothing before the fire, gave them hot drinks and rubbed warmth and life into them, and gave them their own dry things. I got the first-aid box, went down and did my best to fix up their wounds. All except one was wounded. One had a broken leg. Another looked as though he wouldn't last very long. All of them except the pilot could speak English. One of them said that when the Spitfire (sic) had knocked them out, the pilot said he would make a pancake landing near the trawler and said he was certain they would all be picked up...They wanted to know where we were bound for. I told them Grimsby, and said they'd have to put up with things as best they could. They wanted to know how they'd be treated when they got ashore, and I told them 'fair', as I knew they would be. But apart from that, they hadn't much to say until we got into port and I handed them over, when one of them thanked me for the kindness they had received. By that time, the one who had been badly wounded had died...(He was a married man. We found his wife's photograph in the pocket of his flying suit.)

9 February 1940 (off Coquet Island?)

On a day of poor visibility and spasmodic enemy anti-shipping activity, Flight Lieutenant Peter Townsend (L2116), Sergeant Jim Hallowes (L1847) and Flying Officer 'Eddie' Edmonds (L1955), in Hurricanes of

B Flight, 43 Squadron, Acklington, found a pair of Heinkel 111s off Coquet Island.

Shortly after noon, the trio were flying north almost at wave height when they sighted the two enemy aircraft – one flying north, the other going west – both at an altitude of 1,000 feet and just below the cloud base. The Hurricanes turned to intercept the Heinkel flying west and, when they were five miles south-east of Coquet Island, managed to get close enough for Townsend to carry out an attack from slightly below and with full deflection before the bomber was lost in cloud. As he closed in on his would-be victim, Townsend seemingly failed to notice the other enemy machine, which fired on him as he prepared to attack the other. Hallowes followed Townsend into the attack and fired a full deflection burst at the raider. Bits of metal flew off and the Heinkel jettisoned its bomb load before flying unsteadily into cloud and disappearing from view. Hallowes then went after the north-bound bomber and managed a short burst before that, too, took refuge in cloud. Neither of the bombers was seen again by Townsend's section but one of them was claimed as damaged.

At about the time that B Flight was jousting with the Heinkels, five Hurricanes of A Flight were patrolling east of Blyth. One of them (L1744), was being flown by Flying Officer Malcolm Carswell whose engine suddenly failed when the aircraft was five miles offshore. Being too low to bale out, he decided to land close to one of the ships in the convoy he was flying over. His aircraft sank almost straight away but he managed to get out before it went down. However, he could not inflate his Mae West and thus he tried to swim towards the boats – a difficult task at any time, perhaps, but certainly much worse when trying to make headway in freezing, choppy water whilst wearing full flying kit. Inevitably, he passed out before rescuers reached him and he had to be revived by the boat's crew using artificial respiration. According to the Squadron's Operations Record Book, Carswell was picked up by a Swedish vessel, was landed at Blyth and lived to fight another day.

The wreck of He111 TS+OH of 3(F)./Ob.d.L, which crash-landed near St Abbs Head on 22 February 1940 after being attacked by Spitfires of 602 Squadron, Drem.
[The War Weekly, 8 March 1940]

22 February 1940 (off Blyth)

At 11.55 hours on 22 February 1940, three Hurricanes of 43 Squadron, Acklington – Flight Lieutenant P. Townsend (L2116), Flying Officer Christie (L1727) and Sergeant Ayling (L1759) – were patrolling the Farne Islands and were about five miles out to sea at 2,500 feet when Ayling saw contrails at 20,000 feet and heading south. The Hurricanes climbed in pursuit at full boost but Christie was soon forced to give up and return to base when his engine started to overheat.

Townsend and Ayling climbed rapidly towards the vapour trails and the aircraft making them, which was soon identified as a Heinkel 111. When the fighters were at about 19,000 feet altitude the bomber was lost in a thin layer of broken cloud but was again sighted in a clear patch at 20,000 feet. By then it was on the port bow and flying level in a south-easterly direction at 240-250mph. As the two Hurricanes closed in, the Heinkel dived slightly and Townsend swung away to starboard to place himself between the sun and the target. With pursuer and pursued still diving, Townsend made his first approach from slightly astern and a little above the bomber. As he did so, the Heinkel's ventral gunner opened up with a defensive fusillade of tracer or incendiary bullets, but with the bomber diving and with the following Hurricane being slightly above it, there was no way that the German gunner's efforts could be anything more than a gesture. As Townsend was later to put it, 'effective fire was quite impossible'. However, that was the only defensive action the gunners offered for no shots were fired by the dorsal gunner and Townsend subsequently speculated that the height of the Heinkel's tail might have obstructed the field of fire from that quarter.

At 12.15 hours, when the aircraft were some twenty-five miles east of Blyth, Townsend made his move. Closing to within 250 yards of the bomber, he released a sustained burst of machine-gun fire lasting five seconds before breaking away with 150 yards to spare. The undercarriage of the enemy aircraft dropped almost immediately and plumes of bluish white smoke poured from both engines. The Heinkel steepened its dive and increased its speed to 350mph. At 15,000 feet altitude, Townsend attacked again from the same position as before and at a range of 100 yards. By then, the dense vapour belching from both of the bomber's engines almost completely obscured Townsend's vision. The second attack lasted only two seconds – but it was enough. The Heinkel continued its dive but at about 10,000 feet, and at 400mph, the bomber gave a violent lurch forward and portions of both wings broke off about nine feet from the tips. Then the crippled aircraft turned on its back and dived vertically towards the sea.

Both fighters followed the luckless raider until it disappeared from view but neither Townsend nor Ayling saw it strike water because thick mist masked the sea to a height of 500 feet. However, shortly after the aircraft was lost in the mist both pilots saw a column of black smoke rise over the place where the Heinkel was last seen. Thirty years later, Peter Townsend recalled his feelings '...as the fuselage disappeared, followed by a trail of fluttering debris. Only at that moment did I realise what I had done to the men inside. I felt utterly nauseated.'[16]

Although Ayling did not participate in the combat, he had followed it closely and was within 800 yards of the bomber when its wings broke away. During the second attack both Townsend and Ayling were diving at 400mph and are convinced that the Heinkel's final dive was in excess of 450mph.

The writer knows little about this German aircraft or its crew. The Luftwaffe Loss Returns dated 23 February 1940 show the loss of two Heinkel 111P aircraft the day before but the Returns give no crew details. Both of the bombers were reconnaissance aircraft belonging to *Aufklärungsgruppe Oberkommando der Luftwaffe* [(F)./Ob.d.L] One of them, He111 TS+OH of 1 *Staffel* (F)./Ob.d.L was caught by Spitfires of 602 Squadron, Drem, and force-landed at East Coldingham, near St Abb's Head. The other He111 was very probably the one shot down by Townsend. *Blitz, then and now. Vol.1* claims that it crashed into the sea some thirty miles east of the Farne Islands.

Early 1940. A boat crew of the destroyer HMS Griffin *(H31) searches for survivors of a German bomber that had been shot down off the Northumberland coast by Spitfires.* [The War Weekly, May 1940]

27 February 1940 (east of Couqet Island)

Aircraft:	Heinkel 111H-3	1H+?L	w/nr. ?	3./KG26
Crew:	Hptm. Hans-Joachim Helm	?	+	
	Uffz. Heinrich Buckisch	?	missing	
	Uffz. Karl Lassnig	?	+	
	Obfw. Artur Thiele	?	missing	
	Gefr. Walter Rixen	?	missing	

This aircraft was one of two Heinkels on a sortie to the Firth of Forth and the coast of northern England when it was caught ten miles east of Coquet Island by Pilot Officer J.S.B. Jones and Pilot Officer T.S. Wildblood in Spitfires of Blue Section, 152 Squadron, Acklington.[17] Unfortunately, the combined combat report of the engagement fails to name the participants and merely refers to them as Blue 2 and Blue 3 without clarifying which person held each position. Thus the following account is not as clear as it might be.

Shortly before 13.45 hours on 27 February, three Spitfires of Blue Section, 152 Squadron, Acklington, were on patrol off the Northumberland coast and were flying in a step-down echelon left formation. They were flying south, some 400-600 yards apart, just within sight of each other and with Blue 1 at the landward extreme – about ten miles east of Alnmouth but in sight of the coast. Blue 1, at an altitude of 500 feet, was in clear air but Blue 2 and 3, flying at 100 feet and 200 feet respectively, were in mist. A Heinkel 111 was subsequently spotted flying a north-easterly course at an altitude of 500 feet and at a speed of 200mph. The bomber's line of approach took it between Blue 2 and Blue 3. When the Heinkel sighted the fighters it dived to twenty feet above the sea with Blues 2 and 3 in pursuit but thereafter it flew straight and level until Blue 2's third burst of gunfire. Blue 2 attacked immediately because he was afraid that the enemy aircraft might be lost in the mist and as the Spitfire lined up for its first pass, the Heinkel was seen to jettison four or five bombs, none of which exploded on striking the water.

Blue 2 opened his attack on the bomber's starboard quarter from slightly above. Using full deflection at 400 yards' range and shifting from starboard quarter to dead astern before breaking off at 100 yards, Blue 2 fired four bursts of four seconds each. There was no noticeable effect from the first burst, which was met by tracer or incendiary bullets from the bomber's dorsal turret, but that return fire ceased after the Spitfire opened up for the second time. The undercarriage of the Heinkel then dropped and plumes of white smoke were observed streaming from the engines. The bomber dipped after the third burst of gunfire from Blue 2 and the fighter broke away as the bomber changed course to port. Then Blue 3 joined in with an assault that began on the bomber's starboard side and ended up dead astern. Blue 3 fired two bursts, one of seven seconds and one of five seconds. In the interval that separated pursuer

38

and pursued, the enemy aircraft made a steep turn to port while still maintaining speed. However, during the second burst of gunfire from the fighter, a large proportion of the raider's starboard engine was seen to fall away and the engine stopped. The bomber then turned steeply to port and flew towards the coast – but it did not get there. Blue 3 broke away and remained above the Heinkel until it hit the water.

Blue 1, being almost a mile westwards of Blue 2, did not participate in the engagement but he subsequently got close enough to see the enemy pilot ease the Heinkel down on to the sea in a controlled ditching. It sank some three minutes later but not before three of the crew were seen to leave the aircraft by the roof of the front cockpit and climb into an inflatable dinghy.

It is not known what happened to the Germans after they had taken to their rubber boat but none of them survived the ordeal. The body of Karl Lassnig, along with a rubber dinghy, was washed ashore at Whitley Bay on 1 March 1940. The body of Joachim Helm was also subsequently recovered (possibly two days later) and both were later buried in Chevington Cemetery, near Broomhill, Northumberland, under the dates 1 March and 3 March respectively; the three other members of the crew were listed as missing.

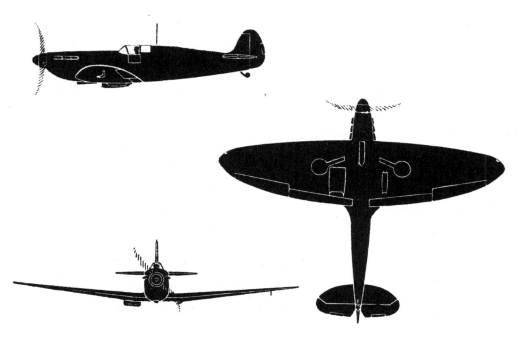

SPITFIRE MKI

39

29 March 1940 (Druridge Bay)

Aircraft:	Junkers 88	4D+AP	w/nr. ?	6./KG30
Crew:	Oblt. Rudolf Quadt	?	+	
	Fw. Gustav Hartung	?	+	
	Uffz. Ernst Hesse	?	+	
	Uffz. Andreas Wunderling	?	+	

Ju88 4D+AP was shot down by naval gunfire on the evening of 29 March 1940 during an attack on a convoy off the Northumberland coast. It crashed in Druridge Bay, a quarter of a mile from the shore, at about 20.30 hours.

Kampfgeschwader 30 (Adler)

The ships had left the Tyne at 17.00 hours and had been ploughing northwards for three hours under heavily overcast skies when the convoy escort sloop HMS *Auckland* warned that German aircraft were in the vicinity. At 20.30 hours, the fleet was off the Northumberland village of Cresswell and in the neighbourhood of the F20 buoy when three loud explosions were heard. Seconds later, the crews of the armed trawlers *Rutlandshire* and *Indian Star*, which were respectively stationed on the port and starboard bows of the convoy, saw a single enemy aircraft crossing 500 yards ahead of the fleet. The bomber was flying in a north-westerly direction at an altitude of 1,000 feet. *Indian Star* opened fire with its .5 gun and managed to fire off one round from its 12-pounder before the aircraft crossed to the port side off the convoy and passed close to the *Rutlandshire*. The latter subjected the fleeing raider to a concentrated barrage of intense fire from its Lewis gun and also managed a number of rounds from its own 12-pounder gun. Although observers on the *Rutlandshire* considered it highly likely that the aircraft had been struck by machine-gun fire from each escort, no damage could be seen in the failing light. However, it seems that some of the defenders' bullets found their mark

According to Middlesbrough's *Evening Gazette* (30 March 1940), a woman living in a nearby village (Cresswell?) said:

> I ran outside when I heard a roaring noise, and saw a huge 'plane travelling towards the sea over the top of my house. I don't know how it missed another street of houses before it went out over the sea. Then it dived down and struck the water with a terrific splash.

A local lifeboat was launched and spent two hours looking for survivors but although patches of oil were found on the surface of the sea, the searchers found no other trace of the aeroplane. The lifeboat continued its search at daybreak on 30 March, but without success. The Germans subsequently admitted the loss of the aircraft but also claimed that a cruiser protecting the convoy had been hit by several bombs and that one of the merchant ships in the convoy had been sunk. Both claims were

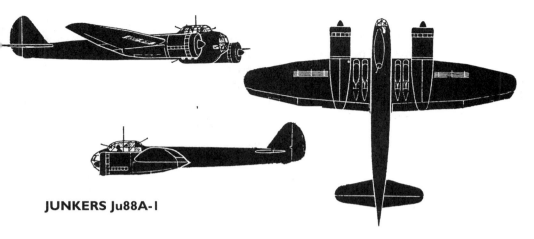

JUNKERS Ju88A-1

denied by the Admiralty.

In spite of the initial lack of success by the local lifeboat, this aircraft was subsequently salvaged from the sea, though precisely when and where is currently not known to the writer. The Summary of Work done by No.60 Maintenance Unit at Shipton-by-Benningborough (Yorkshire) in April 1940 shows that on 9 April 1940, 'In the case of the Junkers 88, assistance was given to the Naval Authority, Blyth, the aircraft being removed from Salvage vessel, dismantled and transported by vehicles of this unit.'[18]

The bodies of three of the crew were found in the aircraft, that of Hesse being recovered from a different location. All four were subsequently buried in Chevington Cemetery, near Broomhill, Northumberland.

First month's operations.
I./KG4 losses over northern England:
June-July, 1940

I./KG4 carried out its first operation against England on 15 June 1940, when its Heinkel 111s laid mines off the south-east coast. During the period from the last week of June to mid-July 1941 the *Gruppe* operated over the English mainland and attacked targets in the Midlands, East Anglia, and the south-west, as well as in the north of England. Targets in the latter area included the chemical works of ICI at Billingham-on-Tees, oil storage installations near Hull, industrial objectives on the Humber and at Middlesbrough, and factories in Sheffield, Leeds and Newcastle.

During that first month of operations over the North, the relatively lighter northern skies of the summer nights favoured the infant night fighter force, the aircraft of which were guided in the pursuit of targets by a combination of radio communications and visual signals (usually searchlights). The defenders were not always decisive in their interceptions but, as far as KG4 was concerned, bullet-scarred aircraft seem to have returned to base after almost every operation. I./KG4 lost four aircraft in the space of one week in the unit's first month of operations over England.

The first loss was Heinkel 111 5J+BL of 3. *Staffel*, which was en route to Birmingham on the night of 25-26 June when it was shot down by a Spitfire of 616 Squadron, Leconfield, and crashed into the sea some fifteen miles off the Humber. The second, Heinkel 111 5J+EK of 2. *Staffel*, was lost on 27 June, during a raid on Middlesbrough, when the bomber was caught by a twin-engined night fighter and was forced to ditch in the sea twenty-one miles east of the Tees. At about the same time, the mechanic of Heinkel 111 5J+DH of 1. *Staffel* was killed when his aircraft was caught by a night fighter over the Humber and he was shot through the head. The third bomber was lost on 30 June after it returned to base from Newcastle on one engine and crashed when the pilot attempted to abort his landing and go round again. The aircraft's observer, *Gruppenkommandeur* Major Hans von Ploetz, was badly injured in the crash. The fourth loss occurred on 1 July 1940, when I./KG4 flew its first daytime sorties against England. It dispatched three aircraft: two of those aborted the operation because of insufficient cloud cover over their intended targets; the third, Heinkel 111 5J+EL of 3. *Staffel*, pressed on to bomb oil tanks near Hull and was shot down off the Humber by Spitfires of 616 Squadron, Leconfield.

Based on *Kampfgeschwader General Wever 4* by Karl Gundelach[19]

26-27 June 1940 (off Blyth – or off the Tees?)

Aircraft:	Heinkel 111H-4	5J+EK	w/nr. ?	2./KG4
Crew:	Fw. Siegfried Gessert	pilot	pow	
	Uffz. Karl-Heinz Beck	?	pow	
	Uffz. Wilhelm Dieter	?	pow	
	Gefr. Horst Filihowski	?	pow	

Gundelach states that this crew failed to return from operations to Middlesbrough on the night of 26-27 June 1940 and implies that 5J+EK was the only loss suffered by KG4 that night. However, he offers no details of the aircraft, its *Staffel*, or the location of the loss. The Luftwaffe Loss Returns for 29 June 1940 provide a little more information and show that a Heinkel 111-4 of 2./KG4 was lost on a raid against Middlesbrough some days before 29 June. However, like Gundelach, the Returns give neither crew details nor the location of the crash. *Blitz, then and now. Vol. 1*[20] confirms the target and the crew details given by

Gundelach and claims that the aircraft crashed off Blyth, Northumberland – but the latter is incorrect. He111 5J+EK did participate in the attack on Teesside on the night in question but it was not lost near Blyth: it ditched into the sea some twenty-one miles east of the Tees at about 01.00 hours on 27 June. According to the German crew, the bomber was damaged by a twin-engined night fighter.[21]

Kampfgeschwader 4 (General Wever)

The Heinkel was one of four from 2./KG4 that had taken off from their base at Wittmundhafen (north Germany) at 22.00 hours on 26 June to attack the ICI chemical works at Billingham, a target familiar to Gessert and his crew for they had visited the plant a week earlier and had dropped twelve 50kg bombs on it. 5J+EK had the same bomb-load on board when it set out from its base on the night of 26 June. During the course of the raid on the Tees area, forty high-explosive bombs were dropped, nine of which failed to explode. Shops were damaged in West Hartlepool, where three people were killed; bombs also fell on ICI's petrol stores while others caused damage to the works' sodium plant, the cooperage plant and a timber yard, as well as to civilian properties in Billingham. A little further east, seven bombs fell in a line from the north bank of the Tees to the Middlesbrough Town Hall and although the platform of the Transporter Bridge was struck, as were industrial properties on the south side of the river, the damage was small-scale.

Siegfried Gessert and his crew had crossed the North Sea at 19,000 feet and were descending to 10,000 feet when they were coned by searchlights in the target area. Shortly after that, they later told interrogators, they were attacked from below and behind by the night fighter.

If Gessert and his crew were correct with regard to the night fighter, it is possible that the Heinkel's attacker was a Blenheim Mk1F of 219 Squadron, Catterick, the only unit in the area with twin-engined fighters on that date. The squadron had three aircraft on patrol at the time the bomber was shot down[22] and any one of them might have been responsible. However, the writer has been able to trace only one combat report submitted by 219 Squadron for that night – the report submitted by Sergeant A.C. Hodgkinson, who claimed to have made an interception at 02.40 hours.

Hodgkinson (with Sergeant Sheppard as his gunner), took off from Catterick (in Blenheim L8720) at 00.10 hours on 27 June to patrol the coast. Sometime afterwards, when the night fighter was near Saltburn and flying northwards towards a cone of searchlights over Teesside, Hodgkinson saw tracer being fired by, what he assumed was, an enemy aircraft. Approaching the raider from astern, he closed to 200 yards range

'Bomben auf England!'

'Bomben auf England!' So heißt es in dem schönen Bombenfliegerlied aus dem Luftwaffefilm *Feuertaufe*. Nun ist es soweit. Jeden Tag und jede Nachtfallen die deutschen Bomben, sie stürzen auf Flugplätze und Eisenbahnen, auf Rüstungswerke und Truppenlager. Was die Briten mit ihren sinnlosen Angriffen auf unverteidigte deutsche Städte herausgefordert, was sie an Töten und Verletzten unter der deutschen Zivilbevölkerung auf dem Gewissen haben, das bekommen sie jetzt in eigenen Lande zu spüren. Mit dem Unterscheid allerdings, daß die deutsche Luftwaffe sich streng an die Befehl ihres Führers und Obersten Befehlshabers hält, nur militärische Ziele anzugreifen und das Leben der Zivilbevölkerung zu schonen. Die Zeichnung von Richard Heß schildert den Angriff deutscher Kampfflugzeuge auf das Stickstoffwerk Billingham.

The Imperial Chemical Industries' plant at Billingham (Teesside), was important enough to attract the attention of the Luftwaffe on eleven occasions in the period June 1940 – July 1942. However, the 106 high-explosives that fell on the site caused relatively minor damage. The above artist's impression of one of the raids was drawn by German war artist Richard Heß and appeared in the Luftwaffe magazine *Der Adler* in the summer of 1940. The caption that accompanies the picture reads as follows:

'Bombs on England!'

'Bombs on England!' So it says in the fine bomber crew song from the Luftwaffe film *Baptism of Fire*. Now is the time. Every day and every night the German bombs fall; they fall on airfields and railways, on armaments factories and military camps. What the British have provoked with their senseless attacks on undefended German towns, and for which they have on their conscience the dead and injured among the German civil population, they must now experience in their own country. With the difference that the German Air Force, under strict orders from their Führer and Commander in Chief, bombs only military targets and spares the lives of the civil population. The drawing by Richard Heß shows the attack by German bomber aircraft on the nitrogen plant at Billingham.

and Sheppard managed to squeeze off one burst of some 300 rounds before losing sight of his quarry.

On his return to Catterick, Hodgkinson made no claim in respect of the encounter but if he was Gessert's attacker his bullets scored hits in the raider's fuselage, cockpit and wings, and also damaged the Heinkel's radiators. Both engines subsequently seized up because of the latter and Gessert was forced to ditch in the sea twenty-one miles east of the Tees, his fiery descent being noted by shore-based observers. The bomber sank within three minutes but that was long enough for the crew, two of whom were wounded, to take to their rubber dinghy. After three hours adrift, they were picked up by an Admiralty drifter and subsequently landed at Newcastle.

Much of the Germans' account of the interception, elicited during interrogation by Air Ministry Intelligence, matches that of Hodgkinson's combat report. The only major point of difference is the time of the occurrence. The Germans stated that they had ditched at about 01.00 hours; Hodgkinson claimed that he carried out his attack at 02.40 hours. If these times are correct, then Hodgkinson is clearly removed from the equation. However, there is a slight complication. 219 Squadron's Operation Record Book (ORB) shows that Hodgkinson landed back at Catterick at 02.15 hours – i.e. twenty-five minutes before the stated time of his interception. If the ORB is correct, the time in Hodgkinson's report must be wrong – which leaves open the possibility that he was the victor.

The assertion in *Blitz, then and now. Vol. 1* that AJ+1K was shot down off Blyth gives rise to speculation that the loss of the Heinkel may have been confused with another incident. Certainly, a German aircraft was claimed in the Blyth area that night but the British pilot responsible for it was under the impression that his victim was a Ju88.

A number of plots appeared off the Northumberland coast on the night of 26-27 June 1940, some of these being He 115 floatplanes which are thought to have placed mines off Blyth and Amble. At 23.57 hours, three Spitfires of 72 Squadron, Acklington, took off to investigate. One hour later, Flying Officer R.A. Thomson (in Spitfire L1078) was on Red patrol line when he saw a very definite cone of searchlight beams in the direction of Newcastle and at just about the time that Sergeant Nielson, at Hirst police station (Ashington), saw an enemy aircraft caught by searchlight beams over the town.

Thomson went to investigate. When he arrived in the Blyth area, no target was visible when the fighter was level with the apex of the cone, but when Thomson reduced altitude by 1,000 feet he was able to see an aircraft clearly illuminated. When he first saw it, the enemy machine was turning from a southerly course to an easterly one and making no effort to evade the searchlights. Thomson identified the raider as a Ju88 and made his approach from astern and below.

At 00.45 hours on 27 June 1940, Thomson delivered his attack at a height of 7,000 feet, when both aircraft were two miles east of Beacon Point, just north of Newbiggin, and just after he had finally positioned himself fifty yards astern and twenty feet below his target. He opened up with two bursts of machine-gun fire, each of some four seconds duration. PC Bruce of Lynemouth police saw the tracers discharged as the aircraft flew between Lynemouth and Newbiggin. After the first burst, Thomson saw smoke issuing from both engines of the Junkers; during the second burst, a blinding white flash occurred and the enemy machine appeared to explode, and it was thought that the fighter's bullets might have struck the German's bomb load. A large number of fragments were clearly visible as they flew off in various directions, some of the pieces striking the Spitfire as Thomson broke away downwards to the left. He did not see his victim again but others witnessed its demise.

The Squadron Operations Record Book points out that the whole combat – and the explosion – was clearly seen from Acklington aerodrome and that observers had no doubt that the aircraft had been destroyed. Thomson was thus credited with the destruction of the bomber, one of the few night victories won by a Spitfire at that stage of the war. The raider is believed to have crashed into the sea some three miles east of Cambois but a subsequent search by a Blyth-based motor launch revealed nothing. Unfortunately, examination of the Luftwaffe's Loss Returns for this date also reveals no information relating to the loss of a Ju88.

Of course, a possible explanation might well be that Gessert's aircraft was not attacked by a twin-engine fighter but was, in fact, damaged by Thomson in his Spitfire. Certainly, the times of the incidents related by Gessert and Thomson are broadly similar – and there is always the possibility that the German was not where he thought he was, but was, in fact, some forty miles north of his target area. If that was the case, the damaged Heinkel might well have staggered on to a point east of the Tees before ditching.

1 July 1940 (east of Hartlepool)

Aircraft:	Heinkel 59C-2	D-ASAM	w/nr.?	Seenotflug.Kdo.3
Crew:	Uffz. Ernst Otto Ielsen	pilot	pow	
	Lt. Hans-Joachim Fehske	observer	pow	
	Obgfr. Erich Philipp	wireless op	pow	
	Uffz. ? Stuckmann	mechanic	pow	

The Luftwaffe's air-sea rescue service was equipped with Heinkel He 59 floatplanes and Dornier Do18 flying boats and these often operated in British waters when searching for downed Luftwaffe crews. Although these rescue aircraft flew under the protection of the Red Cross, they were believed to be armed and were occasionally seen in the locality of British convoys. The British Government maintained that, in addition to rescuing downed flyers, such aircraft were reporting shipping movements and were thus involved in activities inconsistent with privileges normally accorded to the Red Cross. Thus the Germans were warned that such aircraft were liable to be attacked if they were found in our areas where operations were in progress, either on land or sea, or if they were found approaching British territory, territory in British occupation, or British or Allied shipping.

At 03.00 hours on 1 July 1940, Heinkel He 59C-2 floatplane D-ASAM took off from Nordeney to search for the crew of a Heinkel 115 of *Küstenfliegergruppe* 3/106 (Ku.Fl.Gr.3./106) which had been lost off the Yorkshire coast while on a minelaying operation. The air-sea rescue aircraft was off the Durham coast and in the vicinity of a convoy when it was intercepted and shot down by three Spitfires of 72 Squadron, Acklington.

When an unidentified aircraft was detected flying in the vicinity of the

An He 59 floatplane of the German Air-Sea Rescue Service (Deutscher Seenotrettungsdienst). It was an aircraft of this type that was shot down off Hartlepool by Spitfires of 72 Squadron, Acklington, on 1 July 1940. [via Ernst Adolf Schneider]

river Wear at an altitude of 6,000 feet at about 06.00 hours on 1 July 1940, Flight Lieutenant Edward Graham, Flying Officer Edgar Wilcox and Flight Sergeant Harry Steere of 72 Squadron were ordered off to investigate. A few minutes later, at 06.12 hours, Graham sighted a white twin-engined biplane eight miles east of Sunderland and flying south-east at about 500 feet. The speed of the enemy aircraft was estimated at about 130mph and it was soon overtaken.

Graham circled the biplane three times and noted the large red crosses on the upper surface of the top wing and a black swastika on a red background on the tail. He then led his section in a No.1 attack and opened fire with a four-second burst of machine-gun fire at 200 yards, closing to thirty yards. As he broke away, faint greyish smoke or vapour was observed coming from the Heinkel's fuselage. Wilcox followed with another four-second burst from 200 yards. The Heinkel was already losing height when Steere attacked with a simple deflection shot lasting six seconds. Seconds later, his target landed on the water about four miles east of Hartlepool. During the entire engagement, the Red Cross insignia on the Heinkel was clearly visible, there was no return fire experienced by the fighter pilots and the Heinkel took no evasive action.

While Wilcox and Steere circled over the biplane, which was slowly sinking tail first, and watched the four members of its crew clamber into their rubber dinghy, Graham flew to the warship that was leading the convoy and directed the vessel to the spot. The Germans, who later protested most strongly about the violation of the Red Cross, were then rescued by a boat launched by the warship, which turned out to be the destroyer HMS *Black Swan*.[23] By then the Heinkel was in a nose-up vertical position and submerged as far as the trailing edge of the wings. It was subsequently beached and examined for armament but the results of that investigation are not known to the writer.

EYEWITNESS

Daylight attack on the Tyne
2 July 1940

Luftwaffe pilot Hajo Herrmann dropped three bombs over the Tyne in broad daylight at 17.36 hours on 2 July 1940. One fell on Spiller's old flour mill close by Newcastle's High Level Bridge and gave rise to the belief that the bridge was the target of the attack; a view which has persisted to the present day. However, the pilot's autobiography *Eagle's Wings*[24] sets the record straight.

In the summer of 1940, twenty-seven year-old Hajo Herrmann was *Staffelkapitän* of 7./KG4, a Junkers 88 bomber unit based at Schiphol

(Amsterdam). On 2 July, he was ordered to lead a flight of three aircraft to attack the Vickers-Armstrong Elswick works located on the north bank of the Tyne at Newcastle, up-river from the High Level Bridge.

A night attack was the safer option, but because the moon was on the wane, and the sighting of the target was thus less certain, Herrmann decided to attack during daylight with the help of the cloud cover that was forecast. The operation was launched from Bad Zwischenahn, in Schleswig-Holstein.

As the raiders approached the north-east coast, they found the cloud cover as predicted and they were able to take advantage of it in order to escape from two British fighters which attempted to intercept the trio as they crossed in. The Luftwaffe crews lost sight of each other at that point, although they did keep in radio contact.

Herrmann recalls that when he emerged from the cloud layer he was over the Tyne – and the balloon cordon:

> I came out through the cloud ceiling at 1,800 metres (5,850 feet). Fat, horrible, monstrous balloons swept past below me... I flew up the Tyne, past the target area. Despite the balloons, rapid-firing flak got me in its sights. I flew switchback along the lower surface of the cloud – in and out. From below, the gunners could see me only fleetingly.

Herrmann realized that with a cloud base of some 6,000 feet and the presence of anti-aircraft guns along the river bank, the Ju88s would not be able to safely stay in clear air for any length of time when each launched its attack. Thus he radioed his comrades to keep above the cloud and away from the target area while he orbited Hadrian's Wall to the west of Newcastle and planned a suitable strategy. He finally decided to use the protection of the cloud to carry out a timed bombing run to the target, which meant that for much of the run-in he would be unable to see the ground and would thus be without a visual check regarding the accuracy of his approach. It was a strategy calling for great skill and perhaps a little luck. He altered his bomb settings accordingly and

Hajo Herrmann wearing the insignia of the rank of Oberst (Group Captain). [Author's collection]

Ju88s of the type that attacked the Tyne on 2 July 1940.

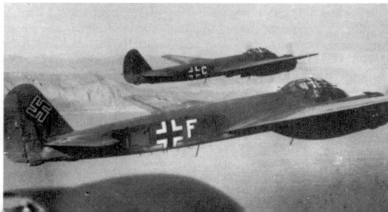

radioed his intentions to his comrades.

He then retraced his route along the river, holding rigidly to his course as he flew from west to east. He flew in cloud, emerging only briefly to locate his objective and to start his stopwatch to measure the flying time from the point at which he would begin his bomb run to the point at which he would release his bombs.

His plan was clear enough. He would approach his target in cloud, having set his stopwatch at the start of his bomb run. When his watch registered the precise moment that he was just short of the Elswick Works he would dip down into clear air for just long enough to sight his target, make minor corrections and release his bombs. Then he would pull up into cloud once again before the ground-based defenders could train their sights on him. His strategy decided, he turned once more on to a westerly heading and commenced his attack.

> The final seconds ticked by. Then – down! The last scraps of cloud flitted past me. There was the Tyne, there was the target… and there were the same plump, odious monsters again – the balloons. Then the flak tracers whizzed past us and disappeared into the clouds. I took hold of my crate. 'Come on, observer, finger out! Finger out! Drop the bloody things! Now, now – it doesn't matter whether you hit the near end or the far end!' He had a long fuse and he stayed calm. His eye was glued to the eye-piece. He didn't have the slightest idea what was going on to the left, to the right, or all around the area.
>
> At last, the bombs were dropped. I hauled the aircraft mercilessly into a climbing turn… Thank God for the clouds! I was enveloped in them. The heavy anti-aircraft fired a few rounds of deterrent flak. As if from nowhere, black wads of cotton wool appeared suddenly… Then, with full throttle, I pulled away, homeward bound.

Military personnel manning the anti-aircraft defences plotted Herrmann's three bombs: one fell in the Tyne, just west of the High Level Bridge; another struck Spiller's old mill on the quayside to the west of the bridge, setting it on fire and the third landed in a nearby yard. Thus Herrmann did not hit his target but, given that defenders reported that the bombs were dropped from 6,000 feet by a raider which was in view 'for only six seconds…', he was not far short. It is believed that two persons were killed in the attack and several injured by flying glass.

Then it was the turn of his comrades. There is some confusion regarding the subsequent actions of Herrmann's companions, although one of them – *Leutnant* Weinrich – decided that he was going to bomb Edinburgh instead! Precisely what the third crew bombed can only be guessed, but the fact that only three bombs fell in the area of Spiller's mill suggests that they did not follow Herrmann's example.

It is possible that they sought an alternative nearer the coast, where more serious casualties were inflicted shortly after Herrmann's effort further up river. At 18.15 hours an enemy aircraft aimed four high explosives at large oil tanks at Jarrow, but the bombs missed and exploded in a working-class district some 300 yards west of their intended target. The final casualty list registered thirteen killed and 123 injured, and many families were rendered homeless.

It is not known for certain whether the aircraft responsible was one of the Ju88s led by Hajo Herrmann. However, Military Intelligence in Newcastle suggested that one of those aircraft had retired out to sea, '...gained height, turned and glided from a bearing of about 70° from Jarrow in a direct line for the oil tanks, which were undoubtedly the target, (but) the bombs were released too late'. They fell some forty yards apart and in a straight line, and wrought destruction which was not intended.

The raid took place at a time when Hitler was hoping to avoid war with Britain. Thus, any actions resulting in civilian casualties were strictly forbidden. When the three crews returned to Bad Zwischenahn they were interrogated by a Provost Marshal, who informed them that information from Hitler's Headquarters indicated that 'German aircraft had carried out a terror raid on the civilian population of Newcastle at about 5.00pm that day' and that the Provost Marshal had been instructed to find out who was responsible.

The result of the enquiry is not known to the current writer, but the fact that Herrmann went on to reach the rank of *Oberst* (Group Captain) suggests that he, at least, suffered no lasting consequences.

Based on *Eagle's Wings* by Hajo Herrmann.

Spiller's flour mill (foreground) after Herrmann's attack on 2 July 1940.
[Courtesy of Newcastle Chronicle & Journal]

13 July 1940

A short report in the Middlesbrough *Evening Gazette* (24 May 1945) states that on 13 July 1940 a light anti-aircraft Bofors gun crew of the 30th Anti-Aircraft Brigade engaged a Ju88 and caused it to crash into the sea off Sunderland. The current writer has found no further details to date.

Fw 200 Condor F8+EH of 1./KG40, which was shot down off Crimdon Dene, north of Hartlepool, on the night of 19-20 July 1940.

19-20 July 1940 (east of Crimdon)

Aircraft:	Focke-Wulf 200C	F8+EH	w/nr. ?	1./KG40
Crew:	Fw. Herbert Külken	pilot	pow	
	Hptm. Roman Stessyn	observer	missing	
	Fw. Karl Nicolai	wireless op	pow	
	Fw. Willi Meyer	mechanic	+	
	Gefr. Silverius Zraúnig	gunner	missing	

This Fw 200 Condor was one of several that started out from Marx on the night of 19 July 1940 on mining operations that were intended to extend as far as the Firth of Forth. F8+EH ventured too close to the Durham coastline and was coned by searchlights. Despite vigorous attempts to evade, the four-engined aircraft was shot down by anti-aircraft fire and crashed into the North Sea off Crimdon Dene, north of

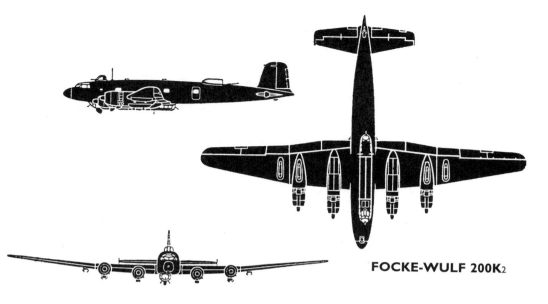

FOCKE-WULF 200K₂

Hartlepool, at 23.55 hours. Meyer's body was subsequently washed ashore on the Yorkshire coast and was buried at Driffield. It was later transferred to the German War Cemetery at Cannock.

7 August 1940 (off Farne Islands)
Pieces of aircraft wreckage were caught in the nets of a trawler fishing off the Farne Islands on 7 August 1940. Small pieces of fuselage and of the nose section suggested that the aircraft was probably an He115.

9 August 1940 (east of Whitburn)

Aircraft:	Heinkel 111H-3	1H+ER	w/nr. ?	7./KG26
Crew:	Uffz. Otto Denner	pilot	pow	
	Fw. Willi Haertel	observer	pow	
	Uffz. Fritz Feinekat	wireless op	pow	
	Uffz. Gustav Karkos	mechanic	pow	

On 9 August 1940, KG26 sent a number of He111s against convoys off the north-east coast but they failed to find them. The raiders therefore dropped bombs on ports in Yorkshire and further north. Three Hurricane fighters of Yellow Section, 79 Squadron, Acklington caught one over the Sunderland area.

The fighters, flown by Flight Lieutenant R.F.H. Clerke, Sergeant J. Wright and Pilot Officer G.H. Nelson-Edwards, had been scrambled in mid-morning, with orders to patrol their base but they were later vectored south. At 11.35 hours, when they were at an altitude of 12,000 feet – and some 5,000 feet above the ten-tenths cloud ceiling – in the area of Newcastle, Nelson-Edwards saw the He111 eight miles to the south, flying in a southerly direction and 2,000 feet below the trio. The bomber appeared to be travelling very slowly and did not appear to see the fighters until just before they attacked.

The Hurricanes each made two assaults on the bomber, the first being launched by Clerke, five minutes after Nelson-Edwards had sighted their quarry. Clerke led his section in a No.1 Attack and encountered heavy, though seemingly ineffective, return fire from the Heinkel's top turret as he himself opened with an eight-second burst of machine-gun fire from 300 yards. Sergeant Wright, as Yellow 2, followed his leader with a four-second burst that caused white smoke to begin streaming from both of the raider's engines as the German began gliding towards the cloud below. Nelson-Edwards was close on the heels of Wright and commenced his attack from 300 yards with a burst of fire lasting six seconds. As the fighter's shells struck home, the Heinkel jettisoned bombs and dropped

In July 2000, Major Alistair McCluskey, RAMC, a keen sub-aqua diver whose parents had witnessed the demise of He111 1H+ER off Whitburn on 9 August 1940, organized an Army expedition to locate the remains of the wreck. The expedition had only limited success and resulted in the recovery of only small finds. However, the team hoped to continue their quest in 2001. The picture shows Major McCluskey with, what is thought to be, pieces of aluminium from the bomber.
[Northeast Press Ltd, Sunderland Echo]

its undercarriage before turning away as it continued its downward path. Clerke, Wright and Nelson-Edwards each managed one more attack of six, two and eight seconds respectively before their victim, now with smoke belching from its engines and fuselage, finally disappeared in the cloud.

Numerous eyewitnesses clapped and cheered when, shortly after machine-gun fire had been heard above the clouds, the bomber was seen emerging into clear air with smoke pouring from its tail. The pilot ditched off Whitburn, close enough to the shore for spectators to watch as the crew climbed on to the wings and shook hands with each other before climbing into their rubber dinghy. Their aircraft sank shortly afterwards. Although Karkos and Feinekat were wounded in the incident, the German crew survived the encounter and were picked up by a Royal Navy patrol vessel within forty-five minutes. They were landed at Sunderland's Corporation Quay, where they were met by an armed guard from the 2/4 Essex Regiment. Karkos and Feinekat were taken to the Royal Infirmary; the others were taken to the Dykelands Road drill hall in Seaburn, before being removed to an interrogation centre.[25]

Rupert Clerke, John Wright and George Nelson-Edwards each claimed one-third of the victory.

In July 2000, a team of Army divers led by Major Alistair McCluskey, RAMC, believed that they had uncovered traces of the wreck when they found some pieces of aluminium alloy in the area where the aircraft was believed to have sunk.

15 August 1940 (off Northumberland-Durham coast)

Aircraft:	Heinkel 111H-4	1H+GH	w/nr. ?	1/KG26 see p59
Crew:	Uffz. Willi Zimmerman	pilot	pow	
	Oblt. Rudolf Roch	observer	pow	
	Gefr. Erwin Kulick	wireless op	pow	
	Gefr. Alwin Machalett	mechanic	pow	
	Flgr. Ernst Henrichsen	rear gunner	pow	

Aircraft:	Heinkel 111H-4	1H+ ?S	w/nr. ?	8./KG26
Crew:	Oblt. Hans von Lüpke	pilot	+	
	Obfw. Karl Hennicke	observer	+	
	Uffz. Max Knauer	wireless op	missing	
	Uffz. Karl Schlick	mechanic	+	

Aircraft:	Heinkel 111H-4	1H+?S	w/nr. ?	8./KG26
Crew:	Oblt. Horst von Besser	pilot	missing	
	Uffz. Franz Brehm	observer	missing	
	Uffz. Alfons Rehm	wireless op	missing	
	Uffz. Eberhard Hofmann	mechanic	missing	
	Uffz. Franz Reichelt	gunner	missing	

Aircraft:	Heinkel 111H-4	1H+?S	w/nr. ?	8./KG26
Crew:	Uffz. Heinz Puschstein	pilot	missing	
	Lt. Wolfgang Burck	observer	missing	
	Uffz. Hans-Karl Klug	wireless op	missing	
	Uffz. Hans Hofmann	mechanic	missing	
	Uffz. Karl Lotz	gunner	missing	

Aircraft:	Heinkel 111H-4	1H+?S	w/nr. ?	8./KG26
Crew:	Fw. Fritz Baldauf	pilot	pow	
	Uffz. Adolf Renner	observer	pow	
	Obgfr. Wilhelm Rössinger	wireless op	pow	
	Gefr. Walter Lorenz	mechanic	pow	
	Uffz. Christoph Schumann	gunner	pow	

Others: Heinkel 111H-4 of 8./KG26. Failed to return. No other details known.

Heinkel 111H-4 (pilot Uffz. Peter Möltgen) of 9./KG26 crashed in sea 100 kms off the German coast. All crew killed.

Heinkel 111H-4 (pilot Oblt. Hermann Riedel) of 8./KG26 crashed in North Sea on return flight. One member of the crew killed; the rest rescued by Danish fishing boat.

Aircraft:	Messerschmitt Bf.110D	M8+?B	w/nr. ?	Stab.I/ZG76
Crew:	Hptm. Werner Restemeyer	pilot	killed	
	Uffz. Werner Eichert	wireless op	killed	

Aircraft:	Messerschmitt Bf.110D	M8+?B	w/nr. ?	Stab.I/ZG76
Crew:	Oblt. Gustav Loobes	pilot	killed	
	Uffz. Xaver Brock	wireless op	killed	

Aircraft:	Messerschmitt Bf.110D	M8+CH	w/nr. 3155	1./ZG76 see p60
Crew:	Oblt. Hans Ulrich Kettling	pilot	pow	
	Obgfr. Fritz Volk	wireless op	pow	

Aircraft:	Messerschmitt Bf.110D	M8+?K	w/nr. ?	2./ZG76
Crew:	Fw. Klaus Ladwein	pilot	pow	
	Obgfr. Karl Lenk	wireless op	fate unknown	

Others: Two further Bf110D aircraft of 2./ZG76 failed to return.
Two further Bf110D aircraft of 3./ZG76 failed to return, one of these being piloted by Lt. Heinrich Kohler.
Two other Bf110D aircraft of 3./ZG76 returned to base with wounded on board.

The Battle of Britain was at its height in August 1940. On Thursday, 15 August, believing that available RAF fighter squadrons were heavily committed in the south, the Luftwaffe launched a two-pronged, daylight attack from bases in Denmark and Norway against aerodromes and industrial targets in northern England. Fifty Ju88s of KG30 were briefed to attack Driffield aerodrome, East Yorkshire (see *Broken Eagles[Yorkshire]*).[26] At the same time, sixty-three Heinkel 111s of KG26 (based at Stavanger, Norway) had the aerodromes at Dishforth and Linton-on-Ouse as their primary targets, with Newcastle, Sunderland and Middlesbrough as alternatives. The Heinkels were escorted by twenty-one Messerschmitt Bf110D twin-engined fighters of I./ZG76.

The bombers and their escorts were detected by radar as they approached the north-east coast shortly after midday. Due to a serious error of navigation, they were some seventy miles north of their intended route, which should have ensured landfall somewhere over the coast of County Durham. When the error was realized, the raiders swung south in search of their targets but by then they were already under attack from seasoned fighter squadrons 'resting' in the north.

Acklington-based Spitfires of 72 Squadron made the first contact, east of the Farne Islands, but as the raiders moved south, over and along the Northumberland and County Durham coast, other fighters joined in. Hurricanes from 79 Squadron, Acklington, 605 Squadron, Drem and 607 Squadron, Usworth, as well as Spitfires from 41 Squadron, Catterick, all exacted their toll, while the anti-aircraft guns around the Tyne, the Wear, and (less often) the Tees made their own contribution whenever raiders were sighted.

The Luftwaffe's attack was a failure. The raiders never expected such a strong airborne defence and the repeated efforts of the fighters had the effect of splitting the enemy formation into a number of smaller units. Most of the Heinkels failed to find their intended targets – though some bombs were dropped (and casualties caused) in the Newcastle and Seaham areas – and most jettisoned their bombs over the coast or the coastal strip of east Durham.

All of the fighter squadrons made claims, as did the guns. According to 13 Group Fighter Command Operations Record Book for 15 August 1940, participating fighter pilots made claims amounting to thirty-one enemy machines 'destroyed', twenty-two 'probably destroyed' and fourteen 'damaged'. In addition, the Tyne guns claimed a further five, and the Tees guns one more. That makes seventy-three enemy aircraft 'destroyed' – almost the entire attacking force!

Although the claims were no doubt made in good faith, they could not be checked conclusively at the time for most actions took place over the sea, the crash site of most of the aircraft shot down.   Later evidence was to show that the claims had been greatly overstated when placed alongside the Luftwaffe's recorded losses of eight He111s and eight Me110s. Even so, the actual losses incurred showed that the Luftwaffe had suffered a major setback over Northumberland and County Durham.

A number of fighter pilots damaged raiders, which then broke away streaming smoke and diving into the cloud layers below the battle zone. The defending fighters were not always able to follow, because of the battle that was raging, and thus a 'damaged' enemy must sometimes have been claimed as 'destroyed'. On the basis of claims made by Spitfire and Hurricane pilots who saw their victims crash, the following does, perhaps, offer a more realistic picture – although, even then, the losses do not exactly match the claims that were made.

72 Squadron, Acklington: Flying Officer Desmond Sheen attacked an Me110, which exploded in mid-air; Pilot Officer Douglas Winter – a native of South Shields – and Flying Officer Oswald Pigg both attacked Me110s and saw them crash into the sea, and Pilot Officer C.H. Robson attacked an He111 and saw it crash into the sea.

79 Squadron, Acklington: Flight Lieutenant Hayson shot down an Me110, which crashed into the sea five miles off Blyth; Pilot Officer Douglas Clift shot down an Me110 some twenty miles east of Coquet Island.

41 Squadron, Catterick: Pilot Officer George Bennions shot down an Me110, which crashed at Barnard Castle; Pilot Officer Eric Lock shot down an Me110, which crashed into the harbour at Seaham; Flying Officer Tony Lovell saw 'his' Me110 disintegrate following his own attack, while Sergeant Frank Usmar had a similar experience when he destroyed an He111.

A bomb-laden He 111 (1H+GH) of 1./KG26 at Trondheim-Vaernes in 1940. This aircraft ditched in Druridge Bay, Northumberland, on 15 August 1940. Its mechanic, Uffz. Alwin Machalett, is on the left. On the right is Uffz. Erich Schmidt, who was captured after his He111 (1H+AH) was shot down over southern England on 11 September, 1940. [via Frau Stefanie Machalett]

607 Squadron, Usworth: Flight Lieutenant W.F. Blackadder shot down an He111, which crashed into the sea near Seaham Harbour; Pilot Officer Welford sent another He111 into the sea some twenty-five miles off Sunderland; Sergeant Burnell-Phillips sent an He111 diving into the sea with both engines burning and then joined Sergeant Cunnington to force an He111 into the sea one mile off Seaham Harbour; Flying Officer Bowen sent another He111 into the sea some ten miles off Saltburn.

605 Squadron, Drem: Pilot Officer 'Bunny' Currant sent an He111 crashing into the sea some eight miles north-east of Newcastle; and Pilot Officer I.J. Muirhead had a part share in the destruction of the He111 he saw ditch in Druridge Bay.

15 August 1940 (Druridge Bay)

Aircraft:	Heinkel 111H-4	1H+GH	w/nr. ?	1./KG26
Crew:	Uffz. Willi Zimmerman	pilot	pow	
	Oblt. Rudolf Roch	observer	pow	
	Gefr. Erwin Kulick	wireless op	pow	
	Gefr. Alwin Machalett	mechanic	pow	
	Flgr. Ernst Henrichsen	rear gunner	pow	

This aircraft is believed to have been shot down by three Hurricanes of Green Section, 605 Squadron, Drem, which were airborne at 12.05 hours and were patrolling the Acklington – Tyneside area at 10,000 feet – 12,000 feet with the squadron's Blue Section.

At 13.12 hours they saw two formations of enemy aircraft approaching Tyneside from the south-east at 12,000 feet, the first formation consisting of some sixty to seventy machines and the second made up of twenty to twenty-five aircraft. While Blue Section climbed into the sun to prepare to attack the larger group, Pilot Officer Christopher 'Bunny' Currant (Green 1) ordered his section into 'Line Astern' before climbing above and behind the second group, consisting of Heinkel 111s. When the fighters were in position behind their targets and some 3,000 feet above them, Currant gave the order 'Echelon Port' and the trio launched their attack. Currant opened fire with a three-second burst on a Heinkel at 200 yards range, putting its starboard engine out of action and forcing the bomber to break formation before Currant broke away to attack another enemy machine. Flying Officer Cyril Passey (Green 2) and Flying Officer James Muirhead (Green 3) then took up the assault on their leader's first victim. By then they were flying a north-westerly course towards Blyth. Passey managed one burst of two seconds from 200 yards closing to fifty yards before breaking away and then it was Muirhead's turn. The Heinkel was climbing with its starboard motor feathered as Green 3 closed in. One short burst aimed at the bomber's port engine was enough to send the bomber spiralling down through clouds to the sea. Muirhead stayed around long enough to watch it ditch

He 111s of 1./KG26, with a side view of 1H+DH. [via Frau Stefanie Machalett]

and to see five of its crew clamber into a dinghy before shortage of fuel forced him to land at Acklington.

Three of the Heinkel's crew had lucky escapes in the encounter. Ernst Henrichsen was caught on his head by a grazing shot that produced more blood than damage. Erwin Kulick had similar luck when a bullet clipped his ear lobe and Alwin Machalett suffered a severe wound to his left leg, which took some six months to heal properly. The five were subsequently rescued by the Fisheries Patrol boat *David Askew* and landed at Amble. Machalett was treated at Newcastle General Hospital, where he stayed for ten days before being moved to a POW camp at Oldham. He was later transferred to Canada, where he spent the remaining years of the war.

15 August 1940 (Streatlam, Barnard Castle)

Aircraft:	Messerschmitt Bf110D	M8+CH	w/nr. 3155	1./ZG76
Crew:	Oblt. Hans-Ulrich Kettling	pilot	pow	
	Obgfr. Fritz Volk	wireless op	pow	

This aircraft was shot down by Pilot Officer George Bennions in a Spitfire of 41 Squadron, Catterick, and crash-landed at Streatlam, near Barnard Castle at 13.36 hours.

As the Luftwaffe's biggest daylight raid on the north of England progressed down the north-east coast, all thirteen Spitfires of 41 Squadron took off from Catterick at 12.40 hours under the leadership of Flight Lieutenant Norman Ryder. However, over Hartlepool it fell to Pilot Officer George Bennions to take over that role when it was realized that Ryder's radio was unserviceable. The raiders were in the area of Seaham Harbour when they were caught by the Spitfires and Bennions dispatched six of his machines to engage the Messerschmitt 110s while he led the remaining seven against the bombers. Following his initial foray, Bennions turned astern of the Heinkels with an Me110 on his tail. Jinking first to port and then to starboard, he escaped his pursuer and found himself 300 yards astern of another Me110. He fired and saw his shells striking home. The twin-engined fighter immediately dived for the clouds with Bennions in hot pursuit: he managed one final burst before his quarry disappeared.

When Bennions emerged from the cloud he was over Barnard Castle; the Messerschmitt had crash-landed nearby. Kettling later stated that his starboard engine had been knocked out (perhaps by Pilot Officer Ted Shipman of 41 Squadron) in an initial foray with fighters and that a second encounter with fighters had stopped his port motor. With both engines dead, the German crash-landed alongside Streatlam Camp, close to Bromielaw station, some three miles from Barnard Castle.

15 August 1940. Hans Kettling's Me110 (M8+CH) at Streatlam, near Barnard Castle. [Author's collection]

61

Shot down over Druridge Bay:
A KG26 air gunner remembers

[In the weeks prior to 15 August 1940 1./KG26 was located at Kristiansand, Norway.]

At the end of July – beginning of August, training flights were intensified. We practised flying in sections of three and in formations. We especially practised flying in a close and tight 'wedge' of all nine machines of the Staffel; we flew almost on top of one another. The idea of this was that during enemy attacks from behind the Staffel could provide stronger defensive fire-power from twenty-seven machine guns firing to the rear. In each aircraft the guns were manned by the wireless operator, the mechanic and third gunner. In addition, our aircraft were fitted with armour plate to protect us from attack from behind. In my opinion, this saved the lives of our crew when we were shot down on 15 August.

At the beginning of August we should also have carried out a night attack against the English coast. We started out at dusk and flew out over the North Sea. The flight was cancelled after about an hour and we were ordered back to Kristiansand.

Then preparations were made to make a daylight attack on northern England. The Geschwader was to fly in close formation towards Newcastle and, if possible, to land at an aerodrome in Germany after the return flight. A similar attack was to be carried out the other way round the day after the first attack.

On 15 August we took off from Kristiansand and flew in formation towards England. When we were over the North Sea and off Stavanger we met up with the rest of the Gruppe that had started from Stavanger. We then all flew in close formation towards the English coast. After some time, we met the Me110s that were to accompany us and provide fighter escort.

In the aircraft I sat a little behind the pilot and the observer and on the edge of the bomb-bays. As we got near to the English coast I went along the aisle between the bomb-bays and into the 'tank' under the fuselage, where the mechanic manned the machine-gun against attacks from the rear. To the left of me Henrichsen stood at a side machine-gun. From the 'tank' I no longer had a view of the direction in which we were flying but I did see how an Me 110 was attacked by an English fighter. In order to be more manoeuverable the Me. jettisoned its auxiliary fuel tank.[27] 'From the 'tank' I noticed that at sometime we had changed course. We were over the mainland and before us was a large factory with water behind it: we were flying towards the North Sea again. Our observer, Oblt. Roch, aimed at the installation and let the bombs go. 'Direct hit!' I reported from my 'tank' when I saw bombs hit the middle of the factory. As I photographed the strikes with the camera, Erwin Kulick, our wireless operator shouted, 'Look out! Fighter from behind!'

I saw the fighter attacking and as I fired several bursts at him I saw the flashes from his eight machine guns. As he fired, the English fighter moved his wings lightly, as if trying to catch us in a spread of gunfire. I thought then that my one machine gun was quite inferior to the eight guns of the attacker and, because the fighter came at us from exactly behind, Flieger Henrichsen, who was manning the left side gun, could not take part in our defence. It did not occur to me at the time that we were not alone and that other squadron aircraft and machine guns were probably also 'dishing it out' to the fighter.

In order that the gunner in the 'tank' could see attackers coming in from behind, there was no armour plate to the left, near my head. A bullet sliced through the 'tank' wall and I felt a dull blow to my left leg. When the fighter broke away, I raised myself and looked around. On my left, stood Henrichsen, his face streaming with blood. It looked terrible but it was in fact a grazing shot along the hairline. Our wireless operator, Kulick, was also injured when a bullet caught his ear lobe. I attempted to make a rough and ready bandage for Henrichsen.

The intercom was out of order but through the bomb racks I saw Oblt. Roch waving me to go forward. When I reached the cockpit I saw the mess: both motors were trailing smoke and oil, one engine had already stopped and the other was stuttering. The pilot, Willi Zimmermann, gave me to understand that we had to make an emergency landing in the North Sea. He had already had practice in doing that because he had ditched in the sea once during the Norwegian campaign. There was no time for me to return to my place and fasten my seat-belt so I lay diagonally across the aisle between the bomb racks and held on firmly to the racks on both sides.

When we struck the water, I was catapulted forward into the cockpit between the pilot and the observer and all I could see was water. The heavy braking effect of the water had pushed the cockpit below the surface but gradually the aircraft righted itself and I was able to open the emergency exit above the pilot. Uffz. Zimmermann, Oblt.Roch and I climbed over the fuselage and on to the right wing, while Kulick and Henrichsen emerged from the wireless operator's cockpit and released the rubber dinghy before joining us. A few weeks earlier, we had practised dinghy drill in the fjord near our base at Kristiansand and what we learned paid off. We inflated the dinghy, climbed aboard and cut the dinghy free.

Fortunately, the North Sea had little swell. Now we could get the first proper look at our 'Gustav' from the outside. There was hardly an undamaged place: the tail unit and the fuselage were covered with bullet holes and I later came to believe that without our protective armour we would have been lucky to escape only with wounds. We could see the coast on the horizon. An English fighter plane came towards us from the sea. As he passed, the pilot waved to us and then disappeared towards the coast. He was probably the one who informed the English fishing boat that picked us up later. Our He111 lay quietly on the water for about 20 minutes and then it sank. We had no bombs on board and the fuel tanks were half empty.

A coastal fishing boat came alongside and the crew helped us to climb aboard. Then I felt an intense pain in my left leg: until then, the excitement of the emergency landing had probably repressed the feelings. I settled myself on the deck and, using English and German gibberish, I pointed at my leg. A member of the boat's crew pulled off my fur flying boot and cut open the leg of my flying overall. My knee and calf were covered with blood. I received an emergency dressing and lay on the deck.

When we put into port, police and many curious onlookers were waiting. We were led through the crowd under guard: first Oblt. Roch and Uffz. Zimmermann, followed by Erwin Kulick and Ernst Henrichsen with their bandages around their heads. I was carried behind on a stretcher. Perhaps it was the sight of Henrichsen, with blood streaming down his face, and me on a stretcher that caused the watching crowd to keep relatively quiet.

I was taken to the yard of, possibly, the police station. On several occasions, various people tried to obtain from me information about my unit and my comrades, and my friends were also questioned. One had to watch out for the concealed catch questions. However, when I stubbornly repeated only my personal details they applied no further pressure. After some time, a doctor appeared and he informed me that I was to be taken to a hospital for treatment. An ambulance took me to Newcastle General Hospital, a civilian hospital. That was probably why the Red Cross initially reported to Germany that there were only four survivors and that I was missing. That is also what my Staffelkapitän, Hptm. Künstler, reported to my parents. On 19 August 1940 my parents were given the news that I had been wounded and that I was a prisoner of war. .

In the afternoon, I was taken into the operating theatre and given a local anaesthetic. From my medical records, which accompanied me through my seven years of captivity and which were handed to me on my discharge, it is evident that a surgeon, Dr Mc Collum, carried out the operation. X-rays showed that a bullet had entered my leg below the left kneecap, had travelled through the calf and had left a large tearing wound at the point where it had exited. After the operation I was placed in a separate room. I was the only German prisoner of war in the hospital and had two soldiers standing guard at the door. After the operation, I had a

15 August 1940. Oblt. Rudolf Roch (observer) and Uffz. Willi Zimmermann (pilot) of 1./KG26 are marched through Amble, Northumberland, after their He111 (1H+GH) was shot down in Druridge Bay. [Beamish Museum Photographic Archive. Neg. 70104]

heavy fever, though that subsided over the following days. Treatment and nursing care by both doctors and nurses were excellent. Naturally, the inquisitive often came into the room, probably in order to see a German flyer. I had the impression that they were astonished to see a clean-shaven and sunburnt young man who was really no different from young English patients.

I stayed in Newcastle Hospital for ten days, then I was taken by ambulance, and under female guard, to POW Camp No.2, a former textile mill at Oldham, near Manchester. I had a plaster cast on my left leg, from the foot to the hip, and I was placed in the camp hospital which was on an upper storey of the building. It was while I was there that I experienced for the first time – from the 'other' side – a Luftwaffe air raid, mainly against Liverpool and Manchester. On such occasions, my healthier German comrades always had the pleasure of carrying me from the upper storey of the hospital area down to the air raid cellar.

After some weeks, the plaster cast was removed. The wound had healed well but it was another six months before I could move my knee free of trouble. In January 1941 we received our marching orders for Canada.

Gefr. **Alwin Machalett**
(He111 1H+GH) 1./KG26

5 September 1940 (Sunderland)

Aircraft:	Heinkel 111P		5J+JP	w/nr. 3065	6./KG4
Crew:	Oblt.Hans-Werner Schröder	pilot	+		
	Uffz. Fritz Reitz	observer	+		
	Obgfr. Rudolf Marten	wireless op	+		
	Gefr. Josef Wich	mechanic	+		

Heinkel 111P 5J+JP was shot down over Sunderland by anti-aircraft fire during an air raid on the town. It crashed on houses in Suffolk Street at 23.18 hours. Marten and Wich crashed with their aircraft but it seems that Schröder and Reitz attempted to save themselves by the use of parachutes. However, they were too near to the ground and both fell to their deaths before their parachutes could fully deploy. Their bodies were found several hundred yards away from the plane: that of Reitz on the roof of a public air raid shelter at Bede Towers in Ryhope Road, and that of Schröder in the front garden of 5 Grange Crescent. The bodies of Marten and Wich were recovered from the wreckage of their aircraft during the following morning. All four were subsequently buried with military honours in Hylton Cemetery, Castletown, Sunderland.

The Heinkel was some 7,000 feet above the town when it was coned by searchlights and although it managed to escape momentarily it was soon caught again. The illuminated bomber then became a target for anti-aircraft fire, which eventually shot away the tail unit. The raider was trailed by searchlights and gunfire as it fell to earth in flames. A Special Constable who witnessed the incident later reported that:

> The bomber was caught in a great concentration of searchlights and, no matter how it twisted and turned, could not escape. Anti-aircraft fire was terrific and suddenly I saw one shell burst right on the tail of the machine. The engine note changed abruptly, and the plane came zooming down, the searchlights following all the way, and shells still bursting round. One of the Germans had fallen on the top of a public shelter and was killed outright. The other had gone through a tree on to the lawn of a garden and was instantly killed.
>
> **(*Consett Chronicle*, 12 September 1940.)**

John and Rachel Stormont, together with their fifteen-year old daughter Jean, were in the brick air raid shelter at the back of their home at 55½ Suffolk Street when the Heinkel plummeted to earth. It crashed on to the Stormont's house and shelter and exploded in flames, trapping the family in their refuge under a blazing mound of rubble and aircraft wreckage. What happened next is recounted in Kevin Brady's book *Sunderland's Blitz*.[28]

Fire Brigade Superintendent T. Bruce was dispatched to Suffolk Street from the Hendon auxiliary fire station with two tenders, additional foam apparatus and three auxiliary fire pumps. The

Heinkel had destroyed a shop and a house and had badly damaged two other houses, and fires were burning furiously at the front and rear of the building. The Stormonts were trapped in their blazing shelter. Superintendent Bruce and Fire Sergeant Patterson were assisted by Chief Inspector Middlemist, Detective G. Cook and Detective Constables Buddles and Simpson, in removing slabs of concrete and other debris from the shelter and managed to rescue the Stormonts. During the rescue, a jet of water had to be played on to the feet of the trapped family to prevent them being burned. Rachel Stormont was found to be dead when brought from the shelter; John and Jean were both seriously injured.

Superintendent Bruce later summed up in his report: 'All the rescuers displayed exceptional courage as rescue operations were greatly hampered by the flames and heat given off by the burning petrol and in addition concentrations of petrol vapour exploding continuously. The men showed complete disregard to the fact that further bombs may have been in the fallen plane and could have exploded at any time during the operation.

Although the crash of 5J+JP caused death and destruction, it was soon realized that the situation could have been much worse because eight bombs from the Heinkel were later found in nearby streets, having failed to explode. Another did explode – in Ward Street – and severely damaged two houses and slightly injured two people. Most of the wreckage was subsequently cleared from the site, but some was too deep in the ground to be easily recovered and it was buried where it lay. It remained there

6 September 1940. Troops inspect the wreckage of He111 5J+JP of 6./KG4 that crashed at Suffolk Street, Sunderland, the night before.
[Northeast Press Ltd, Sunderland Echo]

Personnel from RAF Usworth provide a guard of honour for the crew of the He111 5J+JP of 6./KG4 when they were buried at Hylton Cemetery, Castletown, Sunderland. [Northeast Press Ltd, Sunderland Echo]

until 1986, when it was uncovered by local contractors who were preparing the site for the building of the Suffolk Street Health Centre. One of the engines and a number of other items from the excavation were donated to the North-East Air Museum, Sunderland, where they are now on display.

15-16 September 1940 (north-east of Eyemouth?)

Aircraft:	Heinkel 115C	S4+CL	w/nr.32610	Ku.Fl.Gr. 3./506
Crew:	Oblt. Clement Lucas	pilot	pow	
	Hptm. E-Wilhelm Bergmann[29]	observer	pow	
	Fw. Ernst Kalinowski	wireless op	pow	
	Hptm. Hans Kriependorf		pow	

According to the Luftwaffe Loss Returns, this aircraft was on a sortie to the Firth of Forth on the night of 15-16 September 1940 when it was engaged by naval gunfire and suffered engine breakdown. The pilot, *Oberleutnant* Clement Lucas, made a smooth forced landing on the sea, but precisely where seems to be open to conjecture. Locations of Enemy Aircraft Brought Down (File AIR22/266 in the Public Record Office) gives the location as being some seven miles north-east of Alnmouth, while the A.I.1(k) Crew Interrogation Report No.559/1940 (also

Küstenfliegerstaffel 3./506

in the Public Record Office) puts the site seven and a half miles north-east of Eyemouth. The latter report (erroneously) also gives the unit as *Küstenfliegergruppe* 3./406, an assumption made on the basis of an insignia of '...a white animal's skull with horns' painted on the aircraft.[30]

In initial interrogations, the German crew stated that they had force-landed their aircraft on the sea after the failure of both engines but further interrogations revealed that the crew had, in fact, been carrying out a torpedo attack on a convoy. Seemingly, five aircraft from the unit had started out from the Stavanger seaplane base on an anti-shipping strike and all were armed with torpedoes. Shipping in Methil Anchorage was attacked by floatplanes between 21.29 hours-21.38 hours on 15 September and S4+CL might well have been part of that operation.

The crew of the convoy escort vessel HMS *Vortigen* (I.37) saw at least two He115s that night as the ship steamed northwards at seven knots just south of the Firth of Forth in bright moonlight and good visibility. *Vortigen*, which formed part of the close escort for convoy FN79, was at position 56°03'N/2°21'W and off the coast near Dunbar when the ship's gunners saw the first Heinkel. The escort fired warning shots but the aircraft, which was 500 yards to starboard as it flew passed the convoy at 21.47 hours, made no attempt to interfere and might well have been returning from the operation to the Firth of Forth, having already used its torpedo. Thirty minutes later, the second He115 was seen flying south, seventy degrees to starboard at 2000 yards range and 200 feet altitude. Unlike its predecessor, this aircraft (very probably S4+CL) altered course towards the ships and launched a torpedo from an altitude of 120 feet.

According to *Oberleutnant* Lucas, the German pilot,[31] he had been

c. 16 September 1940. The capsized Heinkel 115c S4+CL of Ku.Fl.Gr. 3./506 beached at Eyemouth. [Author's collection]

briefed to attack an oil tanker that was believed to be approaching the Forth after sailing south from the Moray Firth under destroyer escort. Lucas sighted his target at about 23.00 hours (German Summer Time; 22.00 hours British Summer Time), but postponed his attack and circled the area for an undisclosed period of time until the tanker had rounded the Isle of May and was easing its way westwards towards harbour. Lucas then made his run when the vessel was silhouetted by the full moon to the north-west.

> In case of anti-aircraft fire, we attacked at low-level. About 500m ahead of the ship, I climbed to 50m, aimed at the middle of the ship using my night sights as well as an angle of allowance, pressed the button on the right of my control column and released the torpedo. Now I had to fly straight ahead for thirty seconds so that our slipstream would not affect the torpedo. After dropping the torpedo, I immediately went down to 10m altitude and saw that the tanker had been hit amidships.

Instead of banking away after the attack, the Heinkel continued straight over the convoy and was engaged by ships' anti-aircraft fire. Both of his engines were hit and the consequent damage caused Lucas to make his forced landing on the sea. The Germans later speculated that they had probably been silhouetted in the moonlight before being caught in crossfire. Merchant ships in the convoy subsequently reported that the raider was brought down very close to the *Vortigen*, although the commander of the vessel did not appear to have been aware of it and did not make a claim for the victory.

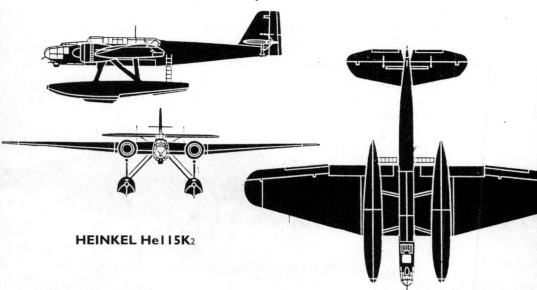

HEINKEL He115K₂

After Lucas had successfully force-landed his aircraft, the crew disposed of most of their documents and maps before getting into their rubber dinghy. They then attempted to sink the plane with the use of detonation devices. However, they succeeded only in part for although the aircraft capsized, it did not sink. Fishermen rescued the crew some three hours later and towed the aircraft to Eyemouth, where it was beached.[32]

In spite of Lucas's claims, it is not known for certain that the Heinkel's torpedo did find its target. According to Lieutenant Commander S. Howlett, the Commanding Officer of HMS *Vortigen*, convoy FN79 lost the Swedish steamer *Holland*, which was sunk by bombs or torpedo at c.22.00 hours, but no explosion was seen by any of the escorts. However, if Lucas carried out his attack as ordered, it is unlikely that the *Holland* was his victim because FN79 was a northbound convoy while Lucas claimed that his target was westbound when he attacked it.

Blitz, then and now.Vol.2 claims that the Heinkel was damaged by anti-aircraft fire while making a torpedo attack on a convoy at 15.00 hours on 16 September,[33] which is certainly at odds with Lucas's version of events. Having said that, there is a problem with the time of the incident. Lucas claims to have sighted his target at about 23.00 hours (GST) and was forced to ditch in the sea at 00.30 hours (GST) on 16 September. Given the ninety minutes difference, one is left to speculate on whether the German circled for that period of time until his target was most advantageously placed – or whether the time of the forced landing is in error.

17 November 1940 (off Whitburn)

Aircraft:	Junkers 88A-5	F6+HL	w/nr. 0426	3.(F)/122
Crew:	Lt. Paul Thallmaier	pilot	missing	
	Uffz. Henry Maisbaum	observer	+	
	Fw. Albert Leise	wireless op	missing	
	Uffz. Paul Hippenstiel	gunner	missing	

This aircraft was shot down by the Royal Navy paddle-driven minesweeper *Southsea* (J133) and crashed into the sea off Whitburn (and six miles north-east of Roker pier)[34] at 08.45 hours on 17 November 1940.

Southsea was sweeping the shipping channel off Whitburn in conditions of overcast skies and deteriorating weather when a twin-engine aircraft was seen two miles to the south and approaching the vessel on a steady course. The aircraft was challenged by Aldis lamp but failed to give the correct response as it continued its approach, gradually losing height from some 700 feet to 200 feet. When the aircraft was 300 yards from the ship it opened up with machine-gun fire and dropped two bombs. The bombs missed but the machine-gun fire caused some

1930. The paddle-steamer Southsea *on her first trip. The vessel, well known to holiday-makers in the Isle of Wight area, was requisitioned for conversion to a minesweeper in the early days of the Second World War. HMS* Southsea *shot down Ju88 F6+HL of 3.(F)/122 off Whitburn on 17 November 1940.* [via Tom Lee]

The gunners of HMS Southsea *who shot down Ju88 F6+HL of 3.(F)/122 off Whitburn on the morning of 17 November 1940.* [Author's collection]

superficial damage to *Southsea's* hull and superstructure. The raider was then engaged by the ship's 0.5 gun crew, who opened fire at point-blank range. They scored an immediate hit and might well have struck the pilot for the bomber nosedived into the sea 800 yards beyond the vessel. There were no survivors.

The success of the ship's gun crew, Able Seaman James Seggie and Ordinary Seaman Percy Preston, who were under the command of Lieutenant Leslie Crammond, RNVR, was later publicly acknowledged when all three were Mentioned in Despatches. The award was posted in

Downed German aircraft were often put on public display and used to raise funds for the war effort. This Me109 fighter was not shot down in the north of England but it was displayed in Derwent Park, Annfield Plain, on 26 October 1940, as part of the town's 'Spitfire Fund' activities. [Newcastle Chronicle & Journal]

the *London Gazette* on 4 February 1941.

HMS *Southsea* was mined off the Tyne on 16 February 1941 and was beached and written off as a constructive loss.[35] It is believed that her remains lie at 55°00′36″N/ 01°25′00″W.[36]

NOTES

1 This from AIR40/2394 (Interrogation of Hilmar Grimm) in PRO.
2 Wynn Kenneth G., *Men of the Battle of Britain*, Gliddon Books 1989 p356.
3 Ramsay, W.G., (ed), *Blitz, then and now. Vol. 1*, Battle of Britain Prints International 1987.
4 Schmidt, Rudi *Achtung-Torpedos Los! Der strategische und operative Einsätze des Kampfgeschwaders* 26, Bernard & Graefe Verlag, Koblenz 1991.
5 Beedle, J., *43 Squadron (The History of the Fighting Cocks, 1916-66)*, Beaumont Aviation Literature 1966 pp124-125.
6 Schmidt, Rudi, op. cit. p349.
7 Bolitho, Hector, *Combat Report: The Story of a Fighter Pilot*, Batsford 1943 p43.
8 Townsend, Peter, *Duel of Eagles*, Weidenfeld & Nicolson 1970 p196.
9 Collings, Peter, *The Divers Guide to the North-East Coast*, Collings & Brodie 1986 p142.
10 Norman, Bill, *Broken Eagles: Luftwaffe losses over Yorkshire, 1939-1945*, Pen & Sword Books 2001.
11 Ramsay, W.G., (ed), op. cit. p67.
12 Bolitho, Hector, op. cit. pp45-46.
13 Report 10/1940. Interrogation of prisoners of war from He.111 1H+GK (AIR40/2398 in PRO).
14 Bolitho, Hector, ibid.
15 Walmesley, Leo, *Fisherman at War*, Doubleday, Doran & Co. New York 1941 pp176-180
16 Townsend, Peter, op.cit. p203.
17 The other aircraft, a He111 (1H+AK) of 2./KG26 was shot down some six miles off St Abb's Head by Spitfires of 609 Squadron, Drem. Oblt. Ernst Heinrich and three others were captured.
18 60 M.U. Operations Record Book, April 1940 (AIR29/1016 at PRO).
19 Gundelach, Karl, *Kampfgeschwader General Wever 4*, Motorbuch Verlag, Stuttgart 1978.
20 Ramsay, W.G., (ed), op. cit. p111.
21 This from AI1(k) Report 154/1940 (Debrief of POWs) in AIR40/2397 at PRO.
22 L1229(Sgt Birkett/Sgt Benn; L1374(F/Lt J.H. Wolfe/P/O Duart) and L8720(Sgt A.J. Hodgkinson/Sgt A.C. Shepperd)
23 Goss, Chris, *The Luftwaffe Bombers' Battle of Britain*, Crécy Publishing Ltd 2000 p32.
24 Hermann, Hajo, *Eagle's Wings: the autobiography of a Luftwaffe pilot*, Guild Publishing 1991.
25 Brady, Kevin, *Sunderland's Blitz*, The People's History Ltd 1999 pp32.
26 Norman, Bill, op. cit. pp56-61.
27 According to Smith/Kay German Aircraft of the Second World War, Putnam 1990 edition, the Bf.110D-0 had a 1,050 litre(231gall) *Dackelbauch* non-jettisonable aux. fuel tank. However, Ivo Nienhaus, a subscriber to the Internet's Luftwaffe Discussion Group (*12 o'clock High*), stated on 15 February 2002 that the tank could be dropped in flight but that the jettison mechanism often failed and thus caused crews a lot of problems.
28 Brady, Kevin, op.cit. pp41-42.
29 Bergmann was the *Staffelkapitän* of 3./506; Kriependorf was the *Staffelkapitän* of another unit and was apparently on the flight to gain experience of torpedo attacks.
30 AI1(k) seems to have made a wrong assumption. The code S4+ was that of *Küstenfliegergruppe* 506 and the insignia was, in fact, used by 3./506, which had been formed from the old 3./406 in October 1939, when *Küstenfliegergruppe* 506 was reorganized.
31 Goss, Chris, op. cit. pp154-155.
32 This choice of Eyemouth tends to lend credence to the AI1(k) report of the location of the ditching.
33 AIR22/266 also gives the time as 3.00pm.
34 Operations Record Book, RAF Usworth, 17 November 1940. (AIR28/870 – PRO).
35 Lenton, H.T., *British and Empire Warships of the Second World War*, Greenhill Books 1998. p326.
36 Collings, Peter, op.cit. p51.

2

A CHANGE OF DIRECTION
(1941)

In the early months of 1941, Germany's bombing campaign against Britain shifted its emphasis. The nightly assaults on the mainland continued until May, but when the possibility of an early victory against Britain faded in the first few months of the year the Luftwaffe's Operations Staff once again focused on blockade and devoted more attention to attacking this country's maritime trade. Consequently, major destructive raids were launched against the principal ports in the south, west, and north-west of England, as well as south-west Scotland. These raids also continued until May, when Hitler's preoccupation with thoughts of Russia ultimately caused a major diversion of effort away from this country.

In Northumberland and Durham things were reasonably quiet in the opening months of the new year and anti-shipping operations, particularly the mining of coastal shipping lanes, remained the principal activity. In January, this was interspersed with occasional scattered (and small-scale) bombing attacks in both counties, with areas near the coast tending to receive most attention. Mid-February saw a slight quickening of raid activity over the north. On 15-16 of the month, high explosives and incendiary bombs fell on coastal areas from Sunderland to Cresswell. Generally speaking, the high explosives were limited to one or two in each locality and did minimal damage, but in Ashington District one of seven parachute mines completely demolished a block of fourteen houses, killing one person and injuring fifty-two others. In the week that followed, the policy of scattered attacks along the coastal strip continued and Sunderland (twice), Seaham Harbour, Hebburn, Morpeth and Durham city all experienced the Luftwaffe's wrath to some degree.

March brought an increase in the scale of bombing over the north. Scattered forays continued over both counties, but on the night of 3-4 March there was a damaging attack on Tyneside's dock and industrial installations by an estimated twenty-two aircraft. It was the area's first raid of any real size and the prelude to a number of highly destructive attacks that both Tyne and Wear would experience in 1941.

In April, the nation's principal ports saw some of the heaviest bombing of the war to date and although there was no activity in the northern counties to match the ferocity of the assaults occurring elsewhere, the Tyne and the Wear suffered some of their most destructive attacks. The month started quietly enough, with only scattered bombing, from Dalton Piercy (Co. Durham) to Kirknewton (Northumberland), in the first week. The following two weeks were different.

On the night of 9-10 April, a large number of enemy bombers operated over the Tyne and unloaded substantial quantities of high explosives and thousands of incendiaries on docks and industrial installations from Newcastle to Tynemouth. There were sixty-eight major fires and widespread damage in Newcastle, where only incendiaries fell, and extensive destruction in Tynemouth (where thirty-five people were killed), Jarrow and South Shields. At least thirty-eight high explosives and 6,000 incendiaries fell on the Tyne Dock and across the town centre at South Shields, and major fires developed in the docks, shipyards and timber yards that lined the riverbank.

This 2,000lb unexploded bomb dropped on Tynemouth on 25 April 1941. The bomb fell on a railway line one hundred yards from the spot where it now stands - in the car park of the Park Hotel, Tynemouth. [Author]

Twenty-two people lost their lives in the attack, which created such devastation that fire brigades from as far afield as Middlesbrough were needed to give assistance. Further south, in Sunderland, a large number of incendiaries dropped on the town centre and caused destructive fires. One such blaze consumed Binns' department store, while high explosives dropped on the Hudson Dock and the Hendon area and destroyed industrial and domestic properties alike.

On the night of 15-16 April, enemy bombers were over the north-east again, a number of them mining offshore and an estimated thirty-eight others unloading bombs on Newcastle, Hebburn, Whitley Bay (fifteen killed), South Shields and Sunderland (eighteen killed). At the latter location, high explosives demolished domestic property in Pallion and damaged the premises of the Sunderland Forge & Engineering Company. Nearer to the centre, the town's first parachute mines demolished the Victoria Hall and damaged the Winter Gardens so badly that the structure had later to be demolished. Bombs also fell on locations further south that night, including Easington, Billingham and Sadberge.

Sunderland was the intended target for fifty-seven bombers and eighty tons of high explosives on the night of 25-26 April. Indeed, German Radio subsequently boasted of the success of the attack, but no bombs fell there. There was, however, extensive bombing in the area, with eight locations being affected in Northumberland and nine others in County Durham. The most seriously affected seems to have been along the Tyne, where the Heaton-Byker-Jesmond-Quayside areas accounted for forty-seven people killed and at Wallsend, where sixteen people succumbed to the onslaught. Across the river at South Shields, a combination of 2,000 incendiaries over the dock area and seven parachute mines over the town also destroyed lives and property. Minor bombing incidents occurred throughout the north-east every night for the remainder of the month but, virtually without exception, they proved to be more annoying than destructive.

The highly damaging attacks on the nation's principal ports continued until mid-May but the situation over the two northern counties eased after the heavy assaults in April. There were, however, some exceptions. On the night of 3-4 May there was some concentrated bombing around the Tyne and there might have been similar concentrations around the Hartlepools on the night of 4-5 May and around ICI Billingham on the night of 11-12 May, if the weather had not intervened. In both cases, some eighteen bombers were targeted on each location but poor visibility gave protection and ensured that bomb loads did not always land where they were intended. However, it was not always necessary for the Luftwaffe to attack in strength in order to ensure a catastrophic effect; sometimes, cruel luck played its part. The saddest example occurred at North Shields on the night of 3-4 May, when a bomb struck Wilkinson's Lemonade factory and killed 105 people who were sheltering in the basement.

After mid-May, the frequency and severity of Luftwaffe operations over Britain fell away markedly, as Hitler prepared to move eastwards. In June 1941, the war against this country was virtually put on hold when Germany embarked on a 'short' pre-emptive campaign against Russia to remove, what the German High Command perceived as, the potential threat to Germany's back door.

The invasion of Russia markedly affected the Luftwaffe's ability to wage war against Britain because some eighty per cent of its frontline aircraft were transferred to the Eastern Front, thus leaving the remaining forces in the West seriously weakened. *Luftflotte 2* moved its main operations from the Low Countries to the east and *Luftflotte 3* – which had itself lost units to the invasion force – was left to fill the gap. Further north, *Luftflotte 5* was forced to extend its boundaries eastwards to include Finland, while much further to the south *X Fliegerkorps* was endeavouring to meet air requirements in the Mediterranean and North Africa. In addition to all of this, the RAF was increasing its bombing operations over Germany, thus making it necessary for the Luftwaffe to increasingly allocate limited resources to home defence.

The months of June, July and August saw only occasional Luftwaffe activity over the northern counties. Offshore, armed reconnaissance aircraft sunk a number of vessels between Alnmouth and the Tees but enemy air activity was only occasional over the mainland. Most of it was also small-scale but the night of 18-19 August saw some concentrations of bombing around Ashington and the Hartlepools, the latter resulting in a number of deaths and the demolition of thirty-one houses.

It was not until the first night of September that a raid of any size was launched against a land target in the area. Twenty-two bombers attacked Newcastle and claimed to have dropped fifty-two tons of high explosives. Although the impact of the raid was much reduced by those aircraft that bombed widely scattered parts of Northumberland and County Durham, the attack costs the lives of forty-nine people in the town and caused considerable damage to property on the banks of the Tyne. Newcastle was targeted twice more in the month. On the night of 7-8 September, poor visibility over the area reduced the concentration of bombing and high explosives fell on diverse locations in both counties. On the second occasion, on the last night of the month, twelve aircraft caused serious damage and casualties when they raided port facilities and shipyards at Newcastle, North Shields and South Shields.

For the remainder of the year, Northumberland (including Newcastle) and County Durham continued to suffer the consequences of spasmodic visits by 'tip and run' raiders, but there were times when the Luftwaffe made more concerted efforts. On 2 October, timber yards, industrial properties and residential accommodation in South Shields suffered widespread devastation, especially in the area of the Market Place, which was described at the time as '...looking like the ruins of Ypres...' in the First World War. The forty-four bombs that fell on the borough killed sixty-eight people and injured 208 others. As on previous occasions, bombs intended for Tyneside also landed elsewhere, including West Hartlepool, Graythorpe and Seaton Carew. On the night of 21-22 October, forty-four enemy bombers searched the area, trying to find Newcastle. However, poor visibility provided a measure of protection and seventy-four tons of explosives ended up being spread over various locations from the Tees to the Tyne. A fortnight later, forty-two bombers aiming for Newcastle and Sunderland squandered most of their sixty-seven tons of bombs around the coastal areas of Northumberland and Durham, although there was some concentration around Sunderland.

Newcastle was again the target on the night of 8-9 December. A number of bombs fell on Heaton and caused both damage and casualties, but the scale of the impact was again much diminished by the raid's lack of concentration. As on previous occasions, many places in both counties, including South Shields and Sunderland, experienced the explosive shock of bursting bombs. However, many of those fell in open spaces and shifted nothing but earth. The last sizeable attack of 1941 took place on the night of 29-30 December, when the docks of the Tyne and Wear were again its principal objectives, but poor weather conditions again proved to be the region's best protector. The thirty-one bombers that made landfall in the area failed to sight their targets; they bombed on dead reckoning and did not observe the results of their widely scattered bombardment.

The transfer of most of the Luftwaffe's aircraft eastwards for the invasion of Russia left basically two units to carry out bombing operations in the West. These units were KG30 (by then relocated from Scandinavia to Holland and KG2, both of Luftflotte 3. Those limited forces were reduced even further towards the end of 1941 when units of KG30 were transferred to Norway to be employed in attacks against Arctic convoys supplying Russia. In effect, this left KG2 as virtually the only operational bomber unit carrying the war to Britain and with aircraft resources roughly equivalent to no more than two or three RAF squadrons. It was an increasingly difficult task – and one that could be attempted only by drawing on crews under training and by 'borrowing' crews from other theatres of operations.

Losses
January 1941 – December 1941

RNLI Records at Poole (Dorset) claim that a German aircraft (type unknown) crashed into the sea five miles north-east of Hartlepool on 15 January 1941. The Hartlepool lifeboat was launched but no service was rendered. The reason why no service was rendered is not given but it was almost certainly because nothing was found. Examination of the Luftwaffe Loss Reports for this date revealed no details relating to this incident.

Sowing aerial mines in coastal waters.
KG4's mine-laying strategy.

In the months of June-July 1940, the Heinkel 111 bombers of KG4 relocated from bases in Germany to airfields in Holland as part of *IX Fliegerkorps*. The *Stab* (HQ) Flight and the three *Staffeln* of I./KG4 were based at Soesterberg, II./KG4 at Eindhoven and III./KG4 (re-equipped with the new Ju88) at Amsterdam-Schipol. According to Gundelach[1], KG4 was the Luftwaffe's only specialist mining *Geschwader* and with the transfer of the *Gruppen* to Holland, KG4's mining operations against the British Isles began in earnest and were on occasion combined with bombing raids on the mainland.

It is known that KG4 mined northern sea lanes – principally around the Tyne and Humber – on a number of occasions in the opening months of 1941 and probably before that, although specific dates cannot always be given. However, it is known that KG4 sent seven Heinkel 111s to mine the Tyne estuary on the night of 15-16 February 1941 (and lost one, which crashed at South Shields) and that on 29 March 1941 He111s of KG4 mined the Humber estuary.

The mines (1,000kg) were dropped into the sea fastened to a green parachute, which was attached to the body of the mine by a firm but soluble, salt plug. On entering the water, the mine sank to the seabed. The plug dissolved quickly in water and thus released the parachute, which was carried away by the current and so did not betray the location of the mine.

The mines had either a magnetic fuse, which exploded the device when a ship with a 'magnetic shadow' passed overhead, or an acoustic fuse, which was activated by the propeller noises of ships passing overhead. If necessary, these fuses could be programmed to become active after a specified time (say, a day or a week) or after a specific number of ships had passed over them.

Mines were sown along coastal shipping routes, in navigable rivers and in the estuaries of the main ports. Although the shipping routes were shown on the charts used by minelaying crews, as a rule the routes were not marked on the sea and, of course, at night they were not illuminated. Therefore precise navigation over the sea was required in order to ensure that the mines were eventually sown in the intended place. Maps and charts had to be meticulously prepared and it was up to the plane's navigator to calculate the points at which the mines were to be dropped.

Although the units within KG4 were responsible for allocating minelaying duties to crews within their respective *Staffeln* they had no influence over the types of mine to be dropped. That decision rested with *IX Fliegerkorps*, of which the *Geschwader* was a part. The *Korps*, which was also responsible for delivering the mines to units, decided the types of fuse to be used, stipulated the heights from which mines were to be dropped, and gave orders regarding self-destruct measures to be programmed into the mine should it fall on land or in shallow water (from which it could be recovered – and examined – by the enemy).

For the mining operations to be fully effective, it was essential that the enemy was unaware that mining had taken place. To that end, KG4's mining operations some times occurred simultaneously with bombing raids on the same general area in order to divert suspicion.

Upon reaching the area to be mined, the minelayer would make a timed run which would start when the aircraft was abreast of a predetermined, prominent fixed point on land (e.g. a lighthouse or headland). The aircraft would then fly at a designated speed (just above stalling speed) along a precise track for a specified time and at a specified height to the point where the mine was to be released.

Upon release, the parachute and its load descended to the water at five metres per second and so it was essential that the weapon dropped at exactly the right time and from the right altitude. Generally speaking, the dropping heights were in the range 400-800 metres and were determined by the wind prevailing at the time. The height had to be such that it was great enough to allow the parachute to deploy and for the rate of descent to be steadied, without being so high that the parachute and its cargo drifted beyond the intended location. In order to protect the secrets of the weapon and its mechanism, the mine was programmed to self-destruct if it landed in shallow water (less than five to eight metres on the ebb), or if it landed on a sand bank.

**Based on *Kampfgeschwader General Wever 4*
by Karl Gundelach.**

15-16 February 1941 (South Shields)

Aircraft:	Heinkel 111P-4	5J+GP	w/nr. 3085	6./KG4
Crew:	Obfw. Wilhelm Beetz	pilot	+	
	Hptm. Heinz Styra	observer	+	
	Uffz. Karl-G. Brützam	wireless op	+	
	Gefr. Franz Janeschitz	gunner	+	
	Uffz. Helmut Jeckstadt	gunner	+	

This aircraft was struck by anti-aircraft fire over South Shields during a raid on the Tyne and lost height before its port wing collided with a balloon cable from a site on the North Foreshore. Contact with the cable caused the bomber to dive into the ground at a steep angle. It crashed at Bent's Park, at the eastern end of Beach Road, South Shields (military map ref. Z8587) at 00.25 hours on 16 February 1941. Four members of the crew were killed when their aircraft exploded on impact with the ground. The fifth member, Beetz, had cruel luck: he managed to bale out but was electrocuted when he landed on trolley-bus wires at the pier head. He hung there until rescued but he was badly injured and died shortly after admission to the Ingham Infirmary. The wreckage caught fire and twenty minutes later a mine that was on board exploded with

RAF ground personnel pose with the wreckage of He111 5J+GP of 6./KG4 that crashed at South Shields on the night of 15-16 February 1941. [South Shields Library]

such force that the blast broke windows in Tynemouth and North Shields. The explosion blew the Heinkel to pieces and killed a policeman and an attendant fireman. A number of other members of the police force and the fire brigade were injured and were admitted to the Ingham Infirmary, where two more fireman subsequently died from their injuries.

Single high-explosive bombs fell on Brodrick Street, on St Aidan's Road, near Redwell Lane and two dropped on the South Sands. Their casualty toll of three killed and seven injured was surpassed by that of the plane crash, which resulted in four killed and seventeen injured. The Germans were subsequently buried in Hylton Cemetery, Sunderland, where they still lie.

3 March 1941

The Luftwaffe Loss Returns record that Heinkel 111H-5 (w/nr.3817) of I./KG53 suffered ten per cent damage due to enemy gunfire while on a raid to Newcastle but the Returns do not state whether a fighter or ground defences were responsible.

13 March 1941 (east of Coquet Island, Amble)

Aircraft:	Junkers 88A-5		M2+JL	w/nr. 2234 Ku.Fl.Gr. 3./106
Crew:	Oblt. H. Voightländer-Tetzner	pilot	+	
	Lt. z. See Rudolf Dietze	observer	missing	
	Obgfr. Walter Wesserer	wireless op	missing	
	Obgfr. Hans Vandanne	mechanic	missing	

This aircraft was on a sortie to Glasgow when it was shot down by Flight Lieutenant Desmond Sheen, 72 Squadron, Acklington. Sheen (in Spitfire K4596) had been ordered up at 21.26 hours. When he reached 10,000 feet he spotted an aircraft silhouetted against thin cloud, which was lit up by the moon. He chased it out to sea and got within 150 yards before he identified it as a Ju88. He made a number of attacks and when he left the enemy aircraft its starboard engine was blazing.

Küstenfliegerstaffel 3./106

At 22.22 hours on 13 March 1941, Police Sergeant Arthur Weallans was on duty at the LNER goods yard at Amble when he saw and heard machine-gun fire from an aeroplane that was flying north-eastwards. The aircraft then flew out to sea in an easterly direction. Weallans subsequently saw five bursts of machine-gun fire and could plainly see tracers in the sky. Then a sheet of flame appeared in the sky to the east of where he was standing. The flame gradually grew larger. He saw and heard six bursts of gunfire and saw the flames develop into a huge size before plunging down towards the sea about three miles north-east of Coquet Island. A short while afterwards, a fighter plane passed over Amble travelling in the direction of Acklington aerodrome. The incident was witnessed by a number of people in the town. At 11.30 hours on 14 March, the Air Ministry confirmed that the crashed aircraft was German and Sheen's claim was confirmed.

On 27 April 1941, Hilderbrand Voightländer-Tetzner's body was recovered from the sea, one mile south-east of the Heugh Light, Hartlepool. He was buried under that date at Acklam Road Cemetery, Thornaby-on-Tees.

EYEWITNESS

Spitfire victory
Coquet Island, 13 March 1941

On the night of 13 March 1941, Flight Lieutenant Desmond Sheen, 72 Squadron, Acklington, shot down Ju88 M2+JL of *Küstenfliegergruppe* 3./106. The German aircraft crashed into the sea some three miles north -east of Coquet Island. The following account of the incident was subsequently broadcast by Sheen on the BBC Home Service on 17 April 1941.

There was brilliant moonlight and I could see the coast for several miles in each direction. The conditions were ideal for night-fighting in a Spitfire. When I first saw the raider, he was about a thousand feet above me, so I opened up and climbed after him. When I was about a hundred yards behind and below, I saw that he was a Junkers 88. As I opened fire, I could see my tracer bullets bursting in the Junkers like fireworks. Soon the old familiar black smoke that you've heard so much about came pouring out of the raider. With it was a lot of oil, which covered my windscreen and forced me to break away. When I turned in for my next attack I saw that one of the Hun's engines was beginning to burn but, just to make sure of him, I pumped in a lot more bullets, then I had to dive like mad to avoid ramming him. I had been so keen on giving him as many bullets as I could that I almost collided with him... In the dive I lost quite a lot of height, several thousand feet, in fact, and when I pulled out I had lost sight of him. But before I went down one of the enemy's wings was burning like a bonfire, so I felt certain that the Junkers would not get home. Actually, confirmation came fairly quickly: members of the Observer Corps had watched the fight and had seen my tracer bullets hitting the raider. I think my first burst must have killed or disabled the gunners, for there was no return fire. Apparently, the Hun went down like a flare; as he hit the sea there was an explosion.

Flt.Lt Desmond Sheen, Spitfire pilot,
72 Squadron, Acklington, 1941[2]

10 April 1941 (off Boulmer)

Aircraft:	Junkers 88A-5		F6+NL	w/nr. 0529	3(F)/122
Crew:	Lt. Rolf Bröse	pilot	missing		
	Uffz. E. Ernst Helmer	observer	missing		
	Fw. Karl Düx	wireless op	missing		
	Fw. Otto Gröbke	mechanic	+		

It is believed that this aircraft fell to Spitfires of 72 Squadron, Acklington, but the names of the fighter pilots responsible might well be open to conjecture. *Blitz, then and now. Vol.2*[3] states that Sergeant Casey and Sergeant Prytherch were patrolling their base as ordered when they intercepted a Junkers 88 on a reconnaissance sortie to Newcastle and destroyed it, the Junkers crashing at Alnmouth at 19.40 hours. However, 72 Squadron Operation Record Books are at variance with this account and record that the enemy machine was seen to crash into the sea further to the north, off Boulmer and about a mile below the low water mark. The time of the crash would also seem to be in dispute, the ORB showing that Casey and Prytherch landed back at base at 19.40 hours – the reported time of the crash.

The apparent conflict may be explained by the fact that 72 Squadron put up four Spitfires at almost the same time on the evening of 10 April. Sergeant Casey (in Spitfire R7069) and Sergeant Prytherch (R6752) took off at 18.44 hours and Sergeant Gregson (X4918) and Sergeant Lack (X4551) followed sixteen minutes later. Like Casey and Prytherch, Gregson and Lack subsequently intercepted a Ju88, '...and probably

'It was an exceptionally low tide on the night of the crash (10 April 1941) and all of the Boulmer boats were on the ground, so they could not be launched...' Just how low the tide can drop at Boulmer is shown in this photograph, which was taken at about the same time of year but in 2001. [Author]

destroyed it...' about ten miles north-east of Longhoughton, certainly north of Alnmouth and probably off Beadnell. However, the final outcome of the encounter was inconclusive, for the weather was cloudy and the results difficult to observe, but when Gregson and Lack last saw their enemy machine (at altitude1,500 feet) it was on fire, disintegrating and diving vertically towards the sea.

The Squadron ORB for 10 April 1941, credits Sergeant Casey and Sergeant Prytherch with one Ju88 destroyed and lists Gregson and Lack's claim '...a moral certainty...' but it also adds that '...The first enemy aircraft could barely have been claimed as damaged had it not been seen to crash from the ground...' However, given that (at the time of writing) only one German aircraft is known to have crashed in the area, it is interesting to speculate on which pair of Spitfires actually deserved the honours. Three of the German crew were listed as missing. Gröbke's body was later found at Amble.

Pensioner and Boulmer resident Jimmie Stanton, in conversation with the writer in June, 2000, remembered that:

At about 7.15pm on the Thursday before Good Friday, an enemy aircraft passed low over the south end of Boulmer. One engine was stopped and the plane was rocking. When it was some 300 yards out to sea and east of the coastguard watch box, the aircraft turned to starboard and ditched just beyond the rocks. It sank quickly: no-one got out. The Boulmer lifeboat was 'off-duty', having been damaged in the SS Somali incident some weeks earlier; it had been within seventy yards of the steamer when it (Somali) had blown up.[4]

It was also an exceptionally low tide at the time of the crash and all the Boulmer fishing boats were on the ground, so they couldn't be launched. Even though the Germans were the enemy, our lads would have gone out for them if they could have done. I think that the Cresswell lifeboat searched without success. About fifteen minutes before that I saw another aircraft going out to sea and on fire. When I saw it, it was in a 45° dive.[5]

Catapult Armed Merchant Ships (CAM Ships)

Following the German invasion of France in June 1940 and the subsequent occupation of the French Atlantic coast, the Luftwaffe's four-engined Fw200 aircraft were employed in anti-shipping operations in areas outside of RAF fighter cover. These activities included reconnaissance flights and cooperation with U-boats, minelaying in Allied coastal waters and attacks on merchant vessels. In the latter instance, the Fw200s operated over the North Atlantic convoy routes up to 1,100 miles from their French base at Brest and by late 1940 – early 1941 they were sinking Allied merchant ships at an alarming rate.

In the absence of escort aircraft carriers available for convoy defence, the idea of allocating converted merchant ships – equipped with radar and a catapult-launched fighter plane – to accompany each convoy, was seriously considered from November 1940. The Catapult Armed Merchant Ships (CAM ships) were to provide a stopgap measure of convoy defence until the first escort aircraft carriers could be introduced.

Selected vessels were merchant ships capable of taking seventy-five feet of steel ramp mounted over the forecastle head. Fitted with a rocket-powered catapult attached to the ramp, the CAM ships were to carry two expendable fighter aircraft, one hoisted on the ramp, the other stored in reserve. The aircraft were usually Mk.I Hurricanes flown by volunteer RAF pilots. The CAM ships were quickly put into service in 1941 (the first one sailed the North Atlantic route in late May 1941) before the first escort carriers appeared, with the aim of driving off or shooting down German bombers or reconnaissance aircraft. Once flown off, the returning pilot usually had to ditch and hope that he would be picked up or, if he were close enough, make for the nearest friendly shore.

From August 1942, the new escort carriers began to enter service and by the summer of the following year the CAM ships had been phased

The Patia *before its conversion to its wartime role.* [via Matt Campbell]

out. It is believed that thirty-five CAM ships made some 170 round trip voyages in two years. Ten of those vessels were lost through enemy action, ten catapult launchings were made, seven enemy aircraft were shot down and a further three were damaged, and one RAF pilot was lost when he baled out and his parachute failed to deploy properly.

Five similar vessels, including HMS *Patia*, were commissioned into the Royal Navy and flew the White Ensign. These vessels were referred to as Fighter Catapult Ships (FCS). They were manned by Royal Navy personnel and were armed with the two-seater Fairy Fulmar or the Hawker Hurricane. Two of those vessels, including HMS *Patia*, were lost through enemy action. Ten catapult launchings were made, one enemy aircraft was shot down and one Fleet Air Arm pilot and his air gunner were lost when their Fulmar struck a hillside in poor visibility following an operational flight.[6]

27 April 1941 (off Beadnell)

Aircraft:	Heinkel 111H-5	1H+MH	w/nr. 3677	1/KG26
Crew:	Obfw. Erich Fenchal	pilot	pow	
	Gefr. Rudolf Klamand	observer	pow	
	Uffz. Siegfried Warko	wireless op	pow	
	Gefr. Johann Schügerl	mechanic	+	

The Luftwaffe Loss Returns list this aircraft as having failed to return from operations against Newcastle-on-Tyne on 27 April and gives the probable cause as ship's gunfire. The Returns also record that Heinkel 111H-5 (w/nr.3572) and Heinkel 111H-5(w/nr. 3674), both of 1./KG26, forced landed at Stavanger-Sola on return from operations, having sustained twenty per cent damage and fifteen per cent damage respectively from flak.

He111 1H+MH was one of three aircraft of 1./KG26 to participate in an anti-shipping reconnaissance operation along the north-east coast of England on the night of 27 April 1941. The bombers set off singly from their base at Stavanger (Norway), Fenchal's aircraft taking off last at 19.30 hours (German Summer Time). 1H+MH crossed the North Sea at an average height of 200 feet and after flying for some two and a half hours the bomber was approaching the Northumberland coast when Fenchal and his crew saw the guns of a ship some way ahead seemingly engaged in battle with attacking aircraft.

The vessel under attack was HMS *Patia*, an Auxiliary Fighter Catapult Ship that had left the Tyne at 18.25 hours en route to Belfast. One of three[7] Elder & Fyffes 'banana boats' to be used as catapult vessels, *Patia* had been converted at Brigham, Cowan's yard, South Shields, and had just been commissioned the day before (26 April) for service with the Royal Navy. Armed with a rocket-powered catapult and allocated the Fairey Fulmar as its weapon, the ship was intended for convoy protection duties on the ocean routes, where the Luftwaffe's FW200 Condor aircraft were active against Allied shipping. However, the vessel was destined to be sunk before it could even embark its aircraft.

1H+MH joined in the attack on *Patia* but the German crew did not see other aircraft involved in the assault whilst they themselves were trying to sink their target. Thus it seems likely that the earlier raider(s) had left by the time Fenchal arrived on the scene.[8] Fenchal made two attacks, using bombs and machine-gun fire in each case. The first attack was across the beam from the starboard quarter: two 250kg bombs were aimed at the ship on the initial run but they missed their target. Fenchal then made a right-hand turn and attacked again, this time from the port quarter. The remaining two 250kg bombs were dropped on that occasion and at least one of them was seen to score a direct hit. However, Fenchal did not have it all his own way. The ship's guns scored strikes on one of the bomber's engines, causing sufficient damage to force the aircraft to ditch close by the vessel, which by that time was on fire.

Fenchal and his crew escaped from the Heinkel with no difficulty and three of them managed to scramble into their rubber boat before their aircraft sank. For reasons currently unknown, the mechanic (*Gefreiter*

The Amble reserve lifeboat, Elizabeth Newton, *helped recover bodies from the wreck of HMS* Patia *on the night of 27-28 April 1941.* [via Bryan Stringer]

James Campbell, coxswain of the Boulmer lifeboat Clarissa Langdon. [via Matt Campbell]

Johann Schürgel) failed to get into the dinghy and although he was supported in the water for some time, he eventually drowned.

The bomb that struck the *Patia* exploded in the area of the ship's engine room, rupturing a bulkhead there and allowing seawater to flood into the engine room and the boiler room. The force of the explosion was violent enough to savagely rock the vessel and to threaten capsize but *Patia* stayed upright. However, she was mortally damaged and as the rocking eased, the ship was on fire and already beginning to sink. The 'Abandon Ship' signal was sounded and boats were lowered. The three German survivors in their rubber boat were close enough to the burning ship to see lifeboats pulling away from it. They also saw a number of men in the water, one of whom they managed to pull into their dinghy before waiting for rescue. After some three hours they, together with twenty-five of *Patia*'s crew, were picked up by the trawler minesweeper HMT *Chassiron* and taken to North Shields.

At least two of the local lifeboats went to the aid of the stricken mariners but they failed to find anyone alive. The Boulmer boat *Clarissa*

The plaque commemorating the loss of HMS Patia *is kept in the lifeboat house at Boulmer.* [Author]

June, 2000. Matt Campbell (son of James Campbell) with a photograph of the Patia *and the plaque that commemorates the loss of the vessel.* [Author]

Langdon, skippered by James Campbell who had been awarded the RNLI Bronze Medal for Gallantry for rescuing crew members of the SS *Somali* which sank off Beadnell Point[9] a month before, recovered five bodies, including that of the *Patia*'s captain, Commander D.M. Baker. The Amble reserve lifeboat, *Elizabeth Newton*, recovered ten corpses. The ship's own lifeboats saved eighty crew members and there is the possibility that the trawler minesweeper *Lord Darling* picked up others, but thirty-seven men of *Patia*'s crew lost their lives. Their names are listed on a commemorative plaque in the lifeboat station at Boulmer. Both the Heinkel and HMS *Patia* eventually sank to the sea bed eight miles north -east of Seaton Point, Boulmer (Northumberland).[10]

29 April 1941 (off Blyth)

Three Spitfires of Green Section, 72 Squadron, Acklington, were practice flying in mid-afternoon of 29 April 1941 when Control reported an unidentified 'bogey' five miles off Blyth. The Spitfires, flown by Pilot Officer Pocock (in P8146), Sergeant Collyer (P8231) and Sergeant Perkins (7376) intercepted the suspect aircraft four miles north-east of Blyth and identified it as an enemy machine. Both Pocock and Perkins got in bursts as the enemy aircraft was going through a gap in clouds but neither could claim to have damaged it. Sergeant Collyer was last seen following the raider into cloud and was heard to say over R/T that his engine had failed and that he was going into the sea. The two other aircraft searched the area but could find no trace of him. Later that day Sergeant Collyer's body was recovered from the sea.

30 April 1941 (off the Farne Islands)

Aircraft:	Junkers 88		S4+JH	w/nr. 715	Ku.Fl.Gr. 1./506
Crew:	Fw. Kurt Pahnke	pilot	+		
	Lt. Hans Jark	observer	+		
	Uffz. Johann Schaare	wireless op	+		
	Hptgfr. J. Schumacher	mechanic	+		

At 14.45 hours on 30 April 1940 two Spitfires of Yellow Section, 72 Squadron, Sergeant White, in P8238 and Sergeant Harrison, in P7968, took off from Acklington on a practice flight. Shortly afterwards, they were ordered to intercept a Junkers 88 flying south from the Farne Islands and they subsequently identified the position of the raider when they saw two bomb bursts in the sea. Soon afterwards, the Ju88 was seen flying eastwards over the sea and at a very low altitude. The Spitfires overhauled the bomber and made numerous attacks on it before finally leaving it with both engines smoking, in cloud and at an altitude of 500 feet. They

Küstenfliegerstaffel 1./506

The wreckage of Heinkel 111 5J+IH of 1./KG4 which was attacked by a Defiant night fighter over the Clyde on the night of 5-6 May 1941. The bomber crashed at Whorlton Park, Newcastle-on-Tyne at 03.00 hours on 6 May. [via Ken Watkins]

did not actually see the aircraft crash and claimed it only as damaged. However, *Blitz, then and now. Vol. 2*[11] claims that the above aircraft was shot down by Spitfires of 72 Squadron whilst on an operation to Whitley Bay and that it crashed into the sea off the Farne Islands at 15.00 hours. It is believed that Schumacher's body was washed ashore at Hornsea, East Yorkshire, on 10 May 1941. He was buried in Brandesburton Churchyard, near Hornsea, under that date.

The Luftwaffe Loss Returns for 30 April 1941 record that this aircraft was lost while on operations to White-Bay (probably a typographical error and should probably read Whitley Bay) but attributes the loss to flak. The Returns also mention that flak killed the mechanic and wounded the observer of another Ju88 (possibly S4+BH) of 1./506 during operations to Newcastle.

5-6 May 1941 (Whorlton Park, Newcastle)

Aircraft:	Heinkel 111H-5	5J+IH	w/nr. 3520	1./KG4
Crew:	Fw. Franz Olsson	pilot	pow	
	Hptm. Eugen Eichler	observer	pow	
	Obgfr. Wilhelm Koch	wireless op	+	
	Gefr. Hans Schiedlinski	gunner	pow	

Heinkel 111 5J+IH crashed in Whorlton Park (military map ref. Q6889), three miles north-west of Newcastle in the early hours of 6 May 1941. The aircraft had dropped bombs on Greenock and was a few miles south-west of Glasgow when it was attacked at 01.44 hours by a Defiant night fighter(T3943) of 141 Squadron, Ayr, crewed by Sergeant G.L. Lawrence (pilot) and Sergeant Hithersay (gunner). Lawrence's report of the incident describes what happened:

On the night of 5-6 May 1941 I was ordered off to patrol according to vectors at midnight. I was airborne at 00.04hours on 6th and was controlled by Vandyke for the first 30 minutes then switched over to GCI, being controlled by them until I was forced to ask for a homing vector because of a faulty microphone and lack of petrol: I had 15 gallons left.I was given a vector of 120°, which brought me to the coast at 12,000ft, a few miles south of Greenock and was asked to call Vandyke for further homing vectors. Shortly after receiving a vector for 140° from Vandyke, my gunner, Sgt Hithersay, saw a twin-engined aircraft some 300 yards behind and some 200 yards to port, flying on a parallel course and silhouetted against some cloud lit up by incendiaries on the ground.

I throttled back to 120mph IAS to allow the aircraft to overtake me. It came up to within 100 yards then altered course and passed behind to my starboard and when next seen by me was some 200 yards away on my beam, flying due south. I recognized the aircraft as a Heinkel 111 and closed in rapidly, intending to take up my position slightly ahead of and to port of the enemy aircraft but my gunner opened fire at approximately 150 yards with a three-second burst while I was still to beam and slightly below. Some of these rounds could be seen striking the fuselage near the tail. The next two bursts, from 50 yards and point blank range, raked the length of the fuselage and port engine.

The De Wilde (an explosive incendiary .303 bullet) ammunition could be seen exploding very plainly. The enemy aircraft then started doing steep turns to port and starboard and I endeavoured to formate, keeping slightly ahead and below while my gunner was firing when he could, all bursts being at close range. By this time the engine was alight and emitting white smoke. I had also seen two small explosions about halfway down the fuselage. We were down to 5,000ft and I decided to break off to check up on my fuel but kept the enemy aircraft in sight... I still had about 9 gallons left so I decided to have another two minutes as I reckoned I was not far from my base. I took up position ahead and to port of the enemy aircraft and my gunner fired a three-second burst into the port engine from a range of about 30ft. He then informed me that his ammunition was expended so I left the Heinkel at less than 3,000ft, flying very slowly in a south-easterly direction with its port engine burning. I landed at Prestwick at 02.10hours with about 4 galls of petrol.[12]

Sergeant Hithersay's shooting caused critical damage to both of the bomber's engines, closing down the left one completely and drastically impairing the operation of the other. The Heinkel struggled on as far as

1942. KG4 personnel in POW Camp 30, Bowmanville, Ontario, Canada.
Hauptmann Eugen Eichler, observer of He111 5J+IH is first from the left on the front
row. [F.W. Koch]

the outskirts of Newcastle before the starboard motor packed in and the
crew prepared to bale out. However, the Heinkel had lost a lot of altitude
by then and was below tree height when one of its wings hit a telegraph
pole and was torn off. 5J+IH crashed to earth 600 yards further on and
was badly damaged. Of the crew, only Franz Olsson emerged unscathed
from the incident. The four fliers were found by pitmen Thomas Dawson
and Ernest Stoker, two members of the local Home Guard, who
subsequently handed them over to the police.

5-6 May 1941 (east of Cresswell)

Aircraft:	Heinkel 111H-5	5J+KL	w/nr. 3794	3./KG4
Crew:	Uffz. Karl Arnold	pilot	missing	
	Lt. Walter Weisslener	observer	missing	
	Uffz. Herbert B'hen	wireless op	missing	
	Gefr. Werner Willeke	mechanic	+	

The Luftwaffe Loss Returns for this date show that this aircraft failed to
return from operations to Greenock on the night of 5-6 May 1941. It
seems highly likely that 5J+KL was the He111 claimed by the Defiant
night fighter crew of Pilot Officer Meredith (pilot) and Sergeant Mott, of
141 Squadron, Acklington, as noted in that unit's Operations Record
Book.

The Defiant (N3430) left Acklington at 23.00 hours to patrol the
Hartlepool area but Meredith was subsequently ordered to patrol

northwards, five miles off the coast and towards the Farne Islands. At 00.20 hours on 6 May, Meredith was off Cresswell and flying northwards at 10,000 feet when he sighted an aircraft flying north-west about 200 feet below and just to the left of his own position. Following a diving turn to port, Meredith placed his aircraft 200 feet below and slightly behind his quarry, which he then recognized as a Heinkel 111.

Both aircraft were four miles east of Cresswell when Sergeant Mott fired one very short burst from almost directly below his target. The result was a blinding flash as his bullets struck home and then the bomber banked to starboard and dived towards the sea. On the way down, Meredith saw one tracer fired from the Heinkel's lower rear gun position but the raider made no other attempt to return fire before it dived into the sea, exploding on impact. The Heinkel's demise was witnessed by another Defiant crew and was also confirmed by ground-based observers.

6-7 May 1941 (Morpeth)

Aircraft:	Heinkel 111H-5	A1+CK	w/nr. 3550	2./KG53
Crew:	Uffz. Karl Raßloff	pilot	pow	
	Gefr. Emmerich Lernbass	observer	pow	
	Uffz. Karl Simon	wireless op	pow	
	Gefr. Walter Schmidt	mechanic	pow	
	Gefr. Heinz Quittenbaum	gunner	pow	

In May 1941, Flying Officer Robert 'Bingo' Day and his gunner Pilot Officer Frank Lanning were the crew of a Defiant night fighter of 141 Squadron, Acklington. During the first week of that month they experienced one particularly successful evening of operations when they were credited with shooting down two enemy aircraft within a couple of hours of each other.

On the night of 6-7 May 1941 bombers of *Luftflotten 2* and *3* carried out a number of attacks on northern Britain. Bombs fell over the Tees and Tyne but the main thrust was

LEGION CONDOR

Kampfgeschwader 53 (Legion Condor)

A Boulton-Paul Defiant night-fighter on patrol.
[from the painting *Stalking the night raider* by Roy Nockolds]

against Glasgow and Clydeside. Among the aircraft detailed to attack the Clyde was Heinkel 111 A1+CK of 2./KG53, based at Vitry-en-Artois. Shortly before midnight on the night of 6-7 May, the bomber was approaching the north-east port of Blyth.

Day and Lanning had taken off from Acklington in Defiant N1796 at 23.25 hours with orders to patrol a line between Blyth and Seaham. After one unsuccessful interception, they were ordered to orbit Ashington. As midnight approached, they were near Ashington and flying south at 11,000 feet when they spotted 'a small black dot' silhouetted against cloud and flying west 1,000 feet below them. Day

Pilot Officer Frank Lanning and Flying Officer 'Bingo' Day c.1941.
[Frank Lanning]

made a diving turn to starboard and positioned his aircraft almost underneath the bomber. Then, as was his usual practice, he slid back his cockpit hood to ensure a clearer view as he formated the Defiant 100 feet below the target while his gunner sighted the four Brownings on the underside of the raider. Three short bursts of gunfire were enough to

L - R: Uffz. Karl Simon, wireless operator of He111 A1+CK of 2./KG53, with his pilot, Karl Raßloff, (second left) and two ground mechanics. [Karl Simon]

The wreckage of He111 A1+CK of 2./KG53, which crashed in the grounds of Morpeth Hospital on the night of 6-7 May 1941. [via Ken Watkins]

Heinz Quittenbaum, (right) ventral gunner of He111 A1+CK of 2./KG53. [Karl Simon]

Gefr. Walter Schmidt, (lower right) mechanic and upper gunner of He111 A1+CK of 2./KG53. [Karl Simon]

Maker's plate from the wreck of He 111 A1+CK that crashed at Morpeth on the night of 6-7 May 1941. [A. Stoker]

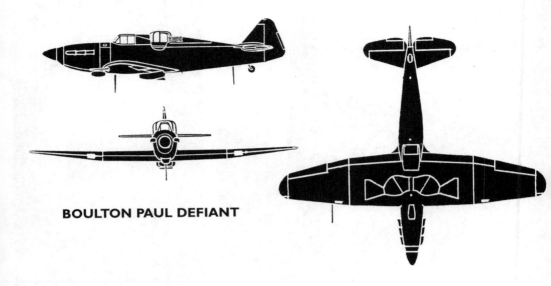

BOULTON PAUL DEFIANT

disable the Heinkel's port engine and set the wing root on fire. The victim dived away sharply, narrowly missing its attacker and spilling incandescent fragments as it spiralled earthwards. The Defiant followed, but Day and Lanning temporarily lost sight of their quarry seconds later when Day had to take violent evasive action after straying into a barrage balloon cordon.

Out of sight of the Defiant, and in spite of the fact that his aircraft was on fire and flying on only one engine, Raßloff seemingly entertained ideas of returning to France. He turned his crippled craft round and headed seawards. At 23.57 hours the RAF Wireless Intelligence Service intercepted Karl Simon's distress transmission: 'CK returning. Engine damaged'.

However, it soon became clear that a return to Vitry-en-Artois was out of the question. Minutes later, Simon transmitted again: 'Landing in England.' The Heinkel crashed in the grounds of St George's Hospital, Morpeth, at 00.05 hours on 7 May. Lanning and Day saw it land in a flurry of sparks before they touched down at Acklington to refuel and re-arm. Hospital attendants were outside when the plane landed and they apprehended the crew of five as they exited from the wreck. Seemingly, the Germans thought that they had fallen victim to two Spitfires.

The Heinkel was on fire when it came down and it was still burning furiously forty minutes later. The crew, who were uninjured, were subsequently taken to Morpeth police station, where they were placed in separate cells pending the arrival of the RAF Intelligence Officer from Kenton (Newcastle).

EYEWITNESS

Shot down over Morpeth, 6-7 May 1941
Uffz. Karl Simon, 2./KG53

Uffz. Karl Simon, wireless operator of He111 A1+CK of 2./KG53 made twenty-nine war flights over Britain between 7 January 1941 – 5 May 1941. His flights included the following operations over the north of England:

25 February 1941	Hull
3 March 1941	Newcastle-on-Tyne
31 March 1941	Hull
9 April 1941	Newcastle-on-Tyne

He made his thirtieth – and final – flight on the night of 6-7 May, and was en route to the Clyde when his aircraft was shot down by a Defiant night fighter of 141 Squadron, Acklington, and crash-landed in the grounds of St. George's Hospital, Morpeth. Fifty-nine years later, he explained to the writer what happened:

> On the night of 6-7 May 1941 we were on our way from Vitry-en-Artois, near Arras, to Dumbarton, near Glasgow. During the flight into England we were attacked by an English Defiant night fighter in the area of Newcastle and repeatedly shot at and hit many times. We could not get away from him; the Defiant was very persistent. A fire was started in our plane, just behind the pilot, and was presumably caused by damaged supply leads. Nearby were oxygen bottles for our

Uffz. Karl Simon, wireless operator of He111 A1+CK of 2./KG53. [Karl Simon]

breathing apparatus and there was also my parachute, which was shot to pieces. The oxygen bottles exploded and blew a hole in the fuselage wall.

The fire in the aircraft could not be extinguished and I could not bale out because of my defective parachute. In these circumstances, Raßloff, an excellent pilot, decided to make an emergency landing in the moonlight and with relatively good visibility. He succeeded in making a good belly landing and none of the crew was injured. I was able to radio an emergency report of our landing and hoped that our HQ would inform my Mother that we had all survived being brought down.

Because the burning plane was in danger of exploding, we all distanced ourselves from the wreck at the double and delivered ourselves to a nearby house, allegedly a hospital. After a short time, the police came and took us away.

In those days our crew was Uffz. Karl Raßloff (pilot), Uffz. Karl Simon (wireless operator and gunner), Gefr. Lernbass (observer, bomb aimer and gunner), Gefr. Schmitz (mechanic and gunner), and Gefr. Heinz Quittenbaum (gunner). Raßloff and I were 23 years old; the rest were 21 years old.

Karl Simon, wireless operator,
He111 (A1+CK) 2./KG53

6–7 May 1941 (Holy Island)

Aircraft:	Junkers 88A-5	4D+EN	w/nr. 7177	5./KG30
Crew:	Uffz. Hans Schaber	pilot	pow	
	Gefr. Heinz Nöske	observer	pow	
	Fw. Paul Graupner	wireless op	pow	
	Gefr. Werner Arndt	gunner	pow	

Following their success over Morpeth (see the preceding entry) and after re-arming and refuelling at Acklington, Day and Lanning were airborne again at 01.15 hours on 7 May. Seventy-five minutes later, they were at altitude 9,000 feet and five miles east of Seaham Harbour when they spotted a Junkers 88 seemingly homeward-bound after visiting Glasgow and the Clyde. The bomber was 'perfectly silhouetted against a bank of cloud...' and 'Bingo' Day manoeuvered the Defiant into a positon 100 feet below and parallel to the bomber's starboard side

When Lanning opened fire, he saw his first burst strike home but observed no obvious damage to the target. However, the vibration of the Brownings was sufficient to throw the gunner's reflector sight out of its socket and against the interior of the turret, thus rendering the sight useless. There was no reply from the German's guns as the bomber swung away to the left on a series of gentle turns to port and starboard – '...the only evasive tactics by the enemy aircraft...' to be noted by the Defiant crew during the engagement.

Day followed and positioned his aircraft almost as before so that Lanning could fire a second (unsighted) burst, again apparently without result. Thus Day resolved to get in closer to allow his gunner the opportunity to fire at point-blank range. As the Defiant drew closer to the bomber, Day threw back his perspex hood to ensure a clearer view – and inadvertantly jammed the muzzle of the lower right gun behind the rear of the cockpit cover. By then, the Junkers was very close but Lanning could not bring his guns to bear. By the time the difficulty had been overcome, the bomber had disappeared. Crestfallen and disappointed, the Defiant crew returned to Acklington, convinced that they had missed a rare opportunity (for 1941) to 'bag' two in one night. Thus they claimed credit for the destruction only of the Heinkel; the Junkers they claimed as damaged.

However, later that day, they learned that a Junkers 88 (4D+EN) had crash-landed on the beach at the north bay of Holy Island, following an engagement with a night fighter, and that the German crew of four had been captured and taken to the police station at Berwick-on-Tweed. The bomber had come down at about 02.45 hours – close to the time of the Defiant's second combat – and, because there were no other defenders in the area contesting the claim, the Ju88 was credited to the Acklington crew.

There must, however, be some doubt about whether Day and Lanning were responsible for the demise of the Junkers. The contemporary combat report submitted by Day and Lanning gave the location of the interception as five miles east of Seaham Harbour (on the coast of County Durham and about sixty miles south of Holy Island) with the

Uffz. Hans Schaber, of 5./KG30, in his Ju88, the front of which carries the Staffel crest. [via Michael Meyer]

raider apparently on its homeward leg. On the other hand, Hans Schaber, the pilot of the Junkers, claimed that the interception occurred within sight of Glasgow and before the bombs were dropped (see Schaber's account below). Such a wide discrepancy is hard to explain – unless, of course, the respective accounts relate to different incidents. When this author first wrote about the incident in *Luftwaffe over the North* he expressed some reservations about the night fighter claim but, on balance, he favoured the odds in support. However, since obtaining a copy of Hans Schaber's full account of the incident from the German pilot's family two years ago, he believes that credit probably lies elsewhere.

EYEWITNESS

Crash-landing on Holy Island, 7 May 1941
Uffz. Hans Schaber, pilot, 5./KG30

Our targets were the port installations at Glasgow. The briefing for the operation took place in the Briefing Room at our quarters at Mariaheim, in Gilze-Rijen(Holland). There our Staffelkapitän gave us our take-off time, told us which wireless beacons would be available, and our route to the target (we rarely flew directly to our objective). As far as I remember, we were to glide in over the Clyde estuary from the North West at our attack height. After dropping our bombs, we could take any route we wanted for the flight home. We wanted a route that would get us away from the area as fast as possible – like I did on both of my previous attacks on Glasgow.

After the briefing, we travelled by bus to the airfield. No-one talked much during the journey: everyone was occupied with his own thoughts. At the airfield, the Staffel was given a short weather briefing at the HQ and then we went to the aircraft. Each machine was stored in its own dispersal and was protected on three-sides by earthen walls spanned by camouflage netting. The Ju88 of my Staffelkapitän, Hauptmann Moog,[13] was located in the next box. The Boss always had his gnarled walking-stick with him and his rear gunner was responsible for ensuring that it was always on the aircraft. When the Boss arrived, he immediately asked for his stick and when the gunner got it for him he went round the aircraft with its dangerous cargo and gave the bomb or mine that was hanging under each wing a light tap with the stick. After that, he climbed into the aircraft followed by the observer and the rear gunner. The wireless operator was already on board and thus it was the rear gunner's task to pull up the ladder and close the hatch.[14] My crew and I also climbed into our machine and we rolled to the start. In the space of a minute we took off and flew alone towards England.

Whenever our targets lay in the southern part of England we did not load so much fuel. Instead, we could take two 1,000kg bombs or mines. But when the objective was in the north, as Glasgow was, we needed a full fuel load and we could take only one 1,000kg bomb and one 500kg bomb. Soon after take-off, I throttled back a little to spare the engines. It was a practice well tried in the whole of my flying experience and I had never had engine damage due to overload.

We had to be at no more than 1,000 metres (1,790 feet) altitude by the time we reached the Dutch coast. It was quiet in the aircraft: only the observer (who was the navigator) occasionally said or asked something. Then we flew over a radio beacon near Den Helder and set our course on Berwick-on-Tweed. Most of our route to Glasgow lay over the North Sea.

The visibility was good as we flew over the North Sea and we could see the English coast on our left and, when we were in the area of the Wash, we saw a convoy following a south-easterly course. Our gunner, Werner Arndt (known as Moritz), had a fear of flak. When we were still 100 kilometres from the coast we could see the guns firing and so every few minutes Moritz would say, 'Hans, flak in front of us'. That was also the case when we were north-east of Berwick-on-Tweed and I turned on to a westerly course and the defences of Glasgow and the surrounding area lay before us. When we were over land, I told Mortiz that the flak could not hurt us but warned him that he had better keep an eye open for night-fighters – but shortly afterwards we got the same call, 'Hans, flak in front of us'.

We flew south of Edinburgh and to the north of Glasgow. The mouth of the Clyde and the port installations could be seen clearly from our altitude of 3,500 metres (11,375 feet). I was turning south-west in order to get on to our attack heading (a south-easterly course) when Graupner shouted, 'Night fighter behind us!' I grabbed the knob and disconnected the automatic pilot with a jerk and dived away – that was my reaction. Our dive angle was about seventy degrees but the fighter still delivered a burst of fire at us. I saw short fiery glow on the left engine and heard a muffled bang.

'He's coming after us!' screamed Graupner. I flew a half roll so that our Ju88 was more on its back as it shot steeply 'downstairs'. I pulled on the stick and we went over the vertical and in the opposite direction. With this manoeuvre we lost our pursuer but I dared not bring the aircraft totally under control too quickly because in the dive – without using brakes – we had reached 750 kilometres per hour (465mph) and the bomb load was still on board. I ordered the bombs to be jettisoned and, after the observer had made the disconnection, I pressed the release button. The bombs dropped free and exploded somewhere in the north or north-east of Glasgow.

After the jettison, I climbed steeply with high speed and full engine power and we soon reached an altitude of over 2,000 metres (6,825 feet). I did not want to go higher. On the climb I had checked the instruments and was satisfied to see that everything seemed to be running normally. Then Moritz reported that the bomb-doors were still open: I told him to crank them up by hand because the lever was near him. And then he reported that we were losing fuel. But it was not fuel, it was coolant. Seconds earlier I had noticed that the pointer on the coolant gauge of the left engine was jerkily nearing boiling point. With the last bit of power, I tried to gain more height but soon I was forced to give up and switch off the left motor to prevent it bursting into flames. To make matters worse, the winding handle for the bomb-doors then jammed and it became impossible to close the doors fully. That created a very unfavourable aerodynamic and a worsening flying situation, especially because we were flying only on one engine. At that time, the Ju88 did not have the powerful engines that were installed on later models, so I could not keep the aircraft in the air without losing some height in order to maintain flying speed. A further complication was that the right motor was not capable of giving extra power because three weeks earlier, during an attack on London, the oil pipe for the left engine had burst and I had to make the return flight using only the right motor.

In order to reduce our overall weight, I ordered that all unnecessary objects should be thrown overboard. These included all of the machine guns and ammunition drums except those of the wireless operator; those were kept in case of emergency. We also jettisoned the bomb-rack. Nöske wanted to get rid of the bomb-sight too but when he tried to unscrew it he got an electric shock – probably because of damage to the mains electrical system.

The plane became easier to fly after I had trimmed it for single-engine flight. We flew southwards of the Firth of Forth and were caught by a group of searchlights. That was particularly unpleasant for me because I could not afford to close my eyes because I needed to constantly observe my flying instruments. For that reason, I determined to fly over the sea. There we were not seen – but we were always getting lower. When we were still 200 metres (650 feet) high – it was in the Berwick area – I informed my comrades, 'We must get out, otherwise we will shortly and suddenly be down below'. The answer that came through the intercom was, as far as I remember, from Nöske. 'We are not baling out. Either we all get down safely together or we all get finished together.' The others said nothing and

I took that to mean that they agreed with Nöske. I was immediately conscious of the additional responsibilty I had taken on – and was also aware of the confidence in me that my comrade's reply had shown. Now it was time to look for a landing place.

I steered over the land and informed the crew that we were going to land on a beach – at night and in bad light. Nöske, being down below, had a better view of the ground. 'We cannot land here: the beach is very narrow and full of rocks!' Because I could still hold the aircraft in the air, I flew on hoping that the beach would be better some kilometres ahead – and so it was. The next beach was straighter and wider than the first one and I prepared to land. I flicked on the landing light – and got a shock. There was a white tower directly in our flightpath and shining in the beam of our light. It was already higher than we were and so there was no alternative but to apply full throttle and turn out to sea once again. Then we were over another beach and I went lower. On my instruction, Graupner jettisoned the cockpit roof and with a hissing sound it flew away behind us. Then, with only a slight easing of the stick, the Ju88 touched its belly on the sand. As it did so, I pushed the stick fully forward to prevent the plane bouncing. The right propeller was still running and it stirred up the fine sand high into the air so that it penetrated all cracks and fell upon us in the cockpit until we finally came to a gentle standstill. I had not lowered the undercarriage for the landing and the electrical alarm was making a great noise to warn us of that. The noise persisted until I switched off the mains' supply, which also closed down the landing light. Then there was silence – followed by a scramble to get out. Although no-one thought to check the time, it was about 02.15 hours when we landed.

Our first priority was to destroy the aircraft so that it would not fall into enemy hands. We had a detonator for this purpose located between our seats and I undertook the task after sending my comrades to take cover behind the dunes. Speed was essential because enemy soldiers could turn up at any time. I took the detonator, removed the adhesive tape from the thread and screwed the charge into position. With a quick glance at my comrades, whose faces I saw in the pale moonlight, I then pulled out the igniter cord to activate the charge and raced off into the dunes.

The charge was supposed to explode after three minutes. We waited expectantly – but nothing happened. Crews were expressly forbidden to return to their aircraft if the detonator failed to explode but after ten minutes of waiting I returned to the Ju88 in spite of warnings from my friends. Because it was dark and I could not see clearly into the cockpit, I had to run my fingers over the device to try to establish what had gone wrong. When I unscrewed the detonator to take a closer look, the top part came away in my hand but the threaded section stayed stuck in the charge. What now? I called my friends over and dropped a parachute on to the sand. I told my comrades to cut out the two shoulder knots on the parachute and to tie them together so that we had one long line. We still had our signal pistol and so I took this and loaded it. Then I opened the filler cap for the wing fuel tanks and stuck the barrel of the pistol into the tank and tied it in place using the chain of the tank cover. I then tied one end of the parachute line to the trigger of the pistol and then went to the other end of the line – a distance of about twenty-five metres (about eighty feet) – and pulled. The pistol fired and a five-metre (sixteen feet) flame shot out of the tank – and with that the fire we had hoped for went out. I repeated the process and achieved the same failure. After a short discussion, we decided to remove the last machine-gun and ammunition drum. We fired the gun at the aircraft from a nearby mound – but still there were no flames from the plane. By this time we were beginning to wonder why we had not been disturbed in our work! Then we made one last try. I climbed into the cockpit once again, this time in order to check that our fuel pumps were still intact. They were and they still worked. We pumped all of the remaining fuel into one tank until it overflowed. Then we soaked the opened parachute in fuel and draped it across the overflowing wing tank and into the cockpit. I used the signal pistol to set the whole lot alight. It burned as high as a house.

In the east it was getting lighter – the start of a new day. We looked into the fire. To our astonishment and regret, the flames were getting smaller and smaller. A German plane on its way home flew over us at about 3,000 metres (9,750 feet) altitude. 'The lucky ones', said Nöske. Meanwhile, the day was becoming brighter. From the south, two men – a policeman and a civilian[15] – came from around a mound and walked towards us. The civilian, who had a gun under his arm, shouted 'Hands up!' and threw a hand in the air in case we did not understand. The policeman removed our remaining weapons from us and then told us to follow him. The civilian with the gun followed on behind.

On the way, we were joined by some of the local inhabitants, including one, perhaps a schoolteacher, who could speak some German: he told us that we were on Holy Island[16]. In the village we were taken to an empty hall – perhaps the dance hall – where we were made to empty our pockets and place the contents on the floor. Some hours passed, during which we were guarded by a member of the local Home Guard, who did not allow us to speak to each other. An officer arrived in the afternoon and he allowed each of us to put our personal belongings in a bag and we were then escorted to a bus, the windows of which had been covered by cloths or blankets. On the short way to the bus, local people shouted loudly at us and these shouts continued until we were driven away.

We did not know our destination, but we later guessed – on the basis of the time taken and the general direction travelled – that we must be in Berwick on Tweed. It was night when we arrived at what seemed to be a police prison and an air raid alarm was sounding. Our soldier escort climbed out of the bus and formed an aisle from the bus to the building. When I arrived at the house door a Sergeant, who was a head taller than me, nearly twice as broad, and who smelled strongly of whiskey, came up to me and grabbed me behind the collar and pulled me to one side so that my comrades could go before me. They were allowed to stay together, but I was pushed into a cell on my own – solitary confinement! Soon after that we had our first meal in England. It was 7 May 1941, our first day in captivity.

On the following day, we were taken to a smaller prison that had corrugated iron huts but no occupants but ourselves. My comrades were again kept together: I was still kept isolated but I did not know why. It was at that place that we met our first interrogator, perhaps an officer, though he was dressed in civilian clothes. Each of us was questioned individually. I had no difficulty answering questions of a personal nature but he received no information of a military nature from me – which perhaps is why I was soon returned to my cell.

It was probably about the 9 May when we were allowed outside to take exercise between the huts. First my comrades for half an hour and then me for half an hour. However, we were always guarded by a sentry with a loaded gun. When I was returned to my cell, I looked out of the window at the sentry, who was still outside. He was speaking to one of his comrades, whom I could not see. He pointed to my hut and said 'Gestapo' and simulated shooting with his gun. That worried me for a while but not for long because I did not have a guilty conscience. The next day we were taken to Edinburgh, where we were questioned by our second and last interrogator (a Captain, I believe) in a camp in which we were again the only inmates. After that, the Englishman must have been convinced that we were harmless because I was allowed to re-join my comrades.

Some days later, about the 14-15 May, we were escorted by two soldiers and taken to the railway station. There, still under guard, we were placed in a reserved compartment in a railway carriage. After a journey of some hours we arrived at a prisoner of war camp at Bury, near Manchester. There we met many of our old friends and so we had much to talk about.

Uffz. Hans Schaber, pilot.
Ju88 4D+EN 5./KG30

"G" or Berwick ....**DIVISION.**

Holy Island ....**STATION.**

16th May, ...19 41.

Divisional No...............

Headquarters No...923..

File No...AA..6/4/5/41.

Subject:—

German plane found at Holy Island.

Sir,

I beg to report that at 4-40a.m. on Wednesday, 7th May, 1941, I received a telephone message from Station Officer Bowen, Holy Island Coastguard Station, to the effect that an aeroplane had landed on the North Shore, Holy Island.

I immediately informed Tweedmouth Police Station by telephone of this message also of the fact that I was going to investigate. I left my lodgings at 4-45a.m. in company with Thomas Walker, an Auxiliary Coast Guard who resides in the same house, and set out for the North Shore which is about two miles from my lodgings. Walker brought with him his Service rifle which he uses in connection with his employment.

I arrived at the North Shore at about 5-10a.m. and there saw a large black aeroplane standing on the shore facing towards the south. Three men, in airmen's clothing, were standing together about 30 to 40 yards away from the machine and as I approached another man came from beside the plane and joined the three. Owing to the darkness I could not see whether this man came from inside the plane or from the far side of it.

I immediately called to the men to surrender as I was of the opinion it was a German plane as I was able to see that there were no Royal Air Force marking on the machine. At the same time I motioned to them to put their hands up by raising my hands and all four raised their hands above their heads.

Examined

Sectional Sergeant.

Walker kept at some distance from the men and I went forward and took an automatic pistol from two of the men and the other two were unarmed. After I had taken the pistols I was about to go over to the plane when one of the men made a signal to me to keep back and motioned with his hands as if the plane was going to explode. We then left with our prisoners to return to the Hut on Holy Island and during the journey kept them covered with the rifle which Walker had with him.

Inspector.

Before leaving the vicinity I saw a red flash in the cabin of the plane which I took to be a fire.

When about half way to the Hut we met some members

Your Ref.........................

FORWARDED for the information of

Police report of the Ju88 crash on Holy Island on 7 May 1941.
[Northumberland Archive Service File NC/6/10]

of the Holy Island detatchment of the Home Guard and I
requested Sergeant George Allison, who was in charge, to
put a guard on the plane and informed him to keep back in
view of what had happened.   Allison agreed to do this.

We continued on our way to the Hut and arrived there
at 5-45a.m. The prisoners were put in the one room together with three members of the Home Guard who were armed
and I requested them to prevent the prisoners from speaking to each other. As I was satisfied the prisoners were
in safe hands I returned to my lodgings and phoned Berwick
Police Station giving a short report of what had happened.

I then returned to the Hut and on my arrival there
found that the Home Guard had been replaced by the Military
who are stationed at Low Lynn; this is the 9th Border
Regiment.   An officer was in charge of the party and
he was engaged in searching the prisoners and he informed
me that he had sent some of his men to relieve the Home
Guard who were guarding the plane.

I then received a telephone message from Inspector
Smith, Berwick Police Station, to the effect that he was
coming to Holy Island as soon as possible with an escort
to take the prisoners to Berwick Police Station.

Inspector Smith, in company with P.C.'s McKenzie and
Davidson, and Special Constable Ross, arrived in an United
Bus shortly after 7-30a.m.   The prisoners were then put in
to the bus, along with the property which had been taken
from them, and I also accompanied them to Berwick Police
Station.

I was on duty in Berwick Police Station until 3p.m.
when I left to return to my station.

I am,
Sir,
Your obedient Servant,

Robert Steel
P.W.R. 172.

Sergt. W. Middlemas,
Police Station,
TWEEDMOUTH.

P.W.R. Steel.

*I have been informed that the prisoners were
found by the Officer of the 9th Border Regiment drinking tea
and eating chocolate. Is this correct.* *Supt.*
17/5.41.

Sir,

A further report is attached.

Robert Steel
P.W.R.172.

2 June 1941 (off Tyne)

Aircraft:	Junkers 88A-5	M2+DL[17]	w/nr. 3422	Ku.Fl.Gr. 3./106
Crew:	Obfw. Bernhard Winse	pilot	+	
	Oblt. z. See Hans Berger	observer	pow	
	Obgfr. Karl Schummers	wireless op	pow	
	Obgfr. Heinrich Forstbach	gunner	+	

This was one of two aircraft from this unit which were lost on 2 June 1941. M2+DL was shot down by Hurricanes of 317 Squadron, Ouston, and crashed into the sea off the Tyne.

In the late evening of 2 June three aircraft from 3./106 took off separately from Amsterdam-Schipol for an anti-shipping operation along the north-east coast of England and each aircraft was armed with four 250kg bombs. M2+DL crossed the North Sea alone at 3,500 feet and on reaching Flamborough Head, swung northwards along the coast. The Junkers was in the area of the Tyne when Winse and his crew were taken completely by surprise by an attack by two fighters.

Between 22.00 hours-22.50 hours eight aircraft of A and B Flights of 317 Squadron were on convoy patrol off Amble and Blyth. After being airborne for some thirty minutes, two Hurricanes of Black Section of B Flight were vectored on to three enemy aircraft on the basis of information provided by the local Observer Corps. The fighters subsequently intercepted one enemy machine and approached in line astern behind the raider before climbing and delivering a diving attack on both beams. Flying Officer Niemlec(?) (in Hurricane V7123) reported that Sergeant Baranowski (Hurricane W9183) practically rammed the enemy machine during the encounter, in which Baranowski used all of his ammunition in one sustained burst. After a very brief engagement, in which Forstbach managed only one burst of gunfire in reply to a withering fusillade that peppered the raider's fuselage and put both engines out of action, Winse was forced to make an emergency landing on the sea.

Confirmation of the fighters' victory came when D Flight, 936 Barrage Balloon (Tyne) Squadron, later reported that a German aircraft had been shot down into the sea at 22.28 hours by a British fighter plane. The location was given as two miles east of the Tyne and although this is nearer to the coast than that given in 317 Squadron's claim (four miles off the coast), it is believed that both reports relate to the same incident.

Three members of the crew succeeded in getting out of the Ju88 before it sank but Forstbach is believed to have been still in the aircraft when it disappeared beneath the waves. Bernhard Winse, who, like Forstbach, may have been wounded in the engagement, managed to evacuate the aircraft but drowned before would-be rescuers could reach him. His comrades Berger and Schummers were picked up by a trawler soon after their aircraft had landed on the sea.

During his interrogation, one of the prisoners from M2+DL recounted the story of the crew of a Heinkel 115 floatplane who took off one night without casting off from their mooring buoy. Unaware of their extra 'baggage', they arrived over London trailing the buoy, a sphere of six feet diameter. The aircraft was subsequently caught by searchlights and the sphere, which was encrusted with cut-glass reflectors, shone in all directions and attracted an increasing amount of hostile attention from ground-based defenders. When the German crew realized that the 'beacon' was attached to their aircraft, the Heinkel's wireless operator climbed out of the aircraft and on to one of the floats, from where he cut the sphere free. The reactions of ground-based witnesses to this 'celestial manifestation' can only be guessed.

2 June 1941 (off the Tyne?)

Aircraft: Junkers 88A-5		M2+BL	w/nr. 6180 Ku.Fl.Gr. 3./106
Crew:	Obfw. Hans Vieck	pilot	missing
	Oblt. z. See Wilhelm Maschmann	observer	missing
	Uffz. Gerhard Emmerich	wireless op	missing
	Uffz. Walter Börge	gunner	missing

There is a possibility that the second aircraft lost by *Kustenfliegergruppe 3/106* on the night of 2 June 1941 was also shot down off the Tyne, by the balloon-carrying drifter *Marcia*, a motor vessel of the Marine Section of D Flight, 936 Barrage Balloon (Tyne) Squadron.

The vessel was moored at the Tyne's North Buoy when an air raid warning 'Red' was received at 23.50 hours. Two minutes later, there was the sound of an aircraft approaching from the north. RAF Corporal W.V. Armstrong, the NCO in charge of the balloon crew on the drifter, was on deck with the *Marcia*'s skipper, John Redpath Burn. Judging from the sound, Armstrong decided that the plane was flying at low altitude. When he saw it seconds later, it was at 1,000 feet – just about at cloud base. He immediately took the plane to be a Junkers 88, because the silhouette showed the engine nacelles projecting unusually far forward of the wings.

A wartime Lewis gun crew 'pose' for action. [Author's collection]

When the aircraft dived towards the *Marcia*, Armstrong thought it was going to attack them:

> I immediately manned the Lewis gun and opened fire at a range of about 200 yards. The aircraft passed to west of the drifter, flying about 300 feet below the clouds, and then climbed into the clouds. In the burst that I fired at the machine I expended one pan of ammunition of ninety-seven rounds.

Seemingly, Armstrong's aim was true for within a minute, he and others on the drifter saw a flash just below the clouds about two miles south-south-east of the Tyne's south pier and then saw a large object dropping into the sea with burning pieces flying from it. A northerly breeze was blowing that night and the machine flew downwind after being engaged. Thus there was no sound of an explosion, but those on board the drifter were in no doubt that they had observed the demise of the Junkers and Armstrong submitted a claim for one enemy aircraft destroyed.

His report was supported by John Redpath Burn, skipper of the *Marcia* and, to some extent at least, by two military officers who had been travelling from Northumberland Dock to Tynemouth at the time of the engagement. They had seen 'an oversized flare' in the sky to the south-east at about the time stated by Armstrong and stated that it '...dropped into the sea at a rate faster than flares normally fall...'. On the basis of the above submissions, on 15 June 1941, Fighter Command credited 936 Balloon Squadron with the 'probable destruction' of the enemy plane.

Examination of the Luftwaffe Loss Returns shows that Junkers 88A-5 M2+BL (w/nr.6180) of *Kustenfliegergruppe 3./106* failed to return from operations that night, although the aircraft's target and area of loss are not stated. However, given that both aircraft were from the same unit, and that the Hurricanes had initially been vectored on to three enemy aircraft, it seems likely that M2+BL was shot down by Armstrong.

24-25 June 1941 (east of Seaham Harbour)

Aircraft:	Heinkel 111H-5	1H+MK	w/nr. 3749	2./KG26
Crew:	Oblt. Heinrich Oswald	pilot	pow	
	Fw. Herbert Dahnke	observer	pow	
	Uffz. Otto Meyer	wireless op	pow	
	Gefr. Werner Ölgarth	gunner	pow	

24-25 June 1941 (east of Blyth)

Aircraft:	Heinkel 111H-5	1H+AK	w/nr. 3671	2./KG26
Crew:	Uffz. Willi Kerney	pilot	pow	
	Gefr. Helmut Ackermann	observer	pow	
	Gefr. Herbert Wolf	wireless op	pow	
	Obgfr. Rudolf Oed	gunner	pow	

On the night of 24-25 June 1941, five Heinkel 111s of 1./KG26 and six Heinkel 111s of 2./KG26 took off from Aalborg to search for a southbound convoy that was reported to be somewhere between the Firth of Forth and the river Tees. Each aircraft was armed with one 500kg bomb and four 250kg bombs. The raiders lost three aircraft on this operation, two of which came down off the Northumberland-Durham coast. The third one (1H+BH; w/nr.3694), piloted by *Feldwebel* Willi Lehmann of 1./KG26, was lost further north.

Lehmann flew low over the North Sea but had difficulty locating the objective because of poor visibility. However, after some time he found a convoy approximately twelve miles south-east of May Island, off the Firth of Forth. The Germans opted to aim for a convoy escort, the destroyer HMS *Versatile* (I.32), and attacked across the beam, dropping all of their

The destroyer HMS Versatile. [Imperial War Museum. Neg No. FL20966]

bombs in salvo from a height of seventy feet. The combined defensive anti-aircraft fire from *Versatile* and other vessels in the convoy, damaged the Heinkel, stopping its port engine and setting the starboard motor on fire. At 01.30 hours on 25 June, Lehmann was forced to ditch in the North Sea about three miles from the convoy. The aircraft remained afloat for thirteen minutes and gave ample time for the crew to get into their dinghy, from which they were subsequently rescued by the destroyer. Heinkels 1H+MK and 1H+AK operated further south – but shared a similar fate.

1H+MK of 2./KG26, piloted by the unit's *Staffelkapitän, Oberleutnant*

Heinrich Oswald, came across a small convoy of eight ships in the area of the Tyne and attacked two freighters, of 3,000 tons and 1,000 tons respectively. The German's 500kg bomb was aimed at the smaller ship and the four 250kg bombs straddled the larger vessel, but none of the bombs found its target. The ships' gunners, however, were more successful; the bomber was hit by light anti-aircraft fire and suffered engine damage. Oswald turned for home but managed to fly only a further twenty miles before (at 00.30 hours on 25 June) he was forced

Launch No.146 of 15 Air-Sea Rescue Marine Craft Unit, Blyth.
[Newcastle Chronicle & Journal]

to ditch his aircraft on the sea some sixty miles east-south-east of Seaham Harbour. The Germans took to their rubber dinghy and were adrift for thirty-seven hours before they were picked up.

Thirty minutes after Oswald had ditched, 1H+AK of 2./KG26 sighted shipping in about the same area as that of Oswald's encounter but the aircraft was damaged by ship's gun fire before it could even launch an attack. Both motors were put out of action and the Heinkel was forced to ditch at 01.00 hours, when it was thirty miles east of Blyth. The crew, who were on their first operational flight, took to their dinghy and were picked up sixteen hours later by an air-sea rescue launch from Blyth.

23 August 1941 (north of Holy Island)

Aircraft: Heinkel 111H-5		1H+EA	w/nr. 3691 Stab/KG26
Crew:	Hptm. Georg Wilhelm	pilot	pow
	Uffz. Hans Hilpert	observer	pow
	Uffz. Otto Siedel	wireless op	pow
	Obgfr. Franz Schmidt	gunner	pow

In the early evening of 23 August 1941, at least six aircraft of 1./KG26 took off from Aalborg on an armed reconnaissance mission to search for a southbound convoy that had been reported off the northern coast of Britain. One of those aircraft was Heinkel 111 1H+EA, which took off at about 19.00 hours armed with one 500kg bomb and four 250kg bombs.

The Heinkel crossed the North Sea in the company of another aircraft and at an altitude of 150-300 feet, partly to aid the easier detection of potential targets but also to reduce the risk of detection by British defences. The latter strategy worked, but only to a point. At about 21.10

He111 of KG 26 being prepared for anti-shipping operations. Note the ship 'victories' painted on the rudder. [Hans Hilpert]

hours, British radar registered three hostile raiders off Middlesbrough and tracked them northwards until they faded off Holy Island.

As it flew northwards, 1H+EA was with another Heinkel 111 and was flying along the coast of Northumberland in sea mist and the gathering darkness when an unseen destroyer opened fire before the German crew was even aware that shipping was in sight. Their port engine was hit but it did not stop and the crew thought that they might be able to make it back home. However, five minutes later the engine began to fail. The crew attempted to lighten the load by jettisoning the 250kg bombs and all moveable gear but they failed to jettison the 500kg bomb. Seemingly, 1H+EA was not their usual aircraft and it appears to have had a bomb-release mechanism with which the crew was not familiar. Thus the 500kg bomb remained in place. Had it been jettisoned, they might have made it home, but with the added weight the aircraft lost height and came down in the sea just north of Holy Island at 21.30 hours.

Fifty-nine years later, Hans Hilpert, the Heinkel's observer, described to the writer what happened that night:

> I do not remember anything special until we were hit by one or more bullets, by which one of the two motors was left stuttering. Our pilot, Captain Wilhelm, tried to hold the plane aloft. This worked for a few minutes. However, slowly we got lower and lower until we reached a height of about fifteen feet above the very calm sea. At this point the crew decided unanimously to risk a soft water landing. It worked perfectly.
>
> We left the plane in a self-inflating rubber boat. I was sure that we could paddle 300 miles east for a landfall in Denmark. However, it

The crew of He.111 1H+EA of Stab./KG26, who were shot down by naval gunfire off Holy Island on the night of 23 August 1941. L-R: Obgfr. Franz Schmidt (gunner), Uffz. Hans Hilpert (observer), Hptm. Georg Wilhelm (pilot), and Uffz. Otto Siedel (wireless operator). [Hans Hilpert]

took me only minutes of paddling to realise that this was sheer wishful thinking. The next thing I realised was that the secret code book was left in the plane so I returned over the wing to the inside of the plane and dived for the code. However, I did not find it so I returned to the boat.

After a while of guessing what to do, there appeared the mighty bow of a man-of-war right in front of our tiny boat. A boat was let down with about eight helmeted soldiers and they took us on board the ship. We were welcomed in a rather friendly manner and taken to a Mess corresponding to one's rank.

We were blindfolded when we left the ship, I suppose at Edinburgh, and were transported by train to London to be interrogated, mainly at Queen's Park, a sort of castle which was said to be owned by Sir Phillip Sassoon.

EYEWITNESS

Attacks on shipping
by KG26

We always started from Aalborg airport after information had been received that a convoy would be on the way near the Firth of Forth. Usually we started in the evening (summer time), early enough for having a minimum of daylight when arriving over the convoy and singling out a ship for the attack.

The attack took place from about 100 feet above the water, releasing a 500kg bomb when a ship appeared well ahead and hoping that it would be hit just below the waterline. It always seemed to me like a sort of unreal happening. Only days later I realized that human beings might have been badly wounded or killed.

During the attack we were surrounded by a firework of tracer-shells from the battle ships. Arriving home again, it was just guesswork when we reported having sunk a ship. The average survival rate for crews was about six attacks on convoys.

Hans Hilpert, observer,
He111 (1H+EA), Stab./KG26

EYEWITNESS

Anti-shipping operations
with KG26

Wing Commander S.D. Felkin was involved with Air Intelligence 1(k), the department responsible for the interrogation of Luftwaffe prisoners

117

of war. The following is an extract from a report dealing with the interrogation of the crew of He111 1H+EA of Stab./KG26, which was shot down by a destroyer off Holy Island on 23 August 1941:

Information as to the movements of British convoys is said to be reasonably accurate and detailed, but owing to cloud and mist it is largely a matter of chance whether aircraft locate their targets, especially as crews usually operate at night. Crews frequently search for convoys for long periods without success, and conversely it sometimes happens that in bad visibility aircraft find themselves on top of a convoy when they least expect it. This occurred in the case of 1H+EA, which was hit by A.A.(anti-aircraft fire) from a destroyer before the crew realised that shipping was in sight. It seems clear from interrogation that the aircraft have no detector apparatus or means of predicting the movements of shipping or of aircraft.

The best conditions for attack were considered to be a rough sea, when A.A. could less easily be brought to bear and a vessel would ship more water if damaged by a bomb. It was also thought that the look-out maintained by ships would be less keen in rough weather.

As a rule, at least two aircraft of the Gruppe operate each night. Flights are taken in turn and each crew flies about once a week.

W/Cdr. S.D. Felkin, Air Intelligence 1(k).
Extract from Report (No.453/1941, dated 4.9.1941)
of debrief of the crew of He111 1H+EA

1 September 1941 (Bedlington Station)

Aircraft:	Junkers 88A-4	4D+BD		w/nr.1064	StabIII./KG30
Crew:	Obfw. Helmut Riede	pilot	+		
	Oblt. Rudolf Elle	observer	+		
	Obfw. Helmut Dorn	wireless op	+		
	Fw. Walter Müller	gunner	+		

On the night of 1 September 1941, the Beaufighters of 406 Squadron, Acklington, opened their score-sheet when Flying Officer R.C. Fumerton (with Sergeant Bing) caught a Newcastle-bound Junkers 88 (4D+BD) of StabIII/KG30 (*Adler Geschwader*) off Blyth and sent it crashing to earth.

Fumerton had been scrambled from Acklington (in Beaufighter R2336) at 21.15 hours and was subsequently passed over to the Ground Control Interception (GCI) controller whose job it was to guide the night fighter close enough to its target to allow Sergeant Bing to get an AI contact. After being given a number of vectors that came to nothing, Fumerton was given vector 290. That was the bearing he was on when, at an altitude of 11,000 feet, Bing got his first AI blip on the radar screen at 5,000 feet range. He held it until his pilot got visual sight of their quarry.

118

A Beaufighter night fighter crew prepares for a night sortie. [The War Weekly, 1941]

The target aircraft was crossing ahead of the fighter, from starboard to port, and in a south-westerly direction that would eventually take it over the Northumberland coastal town of Cambois. Closing in, Fumerton calculated that the, as yet, unidentified aircraft was about 400 feet higher than his own and at some 500 yards range. As his quarry entered a patch of cloud, Fumerton turned to port and followed before easing his machine into a gentle dive to settle himself below the target in order to identify it and to remain unseen, a task made relatively easy because the raider was flying towards the moon.

Shortly afterwards, Fumerton recognized that the 'bogey' was hostile but he mistakenly identified it as a Heinkel 111 and closed to 100 yards behind and below before pulling up the nose of his aircraft and opening fire at fifty yards range. Explosions in the bomber's fuselage and a blazing starboard engine were the first results of the combined fire-power of the Beaufighter's four Hispano 20mm cannon and six .303 Browning machine guns. The planes were over Cambois when the German fell away to port with the fighter following behind. Fumerton moved in for his second attack when the bomber momentarily levelled out and its top rear gunner opened up with heavy but ineffective return fire. Approaching from dead astern and slightly above, Fumerton replied with devastating effect: the enemy machine exploded in mid-air, severing the tail unit and leaving what remained to fall in flaming pieces on to the drying beds of the brickworks (military ref. U7302) at Bedlington Station. The bomber

F/O R.C. Fumerton (left) *and his navigator/ radar Sgt. Bing with a trophy recovered from 'their' Ju88 (4D+BD) of Stab III./KG30 that crashed at Bedlington Station, 1 September 1941.*
[Author's collection]

crashed at 22.11 hours and burned furiously for three hours although appliances from the Bedlington Auxiliary Fire Service were in attendance. The plane, which was subsequently identified as a Ju88, was a complete wreck.

About thirty seconds after the plane crashed, four 250kg bombs exploded in fields behind Burnside housing estate (mil. ref. 768037), Bedlington Station, but caused neither casualties nor damage. The tail of the machine was subsquently found lying in a field near West Sleekburn, north of the crash site, and three oxygen cylinders with German markings, together with several pieces of aeroplane, were found fifty yards south of Moor House Farm, Ashington. On Monday 8 September, J. Pattison, of Red Row Farm, Bedlington, found a number of items in the cornfield behind his house – two oxygen cylinders, one compass and a belt containing five rounds of ammunition. On 26 September 1941 a rubber dinghy with accessories, together with the port tail-plane of the Junkers 88, were found in a cornfield at the side of Brock Lane, West Sleekburn Farm. The dinghy was without its two and a quarter inch compass. That was found seven months later (27 April 1943) in a field north of Freeman's Crossing, Cambois, by George Harvey, of Sinker's Row, Cambois.

RAF personnel began clearing the wreck site on 2 September and over two days they retrieved the bodies of the crew – *Oberleutnant* Rudolf Elle, *Oberfeldwebels* Helmut Riede and Helmut Dorn, and *Feldwebel* Walter Müller – all of whom were later buried in Chevington cemetery, near Broomhill, Northumberland.

7 September 1941 (Newcastle area?)

Aircraft:	Dornier 217E-1	F8+FM	w/nr. 125	4./KG40
Crew:	Fw. Walter Nemming	pilot	missing	
	Lt. Johann Jujowa	observer	missing	
	Obfw. Ernst Elterlien	wireless op	missing	
	Uffz. Helmut Alexander	mechanic	missing	

According to the Luftwaffe Loss Returns for 7 September 1941, this aircraft was lost during an operational sortie to Newcastle but the returns give no indication of the cause or location of the loss. However, 406 Squadron, Acklington, did file a claim for one enemy aircraft damaged

Police report of the Ju88 crash at Bedlington Station on 1 September 1941.
[Northumberland Archive Service F NC/6/10]

"C" or BLYTH .... **DIVISION.**

.... BEDLINGTON .... **STATION.**

2nd., September, 19 41

Divisional No. C. 1983.

Headquarters No. 2747

Ref. No. .......A.R.

Subject:—   AIR RAID REPORT.

Sir,

    I beg to report that at 22.06 hours on Mondaym 1st., September, 1941, the "Alert" was received at this Office and immediately aerial activity commenced in the district.

    At 22.09 hours a short aerial combat was heard over Cambois and a plane was seen to be on fire and in a few seconds this plane crashed on the drying sheds at Bedlington Station Brickyard (Map reference 761039) in flames and burned furiously for three hours. The fire was dealt with by the Bedlington A.F.S..

    The plane was subsequently identified as a German machine; a Junkers 88, 1941 make, and was a complete wreck.

    About 30 seconds after the above plane crashed bombs burst in fields behind Burnside Housing Estate, Bedlington Station (Map reference 768037), and upon examination it was found four H.E. Bombs of about 250 K.G. had exploded in arable fields doing no damage to property or causing any casualties.

    On Tuesday a party of R.A.F. members, working under the direction of Flying Officer McKenzie of Carluke, Techincal Investigation Officer, and Flying Officer Benson, Newcastle Interrogation Officer, commenced to clear the wrecked plane away and at 6 p.m. the badly burnt and mangled remains of one of the crew was recovered and two others were partly uncovered and will be removed tomorrow.

    The tail and rudder of the machine was found shot away, lying in a field near West Sleekburn (Map reference 763058).

I am, Sir,
Your obedient servant,

Inspector.

Examined

Sectional Sergeant.

Inspector.

Superintendent.

Supt. James Cunningham,
    County Police Office,
      BLYTH.

Your Ref.....................

FORWARDED for the information of The Chief Constable, War Department, County Police Office, Morpeth.

CHIEF CONSTABLE'S OFFICE
DIVISIONAL POLICE OFFICE,
MORPETH   BLYTH.

3rd. September, 19 41.

CHIEF CONSTABLE
Superintendent.

that night and this gives rise to speculation that there may be a connection between that claim and the loss of the KG40 Dornier 217 (F8+FM).

Flying Officer R.C. Fumerton (with Sergeant L.P.S. Bing), in a Beaufighter (R2336) of 406 Squadron, Acklington, carried out a three-hour operational sortie on the night of 7 September 1941, and at 22.25

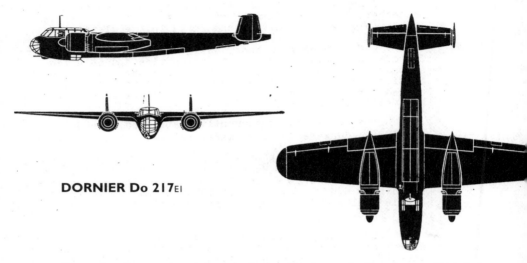

DORNIER Do 217EI

hours they engaged and damaged what Fumerton believed was a Heinkel 111 six miles east of Hartlepool.

The Beaufighter had left Acklington at 21.10 hours for practice interceptions with Ground Control Interception (GCI). At about 22.15 hours raiders were in the area and GCI gave various vectors in a south-easterly direction. At 22.22 hours, when the night fighter was flying at 8,000 feet on a heading of 160°, Bing got his first AI blip at 7,000ft range ahead and below. The enemy aircraft appeared to be making slow left and right turns. Bing maintained AI contact until Fumerton obtained a visual sighting of his quarry at about 1,000ft range. The clear silhouette against a background of cloud was ahead, below and slightly to port of the Beaufighter, which was then at an altitude of 6,500 feet and flying approximately south with the German 1,000 feet below and flying in the same direction as the fighter.

As Fumerton closed in, the German seemingly recognized the danger and dived in a left turn towards the layer of nine-tenths cloud some 500 feet below him. Fumerton followed and managed two short bursts of machine-gun and cannon fire from 200 yards before the enemy machine disappeared in the cloud. Fumerton saw his De Wilde ammunition striking home on the German's fuselage but he saw no cannon shell bursts. The Beaufighter followed the raider down through the cloud by tracking him on AI but the target was lost at 2,000 feet, when the trace disappeared off the tube. There was no return fire from the bomber during the brief engagement.

The Luftwaffe Loss Returns do not show a relevant He111 damaged by enemy action on this date but they do record the loss of the crew of *Feldwebel* Walter Nemming in a Do217E-1 (F8+FM; w/nr.125) of 4./KG40, which was lost on a sortie to Newcastle-on-Tyne. Thus there is the possibility that Fumerton wrongly identified his victim and was more successful than he thought, but there is no proof of any connection between the two incidents.

30 September 1941 (off the Tyne?)

Aircraft:	Junkers 88A-4	4D+MR	w/nr. 3502	7./KG30
Crew:	Lt. Werner Kühnle	pilot	missing	
	Fw. Rudolf Callier	observer	missing	
	Uffz. Heinz Bartelt	wireless op	missing	
	Obgfr. Gustav Petzka	gunner	missing	

Raiders, including twelve Do217 bombers of II./KG2, attacked the Tyne area on the night of 30 September 1941 and South Shields, in particular, felt the effects of at least thirty-four high explosives. A number of those were believed to have been of 1,000kg (2,200lbs) calibre and their devastating impact caused widespread damage to industrial and domestic properties alike. Eighteen people died in the attack, eighty-six others were injured and 300 were rendered homeless.[18]

406 Squadron, Acklington, scrambled seven Beaufighters at various times between 20.15 hours – 22.05 hours. Most of them had no luck but the Squadron CO, Wing Commander Morris (with Sergeant A.V. Rix), chased several enemy machines before catching a Junkers 88 east of the Tyne.

Morris took off from Acklington at 21.16 hours and was operating under Ground Control Interception when, twenty miles east of Tynemouth, Rix got a momentary AI blip of an enemy aircraft slightly above and to starboard at maximum range and flying due east. Under Rix's directions, Morris regained AI contact, which was maintained until a visual sighting was obtained at 3,000 feet range. Morris closed to 100 yards range, with the enemy machine positioned slightly to port and above, and identified his quarry as a Ju88. The Beaufighter attacked the bomber from level and dead astern at 22.09 hours, when both aircraft were at 9,000 feet and some forty-five miles off Tynemouth.

Morris saw flashes – 'one flash very brilliant' – in the raider's fuselage as his own shells struck home. The German dorsal gunner immediately returned the fire and a short, sharp combat took place, during which Morris attacked his target twice more. After the third assault, the return

W/Cdr. D.G. Morris, DFC, commanding 406 (Beaufighter) Squadron.
[Imperial War Museum. Neg No.4884]

fire ceased and the Junkers slowed down so rapidly that the Beaufighter overshot, Morris narrowly avoiding collision when he passed twenty feet above and forty feet to starboard of his victim. Even then, no return gunfire was experienced from the Junkers, but both Morris and Rix saw the red glow of fire in the bomber's cockpit. Seconds later, the enemy machine burst into flames and snapped into an ever-steepening dive to starboard before smacking into the sea.

As he turned for home, Morris discovered that the contest had not been totally one-sided. The port engine of his Beaufighter (R2378) started to throw out sparks and when it began to seriously vibrate, the pilot was forced to close it down and return to base on his starboard engine only. After the Beaufighter had landed, its crew might well have felt that luck had been on their side for not only had the port wing been holed in a number of places by enemy gunfire, the port engine had also been seriously damaged. In addition, the starboard engine had also been hit but not sufficiently to cause a malfunction.

Currently, the writer has no definite details of the Ju88 and its crew, but the Luftwaffe Loss Returns do show that Ju88A-4 (4D+MR) (w/nr.3502) of 7./KG30 failed to return from operations on this date.

However, because the location and cause of the loss of 4D+MR are not given in the Returns, there is no guarantee that this particular aircraft was the one that fell foul of Morris and Rix.

EYEWITNESS

Heinrich Suschake,
wireless operator, 4./KG2

During the period July 1940 – January 1942, Luftwaffe wireless operator *Feldwebel* Heinrich Suschake flew sixty operational flights over England, all of them with 4./KG2 and most of them with *Oberleutnant* Walter Bornschein.

apfer und einsatzbereit gegen England
Neue Bilder von erfolgreichen Flugzeugbesatzungen

Besatzung Oberleutnant Bornschein

Oberleutnant Bornschein   Ofw. Bredtmeyer   Ofw. Lohrer   Uffz. Suschka

Luftwaffe wireless operator Heinrich Suschake flew most of his operational sorties over England as a member of Oblt. Walter Bornschein's crew, the above pictures of whom appeared in the Luftwaffe magazine Adler über Land und Meer *on 30 March 1941. The caption reads:* 'Brave and ready for action against England. New pictures of successful aircrews. Crew of Oberleutnant Bornschein.' *Of the four, only Suschake and Friedrich Lohrer (mechanic) survived the war. Johannes Bredtmeyer (observer) was lost when the Do217 in which he was flying was shot down and crashed into the sea some twenty-five miles off the Tyne on the night of 7-8 July 1942(see p157);Walter Bornschein went on to win the Iron Cross (both First and Second Class) and the Knight's Cross, and had flown over 225 operational sorties before he was shot down and killed while flying a night fighter against a bombing raid on Schweinfurt on the night of 27 April 1944.* [via Rolf Zöphel]

The following extract from his logbook gives the details of fifty-eight of those flights, which included seven sorties to the Humber and one to Newcastle-on-Tyne. In the latter instance, on the night of 30 September-1 October 1941, Suschake's Do217 (U5+AM) was one of twelve Dornier bombers of II./KG2 that dropped a total of forty-eight 500kg high explosives in the area of Newcastle, North Shields and South Shields.

As can be seen from the logbook, Suschake's sorties embraced a range operational activities – armed reconnaissance, attacks on shipping, raids on aerodromes, the bombing of port installations, railways, gun emplacements and industrial targets, and the mining of river estuaries and shipping lanes.

Op	Date	Time up/down	Aircraft	Staffel	Base	Target
1	04.07.40	14.10-15.47	Do17/U5+AM	4./KG2	St Leger	Convoy between Alderney and Dover.
2	07.07.40	20.41-21.55	Do17/U5+AM	4./KG2	St Leger	Convoy off Dover. Emergency landing after fighter attack.
3	24.07.40	08.57-10.14	Do17/U5+CM	4./KG2	St Leger	Convoy between Deal and Ramsgate.
4	25.07.40	19.55-21.16	Do17/U5+DM	4./KG2	St Leger	Convoy SE of Folkestone.
5	11.08.40	12.16-13.22	Do17/U5+DM	4./KG2	St Leger	Nuisance raid over Channel.
6	12.08.40	17.32-19.16	Do17/U5+DM	4./KG2	St Leger	Aerodrome Canterbury.
7	13.08.40	05.51-08.48	Do17/U5+DM	4./KG2	St Leger	Aerodrome Eastchurch.
8	15.08.40	15.00-16.46	Do17/U5+DM	4./KG2	St Leger	Port installations at Dover.
9	18.08.40	17.34-20.06	Do17/U5+DM	4./KG2	St Leger	Rly stations at Southend. Gravesend and Rayleigh.
10	21.08.40	17.34-20.06	Do17/U5+DM	4./KG2	St Leger	Port installations at Lowestoft and Southwold.
11	28/29.08.40	22.05-00.20	Do17/U5+IM	4./KG2	St Leger	Oil storage installations, Thameshaven.
12	29.08.40	03.20-05.37	Do17/U5+IM	4./KG2	St Leger	Port installations at Hull.
13	31.08.40	22.54-00.58	Do17/U5+KM	4./KG2	St Leger	Night aircraft aerodrome.
14	03.09.40	09.46-12..26	Do17/U5+IM	4./KG2	St Leger	North Weald aerodrome.
15	05.09.40	09.27-11.44	Do17/U5+CM	4./KG2	St Leger	Biggin Hill aerodrome.
16	06.09.40	02.15-04.08	Do17/U5+CM	4./KG2	St Leger	Surrey Docks, London.
17	12.09.40	01.38-04.15	Do17/U5+CM	4./KG2	St Leger	Industrial installations, London.
18	15.09.40	13.51-16.45	Do17/U5+CM	4./KG2	St Leger	Docks east of London.
19	16.09.40	07.25-09.44	Do17/U5+EM	4./KG2	St Leger	Nuisance raid, London.
20	04.01.41	03.53-06.32	Do17/U5+AM	4./KG2	Merville	Bristol.
21	05.01.41	03.43-06.40	Do17/U5+AM	4./KG2	Merville	Port installations, Bristol.
22	09.01.41	20.50-00.14	Do17/U5+AM	4./KG2	Merville	Arms industries, Manchester.
23	10.01.41	03.58-06.44	Do17/U5+AM	4./KG2	Merville	Nuisance raid, Derby.
24	21.01.41	11.23-13.12	Do17/U5+AM	4./KG2	Merville	AA positions, Aldeburgh.
25	28.01.41	15.30-17.07	Do17/U5+AM	4./KG2	Merville	Nuisance raid, London.
26	30.01.41	11.38-14.07	Do17/U5+AM	4./KG2	Merville	Nuisance raid, Peterborough.
27	30.01.41	15.30-18.05	Do17/U5+AM	4./KG2	Merville	Ely railway station.
28	31.01.41	14.22-15.40	Do17/U5+AM	4./KG2	Merville	Nuisance raid, London.
29	01.02.41	11.52-14.41	Do17/U5+AM	4./KG2	Merville	Mildenhall aerodrome.
30	02.02.41	10.17-12.12	Do17/U5+AM	4./KG2	Merville	Mildenhall aerodrome.
31	02.02.41	16.02-17.35	Do17/U5+AM	4./KG2	Merville	Nuisance raid, London.
32	03.02.41	09.57-12.00	Do17/U5+AM	4./KG2	Merville	Aerodrome, East Wretham.
33	04.02.41	09.17-10.45	Do1 7/U5+AM	4./KG2	Merville	AA positions, Aldeburgh.
34	04.02.41	20.58-22.54	Do17/U5+AM	4./KG2	Merville	Rolls Royce works, Derby.
35	09.02.41	19.24-22.07	Do17/U5+AM	4./KG2	Merville	Mildenhall aerodrome.
36	10.02.41	18.59-21.36	Do17/U5+AM	4./KG2	Merville	Secondary target, Gt Yarmouth.
37	13.02.41	1944-22.13	Do17/U5+AM	4./KG2	Merville	West Raynham aerodrome.
38	18.07.41	01.20-04.30	Do217/U5+IM	4./KG2	Schipol	Port and industrial installations, Hull.
39	25.07.41	03.32-07.14	Do217/U5+LM	4./KG2	Evreux	Convoy W of Land's End.

40	27.07.41	03.32-07.57	Do217/U5+LM	4./KG2	Evreux	Convoy SW England.
41	03.08.41	22.29-01.35	Do217/U5+AM	4./KG2	Evreux	Shipping, off Orfordness.
42	05.08.41	22.31-02.52	Do217/U5+AM	4./KG2	Evreux	Mining, Humber estuary
43	07.08.41	22.26-01.22	Do217/U5+IM	4./KG2	Evreux	Mining, Thames estuary.
44	12.08.41	23.7-02.35	Do217/U5+IM	4./KG2	Schiphol	Port installations, Gt. Yarmouth.
45	15.08.41	21.38-00.28	Do217/U5+AM	4./KG2	Evreux	Ship, E coast of England.
46	20.08.41	22.31-0052	Do217/U5+AM	4./KG2	Evreux	Mining, Thames estuary.
47	29.08.41	21.00-00.01	Do217/U5+AM	4./KG2	Evreux	Mining, Humber estuary. Landed Schipol.
48	31.08.41	21.30-01.45	Do217/U5+AM	4./KG2	Evreux	Victoria Docks, Hull. Landed Schipol.
49	07.09.41	21.50-23.45	Do217/U5+AM	4./KG2	Schipol	Port installations, Gt. Yarmouth.
50	13.09.41	20.00-23.20	Do217/U5+BM	4./KG2	Evreux	Secondary target, Harwich.
51	23.09.41	23.27-00.23	Do217/U5+AM	4./KG2	Evreux	Shipping, Milford/Pembroke.
52	27.09.41	20.16-23.44	Do217/U5+AM	4./KG2	Evreux	Mining, Humber estuary.
53	30.09.41	20.25-23.58	Do217/U5+AM	4./KG2	Schiphol	Newcastle-on-Tyne.
54	19.10.41	15.23-18.36	Do217/U5+AM	4./KG2	Evreux	Armed recce. E coast England.
55	20.10.41	20.40-00.59	Do217/U5+AM	4./KG2	Eindhoven	Mining, Humber estuary and port of Liverpool.
56	22.10.41	20.18-00.30	Do217/U5+LM	4./KG2	Eindhoven	Port installations (place not given – BN).
57	25.10.41	19.9-23.45	Do217/U5+AM	4./KG2	Evreux	Mining, Bristol and Mersey estuary.
58	11.01.42	18.59-20.37	Do217/U5+FM	4./KG2	Soesterberg	Mining, Thames estuary.

Now eighty-three years old, Heinrich Suschake remembers that most operations were usually carried out with varying degrees of hinderance from anti-aircraft fire, fighters or both, but he confesses that time has taken its toll on his memories of those days. He does, however, recall one particular brush with an RAF Spitfire. On 7 July 1940, his Do17z was on an anti-shipping strike over the English Channel when it was attacked and badly damaged by Sub Lieutenant (Fleet Air Arm) F.D. Paul, flying a Spitfire of 64 Squadron. Suschake's pilot on that day, *Unteroffizier* Wilhelm Pleitz, crash-landed the bomber near Boulogne without injury to any member of his crew.

Suschake knows he was fortunate to survive the war but he may not know that his luck turned out to be better than that of both Wilhelm Pleitz and Dawson Paul. The Spitfire pilot died a fortnight after his engagement with the Dornier and after being severely wounded during combat with Me109s over the Channel. Pleitz was killed four months after his brush with Paul, when the Do17 bomber he was flying was shot down near Newhaven, East Sussex.

2 October 1941 (off the Tyne)

Aircraft:	Dornier 217E-2		U5+GN	w/nr. 5309	5./KG2
Crew:	Fw. Fritz Menzel		pilot	+	
	Fw. Josef Rüth		observer	pow	
	Fw. Horst Schleussner		wireless op	pow	
	Uffz. Arno Herold		mechanic	pow	

Following on their triumph of 30 September 1941, Wing Commander Morris and Sergeant Rix enjoyed further success (in Beaufighter R2307) two nights later, when they claimed two more raiders in bright moonlight

*Kampfgeschwader 2
(Holzhammer)*

during an attack on Tyneside. Aircraft from III./KG40 and KGr.606 of *Fliegerfuhrer Atlantik*, as well as from II./KG2, II./KG40 and III./KG30 from *IX Fliegerkorps*, took part in the raid. Forty-nine of the fifty-five bombers detailed for the attack actually reached the north of England, the units so doing contributing the following numbers and types of aircraft: II./KG2(eleven Do217s); III./KG30 (seventeen Ju88s); II./KG40 (three Do217s); III./KG40 (twelve He111s) and KGr.606 (three Ju88s).[19]

Morris's first claim to victory that night, a Heinkel 111, was seen at 9,000 feet as it crossed in near Lesbury (Northumberland) at 20.50 hours. Despite the German's '...desperate attempts at evasion by swerves and dives...', Morris got the bomber in his sights at 200 yards range over Alnwick, managed one burst of fire and registered hits in the Heinkel's fuselage and starboard wing before the commencement of a diving chase which took them eastwards over Warkworth and the coast. With the German upper gunner returning fire seconds earlier, Morris managed a second squirt at 5,000 feet and saw the flashes on his victim's fuselage as his shells struck home. He lost sight of the bomber near Warkworth, when they were at 2,500 feet and while the Heinkel was still diving. He did not see the bomber's demise, but ground-based eyewitnesses claimed to have seen an explosive flash out to sea off Alnmouth and the Beaufighter crew learned later that one of the German crew had baled out of his burning plane and had been captured in the neighbourhood. The next morning the Hartlepool *Northern Daily Mail* reported that a Heinkel had crashed some three miles off the north-east coast. The newspaper also mentioned that one member of the crew had been captured near 'a small town', and that three others, believed to be from the same plane, had been picked up at sea. However, there is a possibility that the newspaper was confusing Morris's first encounter of the evening with his second.

His second victim is believed to have been Dornier 217 U5+GN (w/nr.5309) of 5./KG2, crewed by *Feldwebel* Fritz Menzel (pilot), *Feldwebel* Josef Rüth (observer), *Feldwebel* Horst Schleussner (wireless operator), and *Unteroffizier* Arno Herold (mechanic).

The attack on the Dornier occurred shortly after Morris's encounter with the first bomber. After the encounter with the He111, Rix reloaded the cannon magazines and Morris climbed to 10,000 feet over base before returning to GCI control. At 21.20 hours Rix got an AI contact on an aircraft approaching Tynemouth from the east, head on at 11,000 feet and slightly to port at 7,000 feet range. Radar contact was maintained while closing to 2,500 feet when Morris made a sharp turn towards his quarry, who was then 400 yards away and forty-five degrees to port. The enemy aircraft, which was turning south and towards Tynemouth from a position roughly east of Acklington, was mistakenly identified by Morris as a Dornier17, when in fact it was a Dornier 217.

Morris slid in behind and closed to 100 yards range before loosing off a one-and-a-half second burst of gunfire, which was immediately returned by the Dornier's upper gunner. The bomber's wireless operator, Horst Schleusser, who also manned the top rear machine gun, had sighted Morris on his approach and though he managed to reply to the Beaufighter's first assault there was no time for his pilot to take evasive action before Morris's shells smacked home. The first attack damaged the Dornier's rudder and severely wounded the mechanic, Arno Herold. A second burst of gunfire from the fighter at the same range was enough to cause the bomber to suffer a terrific explosion and disappear in a blinding flash and a shower of sparks.

As his aircraft slipped into a spiral dive, Fritz Menzel ordered his crew to bale out and then he followed suit. Shortly afterwards, from a height of 11,000 feet over the sea and some three miles off Tynemouth, the Beaufighter crew saw three parachutes, and later a possible fourth, against the reflection of the moon on the sea. Not far away, a mark on the water pinpointed where the Dornier had plummeted to destruction. Fritz Menzel

Feldwebel Fritz Menzel, pilot, 5./KG2, who was killed on 2 October 1941, when his Do217 (U5+GN) was shot down by W/Cdr. D.C. Morris in a Beaufighter of 406 Sqdn, RCAF, Scorton. The Dornier crashed into the sea off Tynemouth.
[via Gunter Bischoff]

was the only one not to survive the encounter. His three comrades, including the wounded mechanic, were subsequently picked up by a trawler but Menzel drowned before he could be rescued. The Beaufighter landed at Acklington with its port glycol tank punctured by gunfire.

On 7 October 1941, Morris was awarded the Distinguished Flying Cross and Rix the Distinguished Flying Medal in recognition of their shooting down three enemy aircraft in as many nights. However, there must be some doubt about Morris's claim in respect of the Heinkel.

The Luftwaffe Loss Returns for 3 October 1941 contain an entry that has a lot in common with Morris's claim in respect of the night before. The entry records that a He111H-6 (w/nr.4313) of III./KG40 was attacked by a night fighter and that the wireless operator baled out. The aircraft, however, did not crash but managed to land at Soesterberg (Holland), having sustained thirty-five per cent damage. The wireless operator, *Gefreiter* Walter Kaiser, had baled out and was listed as 'missing'. The Returns do not detail the Heinkel's operational objective and thus one cannot be absolutely certain of the connection with Morris's claim but the circumstances, coupled with the fact that III./KG40 participated in the Newcastle raid, as well as the closeness of dates, are probably enough to suggest that the incidents are one and the same.

406 Squadron put up five Beaufighters on the night of 2 October. Apart from Morris, only one other crew had contact with the enemy. At 22.00 hours, Flight Lieutenant Hillock (with Sergeant Bell), in Beaufighter R2435, established simultaneous AI and visual contact with a Junkers 88 between Sunderland and Newcastle. They chased it northwards in a diving pursuit, which reduced altitude from 11,000 feet to 500 feet, and managed three one-second bursts of gunfire and a final quarter attack to starboard at fifty yards before they overshot, narrowly missed the enemy's tail and lost sight of their quarry. They claimed, and were awarded, one 'damaged'.

2 October 1941 (south-east of the Farne Islands?)
The Operations Record Book of 43 Squadron, Drem, records that the commanding officer, Squadron Leader 'Tom' Morgan, took off on patrol in his Hurricane (Z3265) at 21.15 hours. When he saw that a raid was in progress over the Tyne he requested, and received, permission to patrol further south than usual. He proceeded down the coast at an altitude of 10,000 feet, twenty miles off shore and keeping a sharp lookout towards land. Twenty miles south-east of the Farne Islands Morgan saw a Junkers 88, 2,000 feet below, about 1,000 yards on his starboard side and flying north-east. He turned and dived below his quarry, coming up dead astern before making the first of three attacks from above and astern. The German top rear gunner returned Morgan's first burst but ceased to retaliate after the Hurricane's second assault. Morgan's third attack brought flames from the raider's starboard wing shortly before the Junkers dived steeply into sea. This incident is also recounted by Beedle[20]. Ulf Balke[21] states that Junkers 88s of *Kampfgruppe* 606 (KGr.606) and III./KG30 participated in this raid and thus it seems likely that Morgan's victim belonged to one of these units. However, as yet, the writer has found no record of the loss in the Luftwaffe Returns.

Aircraft:	Junkers 88	S4+KH	w/nr.694	KGr.1./506[22]
Crew:	Fw. Bruno Schlau	pilot	missing	
	Ofhr. z. See Dieter Kutz	observer	+	
	Uffz. Karl Wilhelm	wireless op	missing	
	Obgfr. Fritz Hölzgen	mechanic	missing	

On 16 November 1941, Squadron Leader Tony Lovell, the newly appointed commanding officer of 145 Squadron, Catterick, shot down a Junkers 88 twenty-five miles north-east of Hartlepool.

Lovell had taken off in his Spitfire at 11.30 hours to practise fighter affiliation with a Halifax bomber in the Scarborough area when he heard the Ground Controller vector 145 Squadron's Green Section away from convoy escort duty and on to 'bogies' between Scarborough and Whitby. Lovell requested, and was granted, permission to investigate. However, he was warned to exercise care because the 'bogies' had not been identified and might well be friendly. Lovell crossed the Yorkshire coast south of Whitby and was ten miles out to sea flying east of north-east when he heard the Controller recall Green Section to resume patrol over the convoy they had been escorting. Lovell also decided to return but then he saw an aircraft to landward, flying at some 270mph and about 100 feet above the waves. Keeping a distance of 1,000 yards to seaward, he drew level with his would-be quarry before pulling up and over the aircraft, which was a Ju88 with roundels on its wings and the German cross on its fuselage.

Lovell turned to starboard and dived on the Junkers from astern. As he closed in, the German began weaving to allow his own rear gunner to fire and Lovell saw flashes of tracer on his port side but the Spitfire was not hit. He then commenced firing, giving two bursts from cannon and machine guns at 500 yards in the hope of silencing the rear gunner. However, the .303 ammunition from his machine guns fell short and he saw it striking the water 100 yards behind the target. Lovell then closed to 250 yards and, with the Ju88 turning to starboard, he fired two more bursts with ten degrees deflection. He saw his bullets strike home around the cockpit, fuselage and engines of the Junkers shortly before its motors sprouted traces of flame. By the time the Spitfire had broken away to port, the bomber's engines were blazing fiercely. It then went into a shallow dive that ended when the bomber hit the sea and exploded. For a while, burning wreckage littered the area and Lovell thought he saw an uninflated dinghy floating among it but he did not see any survivors.

According to the Luftwaffe Loss Returns, two Ju88s of Ku.Fl.Gr. 506 were lost over the English east coast on that day. *Blitz, then and now. Vol.3*[23] claims one of those, (S4+BL; w/nr.1403) piloted by *Oberfeldwebel* Wilhelm Nass of Ku.Fl.Gr.3./506, was hit by anti-aircraft fire and made a wheels-up landing at Mablethorpe (Lincs). The other, (S4+KH; w/nr.

694), piloted by Bruno Schlau, is not listed in *Blitz, then and now. Vol. 3* but it may be the one claimed by Lovell. However, that is nothing more than speculation on the part of the writer.

8-9 December 1941 (east of Newcastle)

On the night of 8-9 December 1941 the Luftwaffe mounted an attack on the Newcastle area during the course of which Sector Control at Ouston scrambled six Beaufighters from 406 Squadron, Acklington. Pilot Officer L. Scargill (with Sergeant R.L. Wilde) had an uneventful patrol, as did Sergeant L. Dumaresqe (with Sergeant W.H. Staines). The rest suffered a catalogue of misfortunes. Pilot Officer H.S.L. Underwood (with Sergeant Horrex), had AI contact and got a visual on what they claimed was a Do17 but a faulty AI set impeded a successful inter-ception. Squadron Leader R.A. Wills (with Sergeant W. Wilcox)

Some years ago, this BMW aircraft engine (stamped 9-801170-08023-14554) was trawled up from the North Sea and landed at North Shields. After treatment, it was subsequently donated to the North-East Air Museum near Sunderland. Given that this power plant spent some sixty years on the seabed, it is in amazingly good condition. [Author]

took off in a spare Beaufighter (their usual aircraft being unserviceable because of an oil leak in the starboard engine) but found their radio to be so loud that they could not understand the controller's instructions. Pilot Officer D.C. Furse (with Pilot Officer J. Downes) found their equipment so unserviceable that no contacts were made and, although they had momentary visual contact with a Ju88, there was no chance to shoot. Pilot Officer Mitchell (with Sergeant Trebell) followed instructions to orbit base – until he was forced to land forty minutes later with one engine dead.

However, in spite of these misfortunes, there seemed to be the possibility of 'good hunting' and the off-duty Squadron CO, Wing Commander Morris, was eager to try his luck. His own aircraft was already in the air being flown by another crew and so, ignoring the protests of the Engineering Officer, he took Wills' unserviceable Beaufighter (R2461) and Flight Lieutenant G.B. Houghton went with

This Jumo 211 aircraft engine was trawled up off the Tyne and is now located at the North-East Air Museum. Unlike the BMW engine opposite, the Jumo looks as if it has been on the seabed for sixty years. [Author]

him as the AI operator. Morris took off at 23.21 hours.

Flying out to sea in a south-easterly direction, Morris was warned that a 'bandit' was near. At a point twenty-five miles north-east of Newcastle, Morris simultaneously got an AI contact and a visual on an enemy aircraft passing some 500 feet behind him. He identified it as a Heinkel 111. As he dived and closed in on the raider, Morris was met by gunfire from the bomber's lower turret. The Heinkel took violent evasive action but Morris managed three or four bursts at 100 yards range and saw a number of strikes. He exhausted his cannon ammunition but continued firing with his Browning machine guns, while his opponent returned very accurate fire from both the upper and lower gun positions. The Heinkel finally disappeared in a dark patch of cloud.

In the course of the engagement, both aircraft had descended from 9,000 feet to 2,500 feet, the latter being too low for the AI to function effectively and so the Heinkel escaped. In any case, pursuit was not an option for Morris: a bullet through the radiator had stopped the Beaufighter's port engine and the starboard motor had been considered 'unserviceable' even before Morris took off. With the inhospitable North Sea below and the risk of a watery conclusion to the night's events, Morris turned for home. The Beaufighter was rapidly losing height as it crossed the coast at no more than 300 feet but it made a safe return to Acklington. The Heinkel was claimed as damaged.

Roof over Britain HMSO 1943, page 58, claims that the first German plane to be brought down by a mixed male and female gun crew crashed in the Newcastle area on this date after being hit when it was a couple of miles away and going out to sea. However, examination of the Luftwaffe Loss Returns reveals no loss around that date other than the one listed below.

9 December 1941 (east of Seaham)

Aircraft:	Junkers 88D-1	F6+CL	w/nr. 1465	3.(F)/122
Crew:	Obfw. Ludwig Volk	pilot	+	
	Lt. Fritz Böhme	observer	+	
	Obfw. Fritz Shackert	wireless op	+	
	Fw. Walter Lentfert	mechanic	+	

This aircraft failed to return from a sortie to Newcastle and is believed to have been shot down by Flight Lieutenant Geoffrey May in a Hurricane of 43 Squadron, Acklington. May (in Hurricane BD715) had left Acklington at 10.50 hours with Sergeant Joe Pipa (BD734) with orders to patrol the Farne Islands. They were later ordered to patrol Blyth at cloud base, from where they noticed anti-aircraft fire south of the Tyne. Shortly after that they found an enemy aircraft ten miles east of Seaham; it was at 7,500 feet and flying south-west at 280-300mph. May made his first assault from astern of the raider (identified as a Ju88), opening fire at 150 yards and closing to fifty yards. He carried out five similar attacks at about the same range and experienced return machine-gun fire from the enemy gunners while the Junkers attempted to evade by diving in and out of cloud. In each attack, May registered hits on the bomber. Following May's second assault, black smoke trailed from the raider's starboard engine. After his fourth attack, the German gunners ceased to react and the bomber dived steeply. After two further attacks, it crashed into the sea.

29 December 1941 (off Cresswell)

Aircraft:	Junkers 88D-1	S4+LH	w/nr.1341	KGr. 1./506
Crew:	Fw. Walter Tschorn	pilot	missing	
	Lt. z. See Heinrich Fleck	observer	missing	
	Uffz. Rudolf Hermann	wireless op	missing	
	Uffz. Axel Reckweg	gunner	missing	

Wing Commander Morris, Commanding Officer of 406 Squadron,

Acklington, chalked up the squadron's first tally of the month on 8 December 1941, when he claimed a Heinkel 111 as 'damaged' (see page 133). The squadron's second success of the month occurred three weeks later, on the night of 29 December.

Bad weather indicated possible inactivity but three crews were put up during the course of the night in response to incoming plots. Two of the patrols made contact, one with a 'friendly' aircraft, but they failed to engage raiders. Pilot Officer J.R.B. Firth (with Sergeant F.G. Harding) did a little better.

They took off at 20.34 hours under Sector Control and Firth was initially ordered to patrol Acklington at 10,000 feet. Later, he was vectored by Sector to a point thirty miles east of the Tyne and then towards a raid approaching Newcastle from the north-east. When he was brought to within five miles of an enemy aircraft, ten miles east of Blyth, he was handed over to Ground Control Interception (GCI). AI contact was obtained at a range of 12,000 feet and sixty degrees to starboard. Several minor corrections of course brought the contact slightly above and directly in front of the Beaufighter, at a range of 6,000 feet. Feeling that he was closing in too fast, Firth throttled back until he got a visual sighting. When he did, he was at an altitude of 11,500 feet and was 2,000 feet behind the enemy aircraft, which turned out to be a Junkers 88.

Firth closed to 500 feet before opening fire; two short bursts from a combination of cannons and machine guns were enough to transform the bomber into a disintegrating, flaming mess. The raider turned to port, stall turned and then dived steeply to earth. Firth thought that both aircraft were over the area between Blyth and Newcastle when the fiercely burning Junkers disappeared through the 6,000 feet ceiling of ten-tenths cloud at 21.10 hours. Because of the cloud, neither Firth nor Harding saw the plane crash but seconds later, the diffused flash of an explosion through the clouds signalled their first victory.

The Ju88D-1 (S4+LH; w/nr.1341) of KGr.1./506 crashed into the sea, the location of the impact being variously reported as two miles south-east of Coquet Island or one mile east of Hadstone Links. A third site was provided by the Special Constable at the coastal village of Cresswell. He reported that the Junkers fell three miles to seaward of the village. It was in flames and in three pieces, the last piece to fall, floating on the surface for ten minutes before the fire disappeared.

RCAF Press Release:
406 Sqdn, RCAF

Wing Commander D.G. Morris DFC of South Africa is one of only three non-Canadians commanding RCAF squadrons overseas. He commands a night fighter squadron equipped with the deadly twin-engine Beaufighters that carry four cannons and six machine guns. The squadron has not long been in operation but it has accounted for at least four enemy aircraft destroyed and several more damaged.

Of the four destroyed, Wing Commander Morris is credited with three – a Ju88, a Heinkel 111 and a Dornier 17 (sic). Flying Officer R.C. Fumerton of Fort Colonge, Quebec, on the Ottawa River, bagged a Ju88 and damaged a Heinkel 111 and Flight Lieutenant F.W. Hillock of Walmsley Blvd., Toronto, damaged a Ju88. Details of the squadron's victories have reached Air Force headquarters at Ottawa.

Wing Commander Morris's first victim was the Junkers 88. 'I got him 50 miles out to sea,' the Wing Commander reported. 'It was a clear night with a three quarter moon. I saw him first 3,000ft away, making for home at 9,000ft. So far as we know, he had dropped his bomb load. We closed up behind and slightly above him to 100yards range. Bright red exhaust flames, two on each side of round engines, positively identified him as a Junkers 88. He apparently was taken by surprise since he made no attempt to evade. He was my first one and I must confess I almost hesitated about firing on him. I had to make myself press the firing button. I gave him a first burst of two seconds and there were flashes on his fuselage – one of them very brilliant. He immediately returned my fire and very accurate he was too. I then attacked again – a one-second burst and another for two seconds. His return fire ceased and he slowed down. I nearly flew into him and I overshot him by about only 20ft above and 40ft to starboard. I could see he was on fire inside. He turned away to the right, burst into flames and went down in a steepening dive into the sea. Then I saw a patch on the water where he went in. We turned for home. The enemy had put a bullet through our port engine and it began to vibrate seriously and throw out sparks. I had to cut it out and fly home on one engine. After landing, we discovered that the starboard engine had been hit too. I was mightily glad to bring the ship home.'

Wing Commander Morris's second was a Heinkel 111. He caught him crossing the coast in the reflection of the moon on the sea. 'I was about 10,000ft up and he was 500ft below me. I was closing up to get in firing position when he spotted me and immediately took avoiding action – twisting and turning. I managed to keep him in sight and I got in a quick burst. He went into a dive, shooting back at us. I had great difficulty keeping sight of him but eventually, at about 5,000ft, I got in another burst. He went into a steep dive and I followed him to about 2,000ft just to make sure. I saw one of his crew bale out and afterwards I learned that his entire crew had been picked up by a trawler.'

The third – a Dornier – was bagged the same night. Wing Commander Morris reloaded and climbed again. 'Twenty minutes later we saw a

Dornier 17 (*sic*) making for home at about 2,000ft. We were on him just before he crossed the English coast. He was obviously making a landfall (identifying his position to set his homeward course) for he turned into what was practically a full moon. I closed in and gave him a good burst, which he promptly returned. Then I missed him with another. But my third burst scored and he blew up. Pieces of his aircraft hit our radiator. We saw his parachutes floating down and we turned for home.'

Flying Officer Fumerton, who won his wings at Camp Borden and has been in Britain for more than a year, served first with a Hurricane fighter squadron but he got his first Hun with the Morris outfit. 'It was a Ju88,' he reported. 'I was over 10,000ft and I saw him 500yards away, crossing directly in front of me. He went into cloud and I followed. We dived a little below to establish his identity and to remain unseen. We closed to 50yards and then I opened fire with a one-second burst. His starboard engine caught fire and I saw explosions on his fuselage. He fell away and then righted. His rear gunner opened up. I got another sight on him as fast as I could and then, from 100yards, let him have a two-second burst. He exploded in the air and pieces of his machine hit our aircraft. Turning for home we saw another Hun fly past with his nose down and going like hell. We gave chase but we never caught him.'

Six days later Flying Officer Fumerton had a smack at a Heinkel 111 but he could not claim it as destroyed. 'We were stooging around one good night at 6,000ft,' he explained, 'and saw him against the moon about 300 to 500yards away. He was a twin-engine aircraft making slow left and right turns. Then we got a clear silhouette of him against a background of cloud. He saw us too and began diving away, spiralling down towards cloud. We followed and at 200yards gave him a one-second burst. He turned right and I gave him another half-second burst. We saw hits all over his aircraft but he disappeared into cloud and we couldn't find him again."

It was about the same time that Flight Lieutenant Hillock got his 'probable'. He too was 'stooging' at about 11,000ft when he saw the enemy 500yards away. But the Hun saw him too and went screaming out to sea, diving steeply. 'We closed to 200yards and opened fire,' Hillock said. 'He was firing back. We gave him three separate bursts of about one second each and we were both losing height. Finally, we were about 500ft over the sea. I saw hits on his wing roots and motor nacelles. We were swerving to avoid his fire. Then I lost him. I don't think he got back but I did not see his end. He was only a probable.'

RCAF Press Release No.546.
3 January 1942

NOTES

1 Gundelach, Karl, *Kampfgeschwader 4 (eine geschichte aus Kriegstagebüchern, Dokumenten und Berichten, 1939-1945* Motorbuch Verlag Stuttgart 1978.

2 quoted by Graeme Carrot in 'Sheen's third off the Northumberland Coast' – the Coquet Island Ju88, March 1941. In Air North vol.40 No.11. Nov 2000.

3 Ramsey, W.G. (ed), *The Blitz, then and now, vol.2* Battle of Britain Prints International 1988. p523.

4 SS *Somali* sank 1½ miles NE of Beadnell on 27 March 1941after being bombed off Blyth the day before. The *Clarissa Langdon* was damaged while effecting a rescue, for which Coxswain James Campbell was later awarded the RNLI's Bronze Medal.

5 Jimmie Stanton believed that the year was 1942 but there are too many similarities with the 1941 incident including the fact that 10 April 1941 was a Thursday.

6 Hague, Arnold, *The Allied Convoy System, 1939-1945* Vanwell Publishing (Canada) 2000 pp77-82.

7 The others were the *Ariguani* and the *Erin* (later renamed *Maplin*).

8 It is interesting to speculate whether the other Heinkels from 1./KG26 were damaged by *Patia* that night.

9 Collings, Peter, *The Divers Guide to the North-East Coast*. Collings & Brodie 1986 p103 gives *Somali*'s position as 55°33'.9"N/01°36'.4"W.

10 This from RNLI reports held by Jimmie Stanton of Boulmer. *Blitz, then and now. Vol 2* (1988) erroneously gives the location as thirty-five miles east of the Tyne. The debrief of the German prisoners (AI1(k) Report 216/1941 (in AIR40/2407 at the PRO) gives *35 miles NE of Newcastle*, which tends to confirm the RNLI records. Collings, op.cit. is more specific with 55°34'N/01°27'W (off Beadnell).

11 Ramsey, W.G.(ed), op.cit. p575.

12 Combat report of Sgt G.L. Lawrence, 141 Squadron, Ayr, for the night of 5-6 May 1941. Kindly made available to the author by Don Aris, 141 Squadron historian.

13 Moog crash-landed at Speeton, nr Filey, on the night of 9-10 July 1941, while flying with *Küstenfliegergruppe* 3./106 (see Bill Norman, *Broken Eagles [Yorkshire]* Leo Cooper/Pen & Sword 2001).

14 Moog's superstitious rituals seem to have had much in common with counterparts in the RAF. For example, see Bill Norman, *Failed to Return*. Leo Cooper/Pen & Sword 1995 and Bill Norman: *No.640(Halifax)Squadron, Leconfield*. Privately published 1999.

15 War Reserve Constable Robert Steel (PWR 172) and Coastguard Thomas Walker.

16 Eyewitness Mrs Margaret Douglas, of Holy Island, has informed the writer that the person concerned was Mr Strickland, the village schoolmaster and member of the island's Civil Defence.

17 The Luftwaffe Quartermastergeneral's Loss Records gives the aircraft code as M2+DL but Air Intelligence 1(k) responsible for debriefing Schummers and Forstbach gives M2+FL. The AI1(k) report is in AIR40/2406 in PRO.

18 Flagg, Amy C., *History of Bomb Damage* (in South Shields). Private mss in South Tyneside Central Library, South Shields.

19 Balke, Ulf, *Der Luftkrieg in Europa. Teil2* Bernard & Graefe Verlag Koblenz 1990 p50.

20 Beedle, J., *43 Squadron* Beaumont Aviation Literature 1966. p187.

21 Balke, Ulf, ibid.

22 Kü.Fl.Gr.506 was redesignated *Kampfgruppe* 506 (KGr.506) on 19 October 1941.

23 Ramsey, W.G., *The Blitz, then and now, Vol.3* Battle of Britain Prints International 1990 p81.

3

INCREASING STRAIN

(1942)

Throughout 1941, the Luftwaffe had concentrated on anti-shipping campaigns, rather than raids on the interior of the mainland, for they believed that satisfactory tonnages of shipping were being sunk or damaged for relatively low losses of aircraft. As far as the north-east coast was concerned, anti-shipping operations included the mining of sea lanes and estuaries (including those of the Tyne and Wear), scattered attacks on coastal shipping, raids on convoys and occasional night attacks on harbours and ports, including those on the Tyne and the Wear in the closing months of 1941. During this period, the total number of bombers participating in a night attack on a port rarely exceeded thirty.

In the months prior to 1942, attacks on shipping targets were often carried out in daylight by single aircraft. However, increasingly effective defensive armament of merchant vessels and improved fighter protection led to mounting casualties among Luftwaffe crews. The scale of losses among bomber crews ultimately forced a change of strategy and by early 1942, attacks on ships usually took place only when natural conditions were considered to be favourable. For example, attacks by day were generally carried out only when cloudy conditions allowed attacking aircraft an element of protection and surprise, otherwise strikes took place during the half-light of early morning and late evening, when light conditions could be utilized to the attacker's advantage.

Apart from the first week in September 1941, there was generally little activity over the interior of mainland Britain between June of that year and the early months of 1942. However, April 1942 saw a reversal of policy regarding Luftwaffe strategy in the West following the increasingly destructive raids by the RAF on German towns and cities. The raid on Lübeck on the night of 28-29 March 1942 triggered the Luftwaffe's reprisal raids on a number of Britain's historic towns, including York, in April 1942. The reprisal attacks, now known to history as the Baedeker raids, were carried out by *Luftflotte 3*, but such was the shortage of Luftwaffe operational bomber units in the West that the attacking forces had to be augmented by crews from training units and from operational units temporarily assigned from other theatres of war.

Although both Northumberland and County Durham could provide examples of 'tip and run' raids on coastal districts and of mining operations offshore during most months of 1942, there seem to have been no attacks in strength until the last night of April. On that occasion, seventy-five aircraft were targeted on Sunderland but bombs were widely scattered over the region and no concentration developed. The Luftwaffe's failure on that night in April 1942 appears to have set the pattern for the rest of the year, as far as Sunderland was concerned. The town was the target on six other nights between August and December (with an average of fourteen aircraft participating in each case). In each instance, most of the bombs intended for Wearside landed elsewhere throughout both counties, although the few that dropped on the town on the night of 11-12 October 1942 caused extensive damage in the area of Corporation Road – Villette Road.

A little further south, ICI's Billingham plant was bombed three times in July, while the Hartlepool district received particular attention on the

The Starfish *bunker (left) and crew air raid shelter at Greenabella (O.S.513263), on the Port Clarence – Seaton Carew Road, Co. Durham. This site was one of several set up around Billingham, Co. Durham to protect the ICI chemical works. On the nights of 6 and 7 July 1942 there were two attacks which were believed to be directed specifically against ICI. On those occasions ninety per cent of all bombing was diverted from the factory.* [Author]

nights of 15-16 April, 4-5 June and 7-8 July, as well as on occasions in September. In most instances, open spaces appear to have been the recipients of the Luftwaffe's wrath, but the nineteen high explosives that fell in the early morning of 8 July caused extensive damage and stopped production at Hartlepool's Cerebos Works for fourteen days. Apart from the latter example, the town also appears to have enjoyed good fortune on the night of 14-15 December, when 'a considerable number of high-explosives' fell in the area of Hart Station, on Hartlepool golf links and on the foreshore at Middleton. There was some damage to miscellaneous properties but no casualties.

This lack of success by Luftwaffe crews was sometimes attributable to the vagaries of the weather, sometimes it was due to the effectiveness of decoy sites and sometimes it was due to successive improvements to Britain's night fighter defence force. By late 1941, the initial problems that had plagued the development of the night fighter had been largely overcome. VHF radio had been developed to give greater clarity and range; blind flying instruments had vastly improved; aerodromes were better lit and good runways had been installed at night fighter bases. In addition a new arrival to the force, the heavily-armed Beaufighter, which was equipped with an increasingly refined airborne radar (AI) to seek its prey, was working in conjunction with Ground Control Interception ground stations to exact an ever-mounting toll on raiders.[1]

During the course of the war, various forms of ruse were developed on a national scale to confuse enemy bombers and thus lure bombs to fake targets. Such decoys were located in rural areas away from the establishment or centre that they were 'protecting', but close enough to trick raiders into believing that they were bombing their intended objective. One such decoy scheme was applied to the protection of civilian and industrial centres at night and involved the use of 'Q' sites. There were two versions of the scheme: 'QL' (where L = lights) and 'QF' (where F = fires). Type 'L' simulated a town or an industrial plant operating under black-out conditions at night but with some lights actually showing; type 'F' simulated a town or an industrial plant under attack at night. The former operated as one might have expected a real target to react when under threat of attack. The town or centre being protected would be in complete darkness but the exposed lights on the 'L' site would remain lit until it was thought that they had been seen by approaching bombers; they would then be extinguished in the way that those on a 'legitimate' site would be. Thus it was hoped that the bomber would be misled and would attack the decoy. The 'QF' scheme (sometimes called *Starfish*) used decoy fires that were electrically lit when bombs fell nearby. Such fires simulated the effects of exploding bombs, as well as buildings on fire, and it was hoped that the ruse would also draw the attack from the intended target. Both lights and fires were controlled from a bunker that was usually located some 300-400 yards from the site, which was always in full view of the controllers.

Although the vagaries of the weather and the use of decoy sites and other forms of static defence (anti-aircraft guns, barrage balloons, etc.) undoubtedly played their part, the biggest single influence in the defence of these islands against the night bomber was very probably the emergence of an effective night fighter force.

By 1942 the British night fighter was the most dangerous threat faced by German bombers in the West, and not only over the United Kingdom. By then, German aircraft were being harassed by British night fighters at almost every stage of bombing operations against the British Isles, even over their home bases. British 'intruder' night fighters operated over German aerodromes in Holland with the intention of shooting at bombers as they took off on operations and that pressure continued as bombers made their way out over the sea and towards their objective. KG2 used to exit from the continental mainland via the radio beacons at Texel and Den Helder but the British night fighters lay in wait there too. Night fighters also patrolled up to 100 miles off the English coast, as well as operating over target areas.

It was a dangerous time for bombers. Even if Luftwaffe crews managed to avoid the hazards of the outward flight and the target area, they still had to run the gauntlet of the return trip, which usually mirrored the hazards of the outward journey. Thus the danger was always present and many fell victim to it. As 1942 drew to a close, the operational strength of the German Air Force was falling further as the replacement rate of crews increasingly failed to make up for those lost on operations.

By mid-June 1942, the three *Gruppen* of KG2, regularly aided by II./ KG40 and with occasional help from two coastal reconnaissance units, were the only units carrying the war to Great Britain. On paper, their total operational strength was 170 twin-engined bombers; in reality, serviceability problems reduced the number of available aircraft to something in the order of half that number. The aircraft that they did have were flown around the clock to give the impression that the Luftwaffe had more aircraft in the West than was actually the case and bomber units were frequently moved around to create an impression of operational strength. For example, targets on the English east coast were attacked from bases in Holland; targets on the south and west coasts were raided from bases in France. However, it was usually the same bomber units that carried out operations in both areas, the units being temporarily relocated to Holland or France in accordance with operational requirements. An additional practice used by the Luftwaffe to create a false impression of overall bomber strength in the West was to temporarily transfer bomber units into Europe from other operational theatres in order to increase the size of the bomber force available for sizeable attacks on the United Kingdom. But even then the average raid strength was no more than forty to seventy aircraft.

Inadequate resources, coupled with the demands placed upon Luftwaffe crews, exacted their price. In January 1942, KG2 was understaffed when it had eighty-eight crews, but by September 1942 it was expected to meet increasing operational demands with just twenty-three crews. It was an impossible task. By September-October 1942, destructive raids on British towns were progressively abandoned in order to spare the units. After that, the chief activity of the bomber was to carry out nuisance raids and mining operations.

NOTES

1 The radar equipment of GCI stations could guide a night fighter close enough to its quarry for the latter to come within range of the fighter's airborne interception radar. An excellent account of the night-fighter war over northern England is given in Lewis Brandon's *Night Flyer*, William Kimber 1969.

Losses
January 1942 - December 1942

15 January 1942 (off the Tyne)

Aircraft:	Junkers 88A-4		S4+EH	w/nr. 1612 KGr. 1/506[1]
Crew:	Uffz. Friedrich Pett		pilot	missing
	Lt. z. See Dieter Andresen		observer	+
	Uffz. Josef Scholze		wireless op	missing
	Fw. Franz Gruschka		gunner	missing

The claim that a Do217 (U5+HS) of 8./KG2 might have bombed Skinningrove Ironworks, near Whitby, in the early evening of 15 January 1942 prior to engaging the steamer *Empire Bay* [see *Broken Eagles* (*Yorkshire*)][2] is challenged by Franz Kurowski.[3] He states that Junkers 88 S4+EH of KGr.1./506 attacked the works on that date and scored direct hits on the blast-furnace, the coking plant and the rolling mill. He also lists Ju88 S4+EH as missing on that operation.

The Luftwaffe Loss Returns do show this aircraft as being lost on 15 January 1942. *Blitz, then and now. Vol.3*[4] claims that S4+EH was shot down by anti-aircraft fire and crashed off Tynemouth at 16.50 hours but gives the date as 16 January 1942.[5] Andresen's body was recovered from Priors Haven, Tynemouth, on 27 January 1942 and was buried at Hylton Cemetery, Sunderland. The crash date in *Blitz, then and now* is wrong but the recovery of Andresen's body near the Tyne suggests that the plane did go down in that area. But was it on its way to or from Skinningrove? Air raid records in Cleveland County Archives show that Skinningrove was bombed at 17.30 hours on 15 January 1942. If the Ju88 crashed at 16.50 hours, as claimed in *Blitz, then and now*, it seems likely that the Junkers did not bomb the ironworks.

15-16 February 1942 (east of Blyth?)

Aircraft:	Dornier 217E-4		U5+BD	w/nr.1167	9./KG2
Crew:	Lt. Konrad Pellar		pilot	missing	
	Maj. Gerhard Klostermann		observer	missing	
	Uffz. Josef Uhl		mechanic	missing	
	Fw. Hans Göggerle		wireless op	missing	

Aircraft:	Dornier 217E-4		U5+NT	w/nr. 5343	9./KG2
Crew:	Uffz. Emil Aster		pilot	missing	
	Uffz. Arnold Neumann		observer	missing	
	Gefr. Hans Lehmann		wireless op	missing	
	Uffz. Karl Thomas		mechanic	missing	

Forty aircraft of *IX Fliegerkorps* laid mines in Tyne Bay on the night of 15-16 February 1942. The attackers included a number of aircraft from KG2, one of which dropped bombs on dock installations in the area. The operation cost KG2 at least two aircraft, U5+BD (w/nr.1167) and U5+NT (w/nr.5343), while a third (w/nr.1149) suffered twenty per cent damage when it force-landed near Rotterdam on its return because of shortage of fuel.

It is believed that U5+BD was shot down by Flying Officer James.G. 'Ben' Benson (with Sergeant Lewis Brandon) in a Beaufighter of 141 Squadron, Acklington, and crashed in the sea four miles east of Blyth. Major Gerhard Klostermann, the Dornier's observer on that occasion, was the Kommandeur of III/KG2. Like the rest of his crew, he was never found. The cause and location of the loss of U5+NT is not known to the writer, although Ulf Balke[6] attributes the loss to either flak or fighters.

141 Squadron put up three patrols at 19.00 hours on the night of 15 February. Two minutes later, Benson (in Beaufighter X7577) was ordered to patrol eight miles east of Blyth at 8,000 feet. Under GCI Control,

Pilot J.G. Benson (left) and his navigator Lewis Brandon who served with 141 (Beaufighter) Squadron, Acklington, in 1942.
[S/Ldr. Lewis Brandon]

Brandon got two unsuccessful AI contacts before the Beaufighter crew intercepted U5+BD. Some ten miles east of Blyth, Brandon guided his pilot into visual range of the Do217 and at about 20.02 hours Benson opened fire from dead astern and slightly below with a two-second burst. No result was observed in this first attack but the enemy machine started to lose height very rapidly. In fact, in the course of the short engagement that followed there was no return fire at all from the raider and no evasive tactics other than the dive. During two further bursts of one-second each from 150 yards dead astern, Benson observed strikes on the Dornier's fuselage and tail and saw a red flash. The bomber was then at 1,500 feet and disappearing into the ceiling of nine-tenths cloud. The Beaufighter crew did not see it again. They claimed 'one Dornier damaged' but the bomber was later confirmed as destroyed following independent reports from the local Observer Corps and staff at St Mary's lighthouse that an enemy aircraft had crashed into the sea four miles east of Blyth at 20.06 hours.

In recent years, divers have discovered the wreckage of what is thought to be a German bomber aircraft five-and-half miles north-east of Blyth's north pier. The wreck lies in forty-two metres of water at map reference 55°09'049"N/001°23'63"W.[7] Although one cannot be certain, it is interesting to speculate whether the wreck has any connection with Benson and Brandon.

EYEWITNESS

Beaufighter Victory
15 February 1942

Lewis Brandon's account of the combat on the night of 15-16 February 1942 is given in his highly readable memoir *Night Flyer* (William Kimber 1961). It is reproduced here to give the reader some insight into the nature of nightfighter operations during the middle years of the Second World War. Brandon takes up the story shortly after his first (unsuccessful) attempted interception of that evening.

The Controller brought us back almost over Acklington, then the excitement started all over again.

'Hello, Rounder three-six. Blackbird Control. We have a bogey for you to investigate. Turn port on zero one zero. Range five miles.'

The term 'bogey' meant that we had to identify with extra care as it might be a friendly aircraft. 'Bandit' meant that it was almost certainly an enemy. In either case, positive identification was essential.

'Hello, three-six. Range now four miles, crossing your port to starboard. Any joy yet?'

'No, nothing yet,' I informed Ben.

A second or two later it was a different story. A quite firm blip showed on both tubes, over to port and slightly below.

'Contact!' I called over the intercom. 'Gently to port and go down. Range three and a half miles.'

As Ben responded at once to my instructions he informed the Controller we had contact.

'Do you need any further help?' asked the Controller.

'Ease the turn now. Range three miles. No, I don't need any more help,' I told Ben.

He passed that information on to the Controller and we went on to intercom.

I could see that the aircraft we were chasing was still slightly over to port but the blip was slowly moving across the time base to starboard. We were flying straight now, so he was crossing us from port to starboard as the Controller had said. I could anticipate this and cut him off by turning now.

'Gently to starboard. Range two and a half miles,' I told Ben.

'Gently to starboard. I'm still going down.'

'Level out now... Keep going starboard.'

Thank the Lord he had reminded me of the height; I had been watching the azimuth tube too closely and had forgotten to watch the elevation tube.

As we levelled out, Ben automatically opened the throttle slightly to keep our speed constant. We were closing in perfectly. The blip showed almost dead ahead now.

'Steady now... Range one and half... We're coming in nicely. Where do you want him?'

'Steady. Put him starboard and above. About ten degrees to starboard. What range now?'

'Just under a mile. Throttle back slightly. Can you see anything yet?'

'No, not yet. Keep giving me the range.'

'About two thousand feet. Gently port now.'

A moment's pause, then explosively: 'Christ! There it is. It's a bloody great Dornier. Here, have a look. I can hold it now.'

I needed no urging but swivelled my seat round and peered into the blackness. My eyes took a moment to become accustomed to the dark, then I saw, just above and to starboard of us, the vague silhouette of an aircraft with pinpoints of reddish lights showing from the exhausts. I could see the pencil-thin fuselage and twin fins. It was a Dornier 217 alright. Ben, who at this time was formating

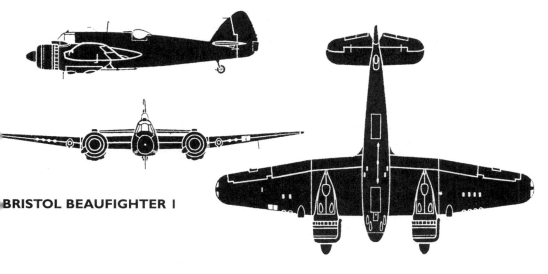

BRISTOL BEAUFIGHTER I

immediately beneath the Dornier and was only two or three hundred feet below him, decided that the time for action had arrived.

The Dornier was weaving gently from side to side as it flew along. Ben throttled back very slightly and lifted the nose of the Beau. It was a little over to port now. It seemed strange that it should be completely indifferent to the presence of a Beaufighter so close. As it drifted in front of us, my heart was thumping so loudly it seemed impossible for the Huns not to hear it. As it passed through his gunsight, Ben turned the Beau almost imperceptibly to follow the Dornier. All hell broke loose as he pressed the gun button and four cannons and six machine guns banged and chattered away. The Beau filled with acrid smoke and the smell of cordite.

Ben had given it a two-second burst of gunfire but although the Dornier began to lose height, we had seen no strikes. We did not use tracer bullets at night in order to retain the element of surprise. We were now following it down in a very sharp dive and Ben gave it two more short bursts from about three hundred feet range. This time we saw strikes all along the fuselage and tail unit, from which there was a great red flash that illuminated the whole aircraft.

Ben was having a devil of a job to keep behind it now. We kept getting into the slipstream, which threw us about violently. Before Ben could get another burst in, the Dornier had entered the clouds, diving into them at a very steep angle. We were about a thousand feet behind it by then and at a height of only two thousand feet Ben pulled out of the dive. We circled the spot where we had last seen the Dornier, hoping that we might see an explosion as it hit the deck. No such luck...

Later, in the crew-room, we were just taking off our flying clothes when the Ops telephone rang. It was the Sector Controller to congratulate us and to tell the glad news that the Royal Observer Corps and St. Mary's Lighthouse had independently reported a plane crashing into the sea four miles east of Blyth... The time and place coincided with our combat. We were told we could claim the Dornier as destroyed.

26-27 March 1942 (east of Tynemouth)

Aircraft:	Dornier 217E-3	F8+KP	w/nr. 0063	6./KG40
Crew:	Lt. Gerthard Westphal	pilot	+	
	Obgfr. Rudolf Bonceck	observer	missing	
	Uffz. Hugo Esslinger	wireless op	missing	
	Fw. IIgnaz Hartl	mechanic	missing	

Dornier 217 F8+KP is believed to have been struck by anti-aircraft fire over Tyneside during a sortie to Sunderland. The body of *Leutnant* Westphal was found in the sea twenty-five miles north-east of Tynemouth on 30 March 1942. His body now lies in the German War Cemetery at Cannock Chase.

25 April 1942 (off the Tyne)

The Operations Record Book of 43 Squadron, Acklington, records that at 13.19 hours on 25 April 1942, Squadron Leader Le Roy du Vivier, Commanding Officer, took off in their Hurricane MkIIC fighters to intercept an incoming raider. When he reached 32,000 feet, du Vivier saw a Junkers 88 3,000 feet below and immediately dived to attack it. The enemy gunners opened fire with machine guns as the Junkers dived away but the German pilot took no evasive action during the combat. Because of the speed of the diving bomber, du Vivier found it impossible to close to less than 400 yards. He opened fire at that range with a series of short bursts in a manoeuvre which tracked the Hurricane from the German's port quarter to astern. The enemy gunners returned fire and du Vivier had a narrow escape when a bullet passed through his windscreen and his Mae West without directly hitting him. However, splinters from the windscreen did inflict superficial skin wounds to his face and neck. The Ju88 was finally shot down and was seen to crash into the sea and explode after one member of crew had taken to his parachute.

J. Beedle, 43 Squadron's historian,[8] gives a somewhat different version

Dornier 217E-2 F8+KP of 6./KG40 prepares to take off for a night sortie. 6./KG40 lost a Do217 with the same code F8+KP (w/nr 0063) off the Tyne on the night of 26-27 March 1942. That aircraft would have then been replaced by another with the same code but not the same serial number (werk nummer). Unfortunately, the serial number of the above aircraft cannot be seen and thus there is no way of knowing whether this aircraft is the one that was lost off the Tyne.
[Ernst Schneiderbauer via North East Air Museum]

of events and claims that du Vivier 'poached' the Junkers from Ouston-based Spitfires. Seemingly, 43 Squadron was not at readiness at the time and Spitfires of 81 Squadron were scrambled from Ouston. According to Beedle, du Vivier took off on what he described as an 'air test', tuned into the frequency being used by the Spitfires and got an idea of the Ju88's position. He climbed out over the sea with the intention of catching the raider on its way home and found it fifty miles east of Tyne. The ensuing chase lasted for several minutes, during which du Vivier failed to close the final gap. He fired a chance long burst, pulling up through the target as he did so. He did not observe any strikes but he must have succeeded for the range immediately shortened. Closing to 300 yards, he delivered a second burst, which set the starboard engine smoking. The Ju88 dived away steeply and the smoke turned to flame. One member of the crew managed to bale out in time but the others were still on board the aircraft when it hit the sea and exploded.

The identity of du Vivier's victim is not known at the time of writing. However, the Luftwaffe Loss Returns for 25 April 1942 show the following two Ju88s missing on operations on that date but locations and causes of loss are not given. The first aircraft was Ju88D-5 F6+ML (w/nr.430006) of 3.(F)/122, *Luftflotte 3*, and piloted by *Feldwebel* Josef Glomb. The second aircraft was Ju88A-4 S4+MH (w/nr. 1540) of Ku.Fl.Gr. 506, *Luftflotte 3*, and piloted by *Unteroffizier* Michael Bartl. In both instances, crews were listed as missing. Both units operated over the north of England during the period in question and thus either aircraft could have been the one shot down by du Vivier. However, in the absence of concrete evidence, the answer must rest with conjecture.

30 April-1 May 1942 (off the Northumberland coast?)

On the night of 30 April-1 May 1942 enemy activity commenced with a number of raids being plotted fifty miles off the north-east coast and travelling in a north-westerly direction. Their intended objective appeared to be the Tyne area and six to eight enemy aircraft did enter the Sector.

Sergeant G. Stephen (with Flight Sergeant C. Bradshaw) of 406 Squadron, Ayr, was one of three crews on detachment at Scorton (North Yorkshire) and was scrambled in Beaufighter R2338 at 01.15 hours. At 02.25 hours, when under GCI Control and at 18,000 feet just off Tynemouth, Bradshaw obtained two contacts. One of them was followed at a range of 12,000 feet.

Losing height and increasing speed, Stephen obtained a visual at 1,000 feet range when his altitude was 17,000 feet. As he closed to 500 feet range, he recognized his quarry as a Junkers 88. Stephen opened fire at 150 feet with a two-second burst from astern. The enemy aircraft

February 1942. Passive defence on the Tyne: a barrage balloon 'at rest'.
[Newcastle Chronicle & Journal]

immediately burst into flames and started a vertical dive from which it never recovered. Sergeant Stephen reported that as it fell, the Junkers appeared to break in half near the dorsal turret before crashing at a currently unknown location. The 406 Squadron Operations Record Book (page 27, 30 April-1 May 1942) states that the aircraft crashed on the outskirts of Morpeth but the writer has so far found no other documented evidence relating to the site of the crash. However, the Ju88 was subsequently confirmed as destroyed, so one can only assume that the wreckage was found or that the aircraft was seen to crash into the sea.

The second Scorton crew, Flying Officer D.C. Furse (with Pilot Officer J.H. Downes) was scrambled at 02.00 hours. They were north of the Tyne and freelancing at 18,000 feet under Sector Control when Downes obtained a contact at 6,000 feet range, below and ahead of the fighter. Furse followed down to a height of 12,000 feet and closed to 500 feet range before obtaining a visual on what appeared to be a Junkers 88 or a Heinkel 111. Furse got in a five-second burst from astern from 300 feet range and a large whitish-red flash appeared on top of the fuselage of the target aircraft. Furse then overshot and lost sight of the raider, which he claimed as damaged but was awarded a 'probable'. Within a few minutes of that engagement, and when north-east of the Tyne, Downes got another contact, which was visually identified as a Ju88. Furse delivered three two-second bursts in a stern attack from 300 feet to 100 feet range and saw the flickering of De Wilde ammunition striking the centre of the fuselage before a brilliant flash appeared on the port engine or wing. The enemy top rear gunner gave fairly accurate return fire but did no damage to the Beaufighter. Immediately after the attack, the Junkers swung violently to port, dived through clouds and disappeared. It too was claimed as damaged. This Beaufighter crew also claimed a Dornier (215 or 17z) damaged forty miles east of Teesmouth on the same night. Furse obtained a visual at 600 feet range at 11,000 feet altitude and managed to squeeze off a three-second burst from 300 feet astern before losing his quarry. As his bullets struck home, Furse saw one brilliant white flash appear on the port engine or wing of the Dornier before the enemy machine turned violently to port, dived through clouds and disappeared. It was claimed as damaged.

The third Scorton crew, Sergeant G. Harper (with Flight Sergeant G. Hardy), was scrambled at 02.25 hours and the Beaufighter was 100 miles north-east of Scorton when Hardy got a visual on what might have been a Dornier 215 or 17z. Harper managed to get within 600 feet range and was preparing to fire when his target dived steeply away. Harper followed and delivered a two-second burst from 250 feet. Strikes seemed to go into the enemy's fuselage and the target swung violently to port as it continued its dive. Harper could not overtake his quarry which, after a drop of 4,000 feet, was still diving and may have been out of control. It was claimed as damaged.

The Luftwaffe Loss Returns show no operational losses of Ju88s from *Luftflotte 3* for 30 April 1942 but they do record that four Ju88s from *Luftflotte 3* failed to return from operations on 1 May 1942. Two were from IV./KG3: Ju88A-5 5K+AU (w/nr.2154), piloted by *Hauptmann* Eduard Kürzel and Ju88A-5 5K+BV (w/nr.4227), piloted by *Oberleutnant* Hans Hübner. The two other aircraft were from IV./KG30: Ju88A-5 4D+TU (w/nr.5129), piloted by *Leutnant* Gerhard Stoll and Ju88A-5 4D+FV (w/nr.200), piloted by *Obergefreiter* Walter Best. *Luftflotten* operating in the North Sea area recorded no losses of Do215 or Do17z for 30 April-1 May 1942.

Blitz,then and now. Vol.3 [9] states that two Ju88s of IV./KG30 and two Ju88s of IV./KG3 were lost on operations against the north-east of England on 1 May 1942, so it might well be that 406 Squadron claims relate to these aircraft – but to date the author has not found proof of this.

EYEWITNESS

Dangerous Encounter
Durham coast, 1 May 1942

Feldwebel Willi Schludecker was a Luftwaffe bomber pilot who began operational flying in the spring of 1941, when he was twenty-one years old. By the time he was twenty-two, he had made 120 war flights with KG2 and had seen service in the Balkans, over Russia and over England.

During the course of his operational career, he was forced to make twenty-three emergency landings, nine of which were crash-landings that resulted in his aircraft being written off. His last crash-landing, on the night of 22-23 July 1942, put him in hospital for six months and ended his operational career, though he later resumed flying in an instructor capacity. He made thirty-two war flights over Britain, including mining operations over the Humber and bombing raids on Hull, York, Middlesbrough and Sunderland.

Luftwaffe pilot Willi Schludecker in the armoured seat of a Do217 during a test flight from Cognac, 1943.
[Willi Schludecker]

During the attack on Sunderland, on the night of 30 April-1 May 1942, Willi was threatened by a night fighter as he neared the north-east coast. As his would-be attacker closed in, Willi dived instinctively for what he thought was cloud below but was, in fact, sea haze. He was over land when he pulled out of his dive and immediately realized a new danger when his aircraft narrowly missed some trees as it was restored to level flight. Shortly afterwards, he dropped his bombs close to a railway line '...possibly in the area of Seaham...' and made good his escape.

Based on a report by Willi Schludecker, pilot, KG2, 1941 -1942

4-5 June 1942 (15 miles east of Tyne)

Some twenty enemy aircraft were plotted entering the Tyne area on the night of 4-5 June 1942 and 141 Squadron, Acklington, scrambled seven Beaufighters at intervals shortly after midnight. Lewis Brandon and his pilot, James Benson, were among those who went up. They were directed out to sea and as they made their way eastwards, they could see anti-aircraft fire in the sky over the Tyne. Thirty miles out to sea and at an altitude of 10,000 feet, Brandon, who was using the new Mk 7 airborne interceptor radar, got a contact at maximum range of seven miles and approaching head on. When the 'bogey' was at range 6,000 feet, Benson, under directions from Brandon, broke hard to port at 180 degrees and dropped 1,000 feet in a controlled manoeuvre that brought the Beaufighter behind and slightly below a Do217. Benson closed to 400 feet, fired a two-second burst at the bomber and saw strikes on the tail unit and a large white flash from the starboard engine. There was some inaccurate fire from the Do217's dorsal turret before the raider dropped its port wing, turned on its back and dived vertically towards the sea. Benson attempted to follow but the Beaufighter just could not keep up. At 5,000 feet the Dornier, still diving vertically, drew away and was lost in the haze. The time was 01.15 hours and the location was fifteen miles east of the Tyne. The enemy aircraft was not seen to go into the sea.

Control then reposted the Beaufighter twenty miles out to sea on a north-south patrol line and at 01.30 hours Brandon got another contact, which was crossing from starboard to port, slightly below and at five miles range. Benson had no difficulty easing his Beaufighter behind his quarry, which was flying level but weaving from side to side, but he had to close to within 1,000 feet before he could identify it as a Do217. A two-second burst produced strikes along the fuselage and prompted fairly accurate return fire from the German dorsal gunner but that response was silenced by a second burst from the night fighter. The Dornier fell away to port and was not seen again. Benson and Branson were credited with a 'probable' for their first encounter and a 'damaged' for the second.

6-7 July 1942 (off Amble)

*see Discussion page 161

Aircraft:	Dornier 217E-4	U5+BT	w/nr. 4270	9./KG2
Crew:	Oblt. Günther Lanz	pilot	missing	
	Fw. Ewald Jörs	observer	missing	
	Uffz. Alfred Engler	wireless op	missing	
	Fw. Johannes Klatt	gunner	missing	

On the night of 6-7 July 1942 *Luftflotte 3* dispatched fifty-two bombers against targets on the Tees. During the course of the raid, twenty-eight tons of high explosives and nineteen tons of incendiaries were dropped over the area, the Luftwaffe subsequently claiming to have inflicted damage on ICI's chemical works at Billingham, Dorman, Long's steelworks in Middlesbrough and the yards of the Furness Shipbuilding Company at Haverton Hill. The raid cost KG2 at least one Dornier 217, which is believed to have fallen victim to a Beaufighter of 219 Squadron, Acklington.

Squadron Leader J. Topham (with Flying Officer H.W. Berridge) took off from Acklington in Beaufighter X8221 at 01.15 hours on 7 July. Under GCI Control, he was vectored 340 degrees at 14,000 feet and Berridge got a contact on his airborne interceptor radar at 12,000 feet range at a point south of Amble. Topham subsequently obtained a visual sighting of a Do217 at a range of 300 yards. Although the enemy machine was taking evasive action in the form of violent jinks to port and starboard and a cycle of 500 feet dives and climbs, Topham closed to 250 yards astern before expending all of his ammunition in one long burst and breaking away at seventy yards range. There was no return fire from the Dornier. Topham observed hits on the tail unit and the mid-fuselage

Members of A Flight 219 Squadron c.1941. Back(L-R): John Willson (third) and Wilbur Berridge (sixth). Front(L-R): John Topham (second).
[219 Squadron Association via Tim Kitching]

of the Dornier before the bomber broke away in a steep dive to port. Topham managed to follow it down to 6,000 feet before he lost it.

Topham then circled the area, slowly losing height down to some 2,000 feet as he looked for signs of the enemy machine on the sea. It was as he was making his second orbit and turning on to a southerly heading that he saw a yellow-orange flash, some three to four miles south of his own position. The flash was followed by about ten small fires, which burned on the sea for approximately half a minute.

Confirmation of the crash was provided by soldiers of 313 Coastal Battery, Amble. They informed Acklington that they had seen tracer fire from an aircraft some distance to the south at 01.45 hours and that this was followed by a mass of flames that appeared and developed in the air before falling towards the sea. They took it to be an aircraft falling in flames and they watched it falling until some intervening land prevented them from seeing it actually strike the water. Topham was awarded one Do217 'destroyed'. It is believed that the Dornier was U5+BT of 9./KG2.

Lt. Johannes Bredtmeyer, observer of the 4./KG2 Do217 U5+BM that crashed into the sea off the Tyne on the night of 7-8 July 1942. This picture was taken when he held the rank of Oberfeldwebel [via Rolf Zöpfhel]

219 Squadron had further success some two hours later, when Flight Lieutenant John Willson (with Pilot Officer D.C. Bunch) in Beaufighter V8325 claimed a Dornier damaged in a combat that began twenty miles east of Seaham Harbour and ended fifty miles east of Whitby.

Willson took off from Acklington at 03.55 hours on 7 July. Under Ouston Control, he was ordered to climb to 13,000 feet on vector ninety degrees before being handed over to Northstead GCI at 04.06 hours. Six minutes later, when the Beaufighter was twenty miles east of Seaham Harbour and still under Northstead's guidance, Bunch got an AI contact on 170 degrees at 13,000 feet altitude and crossing from starboard to port at four miles' range. Bunch then guided Willson close enough to get a visual of a Do217 to starboard and 1,000 feet above the night fighter.

The German gunners were alert and opened fire with twin guns from the lower (ventral) turret as Willson made his approach. That gunfire was the prelude to a series of violent evasive actions – jinking and diving from 13,000 feet to 4,000 feet – which were taken by the bomber and which prevented the Beaufighter from ever getting closer than 400 yards. Willson held his fire for as long as possible in the hope of closing the gap, but when he realized that he was not going to get any nearer he opened fire at 400 yards with four short bursts and one long one with both cannon and machine gun. The Dornier crew retaliated strongly, mostly with tracer, from both the dorsal and ventral twin gun positions and the Beaufighter received hits on the tail and on the port main plane. However, Willson also had some success and strikes with explosive cannon shells on the bomber's tail and mid-fuselage were soon followed by plumes of black smoke. After that, there was no further defensive fire from the Dornier, which dived to 300 feet before being lost by its pursuers. Willson was fifty miles east of Whitby when he broke off the combat. When he landed at Acklington at 04.53 hours he claimed one Do217 'damaged'. The writer believes that this aircraft may have been a Do217E-4 (w/nr. 1199) of II./KG40, piloted by *Oberfeldwebel* Alfred Voigt, that crashed near Soesterberg, killing Voigt and two others.

7-8 July 1942 (off the Tyne or off Scarborough?) *see Discussion page 161

Aircraft:	Dornier 217E-4	U5+BM	w/nr. 5465	4./KG2
Crew:	Fw. Johann Grandl	pilot	+	
	Lt. Johannes Bredtmeyer	observer	missing	
	Uffz. Horst Müller	wireless op	+	
	Uffz. Franz Meindl	gunner	missing	

At 00.40 hours on 8 July 1942, twenty-five raiders appeared seventy miles east of Scarborough, flying north-west at altitudes varying from 12,000 feet to 14,000 feet. When east of the Tyne, they turned south-west and made landfall between Seaham and Scarborough, losing height to between 6,000 feet and 10,000 feet. Four or five enemy aircraft operated between Seaham and Middlesbrough and three others between Middlesbrough and Scarborough. The remainder concentrated over the Middlesbrough area, where the ICI chemical works at Billingham was probably one of the main objectives. High-explosive bombs and incendiaries were dropped, mainly in the Middlesbrough, West Hartlepool and Billingham areas and where damage was done to a dockyard, a powerhouse and a warehouse. The ICI works at Billingham suffered damage and a large fire was started at an oil storage site alongside the Tees.

In June 1942, 406 Squadron had moved from Ayr to Scorton and it was from there that Wing Commander D.G. Morris (with Pilot Officer A.V. Rix) took off at 00.56 hours on 8 July (in Beaufighter Z6) under Sector Control and with instructions to patrol sixty miles off the coast. After five unsuccessful attempts to intercept targets, Morris was two miles out to sea with Middlesbrough slightly to starboard when he was advised that there was a raider two miles south at a height between 10,000 feet and 14,000 feet. Shortly afterwards, the northbound enemy passed nearly vertically below the Beaufighter at a range of 2000 feet.

406 (Beaufighter) Squadron. L-R: P/O. A. V. Dix, Sgt. F. G. Harding, P/O. J. R. B Firth, and W/Cdr. D. G. Morris, DFC, the Squadron CO. Fumerton's souvenir from 1 September 1941 hangs in the window behind Harding. Firth and Harding were killed in the early hours of 29 August 1942 when their combat-damaged Beaufighter crashed on returning to Scorton. [Imperial War Museum. Neg. No. CH4891]

Morris dived hard to port in pursuit and gradually overtook the enemy machine, which appeared to be taking no evasive action but was slowly reducing height. Visual contact was obtained at a range of 1,500 feet, with the German slightly to starboard and 200-300 feet above the fighter, which was flying at an altitude of 12,500 feet. Morris identified it as a Dornier 217. He approached to within 500-600 feet below his target and then slowly climbed before edging up to 300 feet range. Using the German's port engine exhaust as his aiming point, Morris fired one burst of two seconds' duration with cannon and machine-gun fire. Vivid strikes were seen at the root of the port wing, just before the port engine burst into flames and began to burn furiously. In spite of the damage inflicted on it, the enemy aircraft continued for a time on a straight and level course and returned very accurate fire from a distance of 100 yards, the Beaufighter receiving two hits. Then the bomber slowed, its port wing and nose dropped and the aircraft started down in a left-hand turn. Burning parts were seen to fall off the aircraft as it disappeared in a steep spiral through clouds 5,000-6,000 feet below. Although the bomber was not seen to strike the sea, a bright glow was seen reflected through the clouds for a time before it faded out. Morris gave the location of the crash site as being seventy miles east of the Tyne. Fifty minutes later, at 02.55 hours, the Beaufighter landed back at Scorton, where Morris was credited with one Dornier 'destroyed'. There is a possibility that Dornier U5+BM, piloted by *Feldwebel* Johann Grandl, was shot down by Morris.

406 Squadron, claimed four other successes (including one damaged) on the night of 7-8 July and Pilot Officer R.H. Harrison accounted for two of them. Harrison (with Pilot Officer E.P.A. Horrex) took off from Scorton at 00.55 hours under Sector Control before being handed over to GCI and then vectored towards the target area of Middlesbrough. At 01.20 hours, when the Beaufighter was at 16,000 feet, Horrex obtained an AI contact at maximum range on an enemy aircraft approaching head-on at 1,000 feet above. Harrison got a visual when the enemy aircraft was directly overhead. The night fighter turned hard to port and gave chase, Harrison following visually but being aided by AI. At range 1,500 feet, keeping slightly to port of his quarry and with the raider clearly silhouetted against the northern sky, Harrison identified it as a Do217. When the night fighter had closed to 1,000 feet, the bomber started taking the most violent evasive action, eventually turning hard to port and diving on a straight run over the target area. At approximately 01.35 hours, Harrison fired one short deflection burst followed by a longer burst of three seconds from above and with his would-be victim silhouetted against almost daylight conditions during its run over the target. The German responded with some fairly accurate return fire, which did not find the night fighter. In the brilliance of the searchlights, bomb bursts and incendiary flashes over the target, it was difficult for the Beaufighter crew to detect strikes on the Dornier but immediately after the second burst the enemy machine pulled over sharply to port in a very steep dive. It was last seen at 3,000 feet, diving towards the sea at an angle that increased to the vertical. It was impossible for the Beaufighter to follow and so Harrison gave up the chase and returned to Sector Control. He was subsequently awarded a 'probable'.

After his combat over Middlesbrough, Harrison returned to Sector at 01.45 hours and was given vector 140 degrees. Horrex got an almost immediate contact on an aircraft well below and ten degrees to starboard; the enemy machine was reducing height and flying at 280mph. Using full throttle, Harrison slowly gained ground. The fighter was at 12,000 feet when Harrison got a visual sighting at 1,500 feet range and identified the silhouette as that of a Dornier. At 02.00 hours, with both pursuer and pursued at 7,000 feet, Harrison eased to within 300 feet of the raider and, in the face of fairly accurate defensive fire from the enemy machine, managed to squeeze off a three-second burst from his cannons. Immediately, a large cloud of white smoke streamed from his victim and that was followed by a vivid explosion. Oil sprayed over Harrison's windscreen as the bomber went into a steep dive with sparks trailing from its starboard engine. The speed was too great and the angle too steep for Harrison to follow and some thirty miles south-east of Hartlepool he was forced to give up the chase. Seemingly, he did not see the Dornier crash but after he had landed at Scorton at 02.35 hours he was credited with one Do217 destroyed.

406 Squadron's fourth claimed success of the night was provided by Wing Commander G.G. Stockdale (with Flight Sergeant W.R. Dibden DFM), who took off from Scorton at 01.05 hours under Sector Control. At 01.37 hours when at a height of 12,000 feet, Stockdale was handed over to GCI and vectored north-west. After a number of vectors, contact was obtained at a maximum range on an enemy aircraft in a head-on position going to port. Stockdale turned hard left in pursuit and increased speed to 230-240mph. In spite of evasive action by the German, contact was maintained for thirty-eight minutes. At 02.15 hours, when both machines were at 6,000 feet altitude, Stockdale got his first momentary visual, which was soon lost in dark cloud. Dibden, however, kept AI contact and a minute later a second sighting was obtained and Stockdale identified his quarry as a Do217, which he recognized from the position of its exhausts and by its silhouette. Closing in to 400 feet, he squeezed off a two-second burst from astern and slightly below. Immediately, the Dornier emitted a shower of sparks and then a huge sheet of flame. Burning fiercely, it turned to starboard in a slow climb and fell spinning into the sea. Stockdale landed back at Scorton at 03.20 hours to be credited with one Do217 destroyed.

Grandl's Dornier (U5+BM) was the only Do217 acknowledged by the Luftwaffe as having been lost over the North on the night of 7-8 July and Stockdale was the only claimant who saw his victim crash. Thus it would seem that it was he, and not Morris, who caught Grandl.

406 Squadron's fifth claim was submitted by Pilot Officer A.G. Lawrence (with Sergeant H.J. Wilmer), who took off at 01.15 hours and claimed to have destroyed a Heinkel 111 over Hartlepool at 01.30 hours. Lawrence was freelancing at 10,000 feet when Wilmer got an AI contact at maximum range and 600 feet below the Beaufighter. The unidentified aircraft was intercepted and, when the Beaufighter was 1,500 feet astern and 300 feet above, Lawrence identified the silhouette as being that of an He111. Closing to 400 feet, Lawrence fired two short bursts of one second each from dead astern. No results were observed other than the enemy aircraft turning slowly to port. Following a further burst of gunfire, this time of three seconds, the bomber swung slowly to

starboard. At no time was there any return fire. Then Lawrence saw a flash from the starboard engine immediately prior to the raider going into a spin. Lawrence followed his victim down to 8,000 feet before the Heinkel went into a steep spiral dive. It was followed visually until it disappeared into clouds at 3,000 feet, still spinning. The bomber was not seen to crash but Lawrence claimed one He111 destroyed when he landed back at Scorton at 02.40 hours.

Examination of the Luftwaffe Loss Returns shows no Heinkel loss for this date. However, two Junkers 88s of Ku.Fl.Gr.106 returned damaged from operations but it is not certain that they took part in the raid on the north-east of England.

Luftwaffe Losses for 7 July 1942

4./KG2	Do217E-4	U5+BM	(w/nr.5465) pilot / Fw. Johann Grandl
9./KG2	Do217E-4	U5+BT	(w/nr.4270) pilot / Oblt. Günter Lanz
II./KG40	Do217E-4	?	(w/nr.1199) pilot / Obfw. Alfred Voigt [crashed nr. Soesterberg on return from operations.]
Ku.Fl.Gr. 106	Ju88A-4	?	(w/nr. 140022) returned to base with twenty-five per cent damage
Ku.Fl.Gr. 106	Ju88A-4	?	(w/nr. 1650) returned to base with twenty-five per cent damage

Discussion

There seems to be a good deal of confusion regarding losses over the north-east of England on the nights of 6-7 and 7-8 July 1942, with acknowledged authorities putting forward almost diametrically opposed views regarding what happened.

Middlesbrough was raided on the consecutive nights of 6-7 July and 7-8 July. *Blitz, then and now. Vol 3* states that the raid on the night of 7-8 July 1942 resulted in the loss of two Do217s by KG2; U5+BT (of 9/KG2), which crashed into the sea off Middlesbrough, and one from 4./KG2 which crashed off the Dutch coast on its return to the Continent. That source also claims that 406 Squadron, Scorton, was responsible for the demise of U5+BT.

On the other hand, Balke in his history of KG2[1], states that two Do217s (U5+BT and U5+BM) were shot down on the night of 6-7 July. However, Balke would seem to be in error here for the Luftwaffe list of aircrew losses (*Verlustliste*) at the *Deutsche-Dienststelle*, Berlin, shows that Grandl and his crew took off from Eindhoven at 23.34 hours on 7 July 1942 and thus could not have been shot down the night before!

Balke also claims that Squadron Leader John Topham of 219 Squadron, Acklington, was responsible for shooting down both U5+BM and U5+BT. As can be seen above, Topham made a claim (but only one) for a Do217 on the night of 6-7 July, while Flight Lieutenant John Willson (also of 219 Squadron) made a claim for one Do217 damaged. Thus 219 Squadron did submit two claims for the night of 6-7 July 1942, but not quite in the form stated by Balke.

The situation is not helped by the fact that the Luftwaffe Loss Returns for that time show that *Luftflotte 3* lost three aircraft on operations on 7 July. Of course, the latter date could embrace the nights of 6-7 and 7-8 July and might include the claim submitted by 406 Squadron for 7-8 July.

In the Luftwaffe Loss Returns, KG2 is shown as having lost two Do217s on 7 July, U5+BM and U5+BT, while II./KG40 also lost one (w/nr.1199) which crash-landed near Soesterberg on return from operations, killing the pilot *Oberfeldwebel* Alfred Voigt and two of his crew. However, it is not certain that the latter aircraft took part in the Middlesbrough attack, although II./KG40 regularly accompanied KG2 on operational sorties. No operational losses for *Luftflotte 3* could be found for 8 July 1942.

Although there is confusion, what can be said is that the Luftwaffe Loss Returns show three Do217s lost on 7 July, one of which crashed in Holland. 219 Squadron claimed one destroyed (which was seen to crash) and one damaged on the night of 6-7 July; 406 Squadron claimed four destroyed on the night of 7-8 July. However, only one of those was actually seen to crash, namely, the Dornier claimed by Wing Commander Stockdale [see *Broken Eagles (Yorkshire)*],[11] although Morris observed a glow which he interpreted as a crashing aircraft. Thus the combined claims do not match the Loss Returns but the 'sighted' claims do match. However, although the writer has offered possibilities regarding victors and victims, it cannot be said with certainty which claim relates to which loss.

25-26 July 1942 (off the Northumberland coast?)

On the night of 25-26 July 1942 twenty-two Dornier 217s of KG2 set out from their Dutch bases to raid the Middlesbrough area. Twenty-two tons of high explosives and six tons of incendiaries were dropped from altitudes of 2,000 feet – 4,500 feet over the area of West Hartlepool, Middlesbrough, Billingham and Haverton Hill. Numerous fires were started and some damage inflicted, mainly to domestic properties. The aiming point of the attack was the Haverton Hill shipyard on the Tees loop and returning crews claimed to have seriously damaged six important armament factories in that area, as well the ICI chemical works at Billingham. Thirteen RAF aircraft were involved in night fighter operations over the target; four Beaufighters from 406 Squadron, Scorton, three Beaufighters from 219 Squadron, Acklington, five Hurricanes from 1 Squadron, Acklington and one Havoc. It is known that 406 Squadron had no combats that night but Squadron Leader J.G.

Topham, (with Flying Officer H.W. Berridge) of 219 Squadron claimed two enemy aircraft shot down in fifty minutes.

Squadron Leader Topham (with Flying Officer Berridge) took off from Acklington at 00.20 hours. Under GCI control, Topham was vectored out to sea, where Berridge got a contact at 10,000 feet and at nearly three miles range. Topham closed to 200 yards and got a visual on a Do217 before firing cannon and machine gun. Strikes were seen all over the enemy aircraft, which did not offer any defensive gunfire but which twice turned completely over. Then it caught fire, lost its tail and dived steeply. Topham followed for 3,000 feet before breaking away. He did not see the Dornier hit the sea.

Later, again under GCI, Berridge got a contact on an enemy aircraft 4,000 feet below. Topham got close enough to identify it as another Do217, but unlike its predecessor, this one took unusually violent evasive action and retaliated with gunfire from its dorsal turret. Topham opened fire with cannon and machine gun at 200 yards dead astern and saw strikes on his target's fuselage and mainplane. Shortly afterwards, the Dornier turned to port and dived steeply towards the sea, leaving a stream of flaming debris in its wake. Topham followed long enough to see the bomber explode when it struck the water. The Beaufighter landed back at Acklington at 01.35 hours.

Unfortunately, the available documents recording Topham's claims do not give the locations of the crashes. Equally unfortunate is the fact that examination of the Luftwaffe Loss Returns reveals no record of such losses being sustained on the night of 25-26 July 1942.

8-9 August 1942 (north-west of Newcastle?)

Flight Lieutenant Beaumont (with Sergeant Andrews) of 219 Squadron, Acklington, took off at 21.55 hours on a practice flight under Northstead GCI when he was informed that there were 'bandits' in the area. He was ordered to patrol south-east of Acklington at 15,000 feet. After one failed interception, AI contact was made with a second raider flying at 10,000 feet. Under Andrews' guidance, Beaumont closed to 800 feet and identified the 'bandit' as a Junkers 88 before the enemy aircraft began a series of evasive manoeuvres consisting of violent 'jinking' and semi-stall turns. The fighter's speed was then 280 IAS and because Beaumont thought he was unable to close in any further than 250 yards, he opened fire from astern and slightly above his target. Explosions were seen on the wing of the Junkers, which appeared to reduce speed. Return fire was experienced from the raider's dorsal gun, but this ceased during a second burst from the fighter. The continuation of this second burst from the fighter caused fire to break out in the bomber's port engine, the port wing and part of the fuselage. The blazing aircraft dived away to port, close enough to the Beaufighter to force Beaumont to pull away sharply to starboard in order to avoid collision. The enemy machine was last seen going down slightly north-west of Newcastle at 23.30 hours but the night fighter crew did not see it crash. A 'probable' was claimed but examination of the Luftwaffe Loss Returns for this date revealed no listing of such a loss.

15-16 August 1942 (off Sunderland?)

Flight Lieutenant D.C. Furse (with Pilot Officer J.H. Downes) of 406 Squadron, took off on patrol from Scorton in Beaufighter X8226 at 22.35 hours on 15 August. Between 20.30 hours and 00.25 hours on the night of 15-16 August approximately twelve enemy aircraft approached the Sector area, chiefly between Whitby and the Farne Islands. One of them was a Do217E-4, U5+IM (w/nr.4268) of 4./KG2, which was based at Eindhoven (Holland) and which was sortied to make a nuisance raid on Sunderland.

Under GCI control, Downes subsequently made contact with an unidentified aircraft which was not displaying its IFF (Identification Friend or Foe). The weather '...was extremely thick...' and Furse could not see the silhouette of the suspect aircraft when Downes guided him close to the 'bogey'. However, he could see its exhausts well enough to take aim. In the absence of IFF, which would have identified the suspect as an Allied aircraft, it was presumed to be an enemy. Furse fired a three-second burst from 150 feet range. A large ball of flame erupted at the point of the strikes and a piece of aircraft flew up from the victim's left side and another piece dropped from the right side. Contact was lost immediately and nothing more seen of the Beaufighter's (unidentified) target, which Furse claimed as 'damaged'.

The night fighter's victim was probably the Do217 U5+IM (*Ida Marie*), the pilot of which is not known at the time of writing. The night fighter's combination of bullets and cannon shells struck home 4,000 feet over Sunderland. Furse's attack did not destroy the raider but it did tear away large holes in the cockpit roof of the bomber before damaging the instrument panel, destroying the course-setting compass, damaging the right engine, and adversely affecting the controls so that the Dornier plunged 3,000 feet before the pilot managed to force a sluggish response from the joystick. Additional damage to the hydraulics caused the bomb doors to drop open as the Dornier plummeted earthwards. It is believed that the bombs dropped harmlessly into the sea, but it is not known whether they were jettisoned or whether they dropped of their own accord. Only the unnamed German pilot, protected by the armour plating of his seat, survived unscathed. *Unteroffizier* Fritz Aigner (observer) was wounded in the thigh, *Unteroffizier* Heinz Niegisch (ventral gunner) was badly wounded in the left arm and lost a finger from his right hand and *Unteroffizier* Walter Schmidt (wireless operator) was killed instantly when he was shot through the head.

After Aigner had succeeded in cranking up the bomb doors by hand, the Dornier eventually managed to make its way back to Eindhoven, where it crash-landed with little fuel to spare. A subsequent assessment showed that the bomber had suffered thirty per cent damage.

28-29 August 1942 (off Seaham)

Aircraft:	Junkers 88A-4	3Z+CB	w/nr. 144146	StabI./KG77
Crew:	Obfw. Alfred Riedel	pilot	pow	
	Fw. Josef Pfeffer	observer	pow	
	Obfw. Paul Kolodzie	wireless op	+	
	Gefr. Josef Sanden	gunner	+	

Dornier bombers of KG2, augmented by aircraft from I./KG77, were detailed to attack Sunderland with twenty-one tons of bombs on the night of 28-29 August 1942. Balke[12] claims that twelve aircraft from KG2 reached their target, with two others attacking alternatives in Middlesbrough and County Durham. However, it would appear that the raid was more scattered than intended. The Operations Record Book of the Scorton-based 406 Squadron records that between 22.09 hours and 23.50 hours bombs were dropped in the areas of Sunderland, Seaham, Alnwick and Acklington. Both 219 Squadron at Acklington and 406 Squadron at Scorton, scrambled Beaufighters in response to the threat and both squadrons subsequently claimed victories but it is not clear who shot down what and where.

Junkers 88 3Z+CB is recorded as having crashed into the sea at position 54°50'N/01°08'W[13] (off Seaham) at 23.04 hours on 28 August 1942. During the course of their interrogation, the German survivors explained that nine aircraft from KG77 had taken part in the raid, which was aimed at Sunderland's docks and shipyards. Apparently, it was an operation which gave rise to a measure of dissatisfaction among participating crews, who believed that the distance to Sunderland from their temporary base at Soesterberg[14] was just too far to allow their usual twenty per cent safety margin of fuel. Despite their reservations about the trip, the crew of 3Z+CB had taken off, loaded with four 500kg bombs and had flown towards the Norfolk coast while climbing steadily to 3,000 feet. When they were twenty miles off Great Yarmouth, they were intercepted by a night fighter but they managed to escape when Riedel flew a 360 degree turn and dived to sea level before continuing northwards on a course that paralleled the coast.

Climbing steadily to 14,000 feet, Riedel continued northwards until, at 22.47 hours and when he was forty miles east of his target, he turned to port for the run into Sunderland. As he flew westwards, the German continually changed height within the altitude range 14,000 feet – 17,000 feet as a precaution against night fighters but it was not enough. At 23.00 hours, when searchlights could just be glimpsed operating over the still-distant coast, Paul Kolodzie shouted the warning, 'Night fighter at two hundred metres!' a split second before attacker's shells struck home between the bomber's port engine and fuselage, wounding the rear gunner, *Gefreiter* Josef Sanden, in the process.

Fire started immediately and soon enveloped the port engine. Riedel jettisoned his bombs and made a diving turn to port, losing height rapidly in an effort to escape his assailant. Within seconds, he was forced to switch off the damaged motor and continue his hasty descent on one engine only. After three minutes, the night fighter had gone but the Germans' predicament was no less serious; the Junkers was then at only 3,000 feet and in a shallow glide towards the sea. In addition, the flames were spreading, the inner fuel tanks were full and an explosion was a distinct possibility. Riedel swung towards the coast in the hope of making an emergency landing there but the threat of aerial incineration proved too serious to be ignored and the order was given to bale out. The pilot was the last to go and his parachute scarcely had time to open before he touched the water.

Riedel and Pfeffer were lucky enough to be picked up by a south-bound convoy some thirty minutes after landing in the sea and were set ashore at Sheerness three days later, but the other two members of the crew drowned. Kolodzie's body was retrieved from the sea off Crimdon Dean, north of Hartlepool, on 31 August and Sanden's body was recovered from Blackhall Rocks on the same day. Both Kolodzie and Sanden were buried in Acklam Road Cemetery, Thornaby-on-Tees, where they still lie.

Blitz,then and now Vol.3[15] maintains that 3Z+CB was shot down by Flight Lieutenant J.R.B. Firth (with Pilot Officer R.G. Harding) of 406 Squadron but this is questionable. Doubt is raised, firstly, by the time of Firth's take-off (given as 23.00 hours in the Squadron Operations Record Book) and the time of the crash of the Junkers 88 (23.04 hours) and, secondly, by Firth's radioed report . The 406 Squadron Operations Record Book records that, following take-off under GCI Control, the Beaufighter crew '...soon obtained an AI contact which quickly led to a visual. A long and exciting combat followed, ending with the destruction of an enemy aircraft 30 miles east of Whitby at 23.30hours...', the wreck being observed burning on the water. The writer believes that Firth's victim was probably Do217 U5+FH, piloted by *Leutnant* Josef Weigel of 1./KG2. (see *Broken Eagles* [*Yorkshire*]).[16]

The Beaufighter was damaged during the engagement and Firth had to return to Scorton with his starboard engine dead. On his return, a heavy ground mist increased the hazard of landing, the Beaufighter overshot and crashed into a house near the end of the runway at 00.15 hours. Sadly, neither Firth nor Harding survived the impact.

In the writer's view, Ju88 3Z+CB was probably shot down by Flight Lieutenant Horne (with Sergeant Alcock) in a Beaufighter of 219 Squadron, Acklington, whose combat report of an encounter off Blyth bears striking similarities to Riedel's account. Horne took off at 22.35 hours under Northstead GCI. After various GCI vectors, Alcock got a contact two miles ahead while on vector 330 at an altitude of 14,000 feet. Contact was maintained until a visual was obtained (at 23.05 hours), when the target aircraft was 2,000 feet ahead. Horne identified the raider by its exhaust and its silhouette and believed it to be a Heinkel 111 – mistakenly, in the current writer's view. When pursued and pursuer were in the area of Blyth, Horne closed to 150 yards and fired a two-second burst of gunfire from astern and slightly below. Immediately, a bright explosion was seen between the enemy's port engine and fuselage and then the raider went into a steep dive to the left with white vapour streaming from the port engine. Horne followed his victim down to 8,000 feet before breaking off the chase but the bomber was still diving when it was last seen by its attackers. Horne submitted a claim for one He111 'damaged' but he was subsequently awarded one 'destroyed'. The writer could find no relevant reference to the loss of a Heinkel in the Luftwaffe Loss Returns for that night but the loss of the Ju88 is listed.

As can be seen, Horne's version of events shares much common ground with the Germans' account, in terms of location, time and the altitude at which the interception took place, as well as in relation to the damage inflicted in the attack. On the basis of this evidence, the writer believes that Horne misidentified his victim and that he (Horne) was, in fact, responsible for the demise of 3Z+CB.

1942
The Luftwaffe's efforts to conserve aircraft and crews

In July 1942, I./KG77 was transferred from the Russian Front to Creil, north of Paris, to be used in operations against the United Kingdom and to offer a measure of reinforcement to the Western Front in case of invasion. The unit had been reinforced by twelve crews from III./KG51, all of them being very experienced in war operations for they had flown numerous war flights in Russia. During the summer of 1942, KG77 raided both northern and southern areas of England, southern targets being attacked from Creil (France) while those in the north necessitated a temporary move to Soesterberg (Holland).

In the middle of 1942, Air Ministry Intelligence personnel engaged in the interrogation of captured aircrews were moved to remark that recently captured Luftwaffe crews tended to acknowledge that they were fighting on the defensive in the West. The interrogators also formed the opinion that because of this, the general policy of the German Air Force in the West seemed to be to conserve aircraft and crews at the expense of maximizing their effectiveness in raids on targets in Britain.

This was a view which also emerged strongly during the interrogation of the survivors of the crash of Ju88 3Z+CB (StabI./KG77), which was shot down off Seaham (probably by Flight Lieutenant Horne, 219 Squadron, Acklington), on 28 August 1942, and by the crew[17] of Ju88 3Z+OH (1./KG77), which force-landed near Grimsby on the night of 2 September 1942. Following the interrogation of both crews, the interviewing officer reported that:

> The *Gruppenkommandeur* of I./KG77, Major von Scheliha, appears to be far more concerned with getting his crews back safely than with destroying the target which they are sent to attack. He has even gone to the length of telling crews that if the objective looks particularly dangerous and well defended they are to go to the alternative target or even to attack any likely objective they may find. Those crews of I./KG77 which have recently joined the unit from the Russian Front have been intensively engaged since the beginning of the Eastern campaign and are to some extent operationally tired. They have found that flights over England are very much more dangerous than those over Russia and, judging from the present prisoners, their reaction appears to be to seek out the easiest alternative target or even to jettison their bombs into the sea.

To support their claim, the interrogators offered examples from operations undertaken by 3Z+CB and 3Z+OH, though one wonders whether fuel considerations, aggravated by defensive tactics, proved to be a more relevant factor in aborted missions. The flights included a raid on Portsmouth on 20 August 1942, when the crew of 3Z+OH claimed to have found the searchlights and anti-aircraft fire so menacing that they aborted the attack and jettisoned their bombs in the sea before returning to Creil. Seven days later, 3Z+CB was among a number of KG77's aircraft detailed to raid Leeds, and was one of at least two aircraft which aborted their mission because evasive manoeuvres (constant changes of course and height on approaching the English coast and beyond) was so costly in fuel. Even though Riedel was in sight of Leeds at the time, he opted to drop his 2,000 incendiaries nearer the coast and return to Soesterberg. The other aircraft, in which the observer of 3Z+OH was flying as a 'spare', aborted after its attempts to escape the searchlights around Leeds consumed too much petrol and the crew decided to jettison their bombs in the sea and return to base. A further example was provided during the raid on Sunderland on 28 August 1942, during which 3Z+CB was shot down. On that occasion, the crew of another (unidentified) Ju88 from the same unit was also intercepted by a night fighter and used up so much fuel escaping their pursuer that the attack on the town was abandoned.

Based on AI1(k) Report No.292/1942 in AIR40/2411/ PRO

6-7 September 1942 (off Sunderland)

On the night of 6-7 September 1942, fifteen aircraft of *IX Fliegerkorps* attacked Sunderland. The raid included a number Do217s of KG2, which took off from their Dutch bases at 22.50 hours local time. Crews claimed to have bombed the designated area and noted a number of explosions and resultant fires. Bombs also fell on the Cargo Fleet Ironworks on Teesside, as well as at Eston and in Middlesbrough.

The operation got off to a bad start for the attackers when the Do217 U5+LT (w/nr. 4275) of *Unteroffizier* Steudal (9./KG2) crashed at Harderwijk shortly after take-off, killing all four members of the crew. Further misfortune awaited KG2 as they approached the north-east coast. Some twenty miles east of Sunderland, Dornier 217 U5+DP (w/nr. 5544) of 6./KG2 (based at Eindhoven, Holland) was caught by a night fighter and did not escape until its mechanic, *Oberfeldwebel* Heinrich Müller, had been killed. This machine, together with one other, Do217E-4 (w/nr. 4927) from Deelen-based III./KG2, managed to return to their bases but both suffered damage when they crash-landed.

Beaufighters of 219 Squadron, Acklington and 410 Squadron, Scorton, were operational on the night of 6-7 September 1942. 219 Squadron was involved in several chases but did not manage an interception. However, it is conceivable that the following engagement by 410 Squadron might have a bearing on the fate of Do217 U5+DP, but in the absence of more specific information such a connection is no more than speculation.

Between 21.32 and 21.45 hours, Pilot Officer F.R. Ferguson (with Pilot Officer D. Creed) in Beaufighter T3428 of 410 Squadron, Scorton, obtained a contact at 13,000 feet near the mouth of the river Tees. Ferguson closed in from behind and identified what he thought was a Ju88 before firing a three-second burst from machine guns and cannons at 150 yards range. His next three-second burst appeared to strike the top of the enemy's starboard wing, both inboard and outboard of the engine. Directly after that, the raider dived out to sea and although Ferguson attempted to follow, contact was lost. According to the Squadron reports, subsequent information received suggested that the enemy aircraft had crashed in flames into the sea. However, the source of that information is not given.

On the same night, Flight Lieutenant E.P. Sharpe (with Sergeant A.F. Watson) took off in Beaufighter T3381 of 410 Squadron at 22.55 hours. He was vectored on to a 'bogey' and made first contact straight ahead at range 10,000 feet when he was at an altitude of 15,000 feet. Sharpe closed to within 200 feet and identified the 'bogey' as a Do217. As the bomber took violent evasive action and crossed in front of the Beaufighter from starboard to port, Sharpe opened fire with a two-second burst but no hits were seen and visual contact was then lost.

19 September 1942 (off Tynemouth)

Aircraft:	Dornier 217E-4	U5+KR	w/nr. 4262	7./KG2
Crew:	Obfw. Helmut Ahrendholz	pilot	+	
	Uffz. Edgar Moll	observer	+	
	Uffz. Peter Hartmann	wireless op	+	
	Uffz. Hans Woelke	mechanic	missing	

On the night of 19 September 1942, 219 Squadron, Acklington, put up four Beaufighters between 21.15 hours and 22.10 hours to meet incoming hostile aircraft making for Sunderland but only Squadron Leader John Topham (with Flying Officer H.W. Berridge) had any luck. He caught Dornier 217 U5+KR off Blyth at 22.04 hours and shot it down. The bomber crashed into the sea near the mouth of the Tyne.

Topham had taken off in Beaufighter X8217 on a practice flight under Northstead Control when he was notified that there were 'bandits' in the area. With Northstead's help, Berridge got a contact a few seconds later, when the German was to port of the Beaufighter and at 9,000 feet range. Topham turned and dived in pursuit and obtained a visual of an anonymous silhouette against a moonlit cloud when he was 2,000 feet below his target. The raider was travelling very slowly, at a speed estimated at 160-180mph, and Topham had to reduce his own rate of progress by lowering wheels and flaps in order to keep the enemy aircraft ahead of him.

The German was completing a series of violent evasive actions consisting of long 'jinks' to port and starboard as well as up and down between the altitudes 9,000 feet and 12,000 feet. In spite of these defensive tactics, Berridge continued to maintain AI contact as Topham slowly eased his aircraft to a point 500 feet below and 2,000 feet behind his intended victim. When the range had been reduced to 600 feet and the fighter was poised 200 feet below the raider, Topham identified it as a Do217 and opened fire with a burst of gunfire that lasted five-six seconds. He saw bullet and cannon strikes on the bomber's fuselage and both engines. The clouds of black smoke that followed were momentarily speckled with showers of red sparks but these were soon transformed into a ball of fire. The enemy machine flew parallel to the coast until it reached a point off Tynemouth. Then it burst completely into flames and dived straight into the sea from an altitude of 8,000 feet. It crashed at about 22.10 hours. Both Topham and Berridge saw it burning on the water but further confirmation came later from police at North Shields, the coastguards at Blyth and the Royal Observer Corps at Newcastle. During the course of this engagement, the Beaufighter was twice illuminated by searchlights but it was not engaged by anti-aircraft defences.

The body of *Oberfeldwebel* Helmut Ahrendholz was recovered from the sea four miles off the river Tyne on 20 September 1942 and was buried in Preston Cemetery, North Shields. In the 1960s, it was reburied in the German War Cemetery at Cannock Chase, Staffordshire.

EYEWITNESS
Feldwebel Günter Bartnik
wireless operator (8./KG2)

Günter Bartnik was the wireless operator in the crew of *Leutnant* Helmut Ueberson of 8./KG2, based at Deelen (Holland). During the period July 1942–March 1943, Ueberson's crew took part in fifteen raids over northern England:

1942				1943			
	6-7	July	Middlesbrough		9	January	Humber (mining)
	7-8	July	Middlesbrough		2	February	Humber (mining)
	25	July	Middlesbrough		3	February	Sunderland
	1	August	Hull		9	March	Hull
	27	August	Leeds		11	March	Newcastle/Tyne
	28	August	Sunderland		12	March	South Shields
	11	October	Sunderland		14	March	Sunderland
	12	October	Humber (mining)				

In the paragraphs that follow, Günter Bartnik comments on some of those operations.

Land targets were generally specified as port installations, docks or factories. Night bombing attacks on such targets followed the same pattern on each occasion. At briefing, details of the target were given, as well as attack height and allocated time over the target. Weather details were provided by the weatherman and course details given to the Observer. A few aircraft took off to act as target markers (using flare bombs) and the bombers took off at one or two minute intervals.

The flight across the North Sea was always made at low level in order to keep below British radar. Threats and dangers were ever present from night-fighters, ships' flak (if we accidentally over-flew them), or engine failure.

When in sight of the English coast we began to climb to our attack height. Now began our defensive manoeuvres: continuous deviations around our main course, as well as changes in altitude – all of which made it difficult for the ground (radar) station to lead the night fighter to us. While these manoeuvres were going on, the wireless operator (above) and the mechanic (below) constantly watched for night fighters in the airspace behind.

Near the target we saw the placed target markers or fires already burning on the ground (or man-made decoy fires). Dazzling searchlights and the explosions of flak shells brought new dangers, against which we were powerless. Abrupt defensive manoeuvres by the pilot helped as we approached the searchlight beams – and to disturb the searchlight tracking equipment our mechanic would sometimes release aluminium strips (Düppel). In this pandemonium it was then: 'Bomb doors open...Bombs dropped... Bomb doors closed'. The bombing procedure was carried out by the pilot or by the observer (depending on whether that aircraft was in level flight or diving). The mechanic, lying in the ventral turret, confirmed that the bombs had gone. Then we left the 'inferno' as quickly as possible.

The homeward flight was again dangerous because of night fighters. Always one saw a chain of tracer in the dark night sky and after that the sight of a blazing machine falling earthwards. Thus an exhortation from the wireless operator or the mechanic was particularly good at the right time because the night fighter, more often than not, struck from behind and from under. This danger persisted over the North Sea – and a few machines were even attacked by night fighters while on their final approaches to their home base.

Mine-laying operations were somewhat quieter and not so hectic as

L-R: Lt. Helmut Ueberson (pilot), Fw. Josef König (mechanic), Ofhr. Kürt Kühling (observer) and Fw. Günter Bartnik (wireless operator). This crew operated over northern England fifteen times during 1942-1943. Ueberson and his colleagues were the longest surviving crew in their unit by March 1943, when they were taken off operational flying and employed as 'instructional crew'. They returned to operations in April 1944. This picture was taken at Melun-Villaroche in March 1944.
[Günter Bartnik via Peter Kirk]

bombing operations. We flew at low level to the target area then we had to find and identify the estuary we had been ordered to mine, before laying the mines and returning at low level across the sea. Minelaying was not so dangerous because we didn't fly at high altitude and we didn't fly over land – so we didn't have to reckon with flak.

We had two types of mines: the LMB1000 and the BM1000. The LMB was a sea mine, dropped by parachute; the BM fell like a bomb into the water. Both were 1,000kg. Two mines were carried and were laid in shipping channels and convoy routes, principally in the Humber and the Thames but also off Portsmouth and the Isle of Wight.

Günter Bartnik, wireless operator, 8./KG2

16 October 1942 (east of Roker)

Flying Officer Farrar (with Sergeant Crozier) of 219 Squadron, Acklington, took off in a Beaufighter at 20.20 hours on 16 October with the intention of participating in a GCI exercise under Northstead Control. After some time, Farrar saw flares and incendiary fires south of the Tyne, where Sunderland was under attack from nine Do217s of KG2. Shortly after investigating, and when the Beaufighter was at 10,000 feet, Crozier got an AI contact to starboard at 9,000 feet range. Under Crozier's direction, Farrar had closed the range to 2,500 feet when the 'bogey' was caught by searchlights and Farrar was able to identify it as a Do217. The enemy machine was then to starboard and 600 feet above the fighter. As Farrar edged nearer, both the Beaufighter and the Dornier were momentarily illuminated by searchlights some considerable distance away to starboard but the German crew failed to see the danger as Farrar closed in from below and to port. He opened fire at 21.40 hours and from 700 feet range. Three short bursts were enough to cause the bomber to burst into flames before it plummeted into the sea off Roker, its burning wreckage floating for some time before settling to the seabed. The demise of the enemy machine was witnessed by members of the local Observer Corps and the police, who provided the confirmation of Farrar's claim. However, no record of this loss could be found in the Luftwaffe Loss Returns. Farrar landed back at Acklington at 22.20 hours, a wing of his aircraft slightly damaged by flying metal shed by the Dornier as it fell.

13 December 1942

Dornier 217s of KG2 raided the port installations at Sunderland in the early hours of 13 December 1942. Twenty-three crews started taking-off from their bases at 03.05hours (local time) but a number of those, including three crews from III./KG2, returned early because of technical problems. A Do217 of I./KG2 (w/nr. 5570) suffered twenty per cent damage on landing at Gilze Rijen on its return from Sunderland while

Do217E-4 U5+AK (w/nr. 4348) of 2./KG2 failed to return at all, the crew *Leutnant* Georg Ratzke (pilot), *Feldwebel* Paul Köhler (observer), *Obergefreiter* Wolgang Mertz (wireless op) and *Unteroffizier* Gerhard Krüger (gunner) being posted as 'missing'. The location and cause of the loss are not known at the time of writing.

14 December 1942

On 14 December a further attack was made on the British north-east coast between Middlesbrough and Sunderland, the focal point of the attack being the dock installations at Hartlepool. Twenty-seven bombers of *IX Fliegerkorps* took off at 18.15 hours for the attack on the port but only twenty-four actually claimed to have reached the target. Flare bombs were used to illuminate the area and in conditions of favourable visibility, the raiders dropped their loads of high explosives and incendiaries from heights ranging from 3,000 feet to 7,000 feet. Three high-explosive bombs also fell on Warrenby ironworks.

Despite the favourable visibilty and the use of flares, the expected concentration in bombing was not achieved. The attack was widely scattered and little damage was inflicted, although the attackers claimed hits on the Dorman, Long iron and steel works at Middlesbrough and Redcar, as well as South Durham steelworks at Hartlepool. Participating KG2 crews described the northern defences of anti-aircraft fire, searchlights and night fighters as 'fierce' but all aircraft returned to their bases. However, not all landed unscathed. A Do217E-4 (w/nr. 4377) of I./KG2 suffered fifteen per cent damage when it crash-landed at Gilze-Rijen (Holland) following 'an operating error' by crew members, while a Do217E-4 (w/nr. 4363) of III./KG2 suffered thirty per cent damage when it crash-landed at Deelen. Three members of the crew are recorded as being wounded in the latter incident but the cause is not stated.

NOTES

1 Kü.Fl.Gr.506 was redesignated *Kampfgruppe* 506 (KGr.506) on 19 October 1941.
2 Norman, Bill, *Broken Eagles(Luftwaffe losses over Yorkshire, 1939-1945)* Pen & Sword Books Ltd. 2001.
3 Kurowski, Franz, *Seekrieg aus der Luft*. E.S. Mittler & Sohn, Herford 1979 p186.
4 Ramsey, W.G., (ed), The *Blitz, then and now. Vol. 3* Battle of Britain Prints International 1990 p94.
5 Alan White of Houghton-le-Spring believes that this aircraft was shot down by his father's gun crew of the Tyne-based 'C' Troop, 278 LAA Battery/68 LAA Regt. RA. Alan still has the small trophy he says was awarded to each member in recognition of their achievement. However, as yet there is no conclusive evidence as to who was responsible for the loss of S4+EH.
6 Balke, Ulf, *Der Luftkrieg in Europa Vol.2* Bernard & Graefe Verlag, Koblenz 1990 p82.
7 Young, Ron, *The Comprehensive Guide to Shipwrecks of the North East Coast*, Tempus 2001 p189.
8 Beedle, J., *43 Squadron*, Beaumont Aviation Literature 1966, p194.
9 Ramsey, W.G., (ed), op.cit. p124.
10 Balke, Ulf, op.cit. pp127-128.
11 Norman, Bill, op.cit. p144.
12 Balke, Ulf, op.cit. p147.
13 AI(k) Report 292/1942(Debrief of POWs) in AIR40/2411 at the PRO.
14 I./KG77 had transferred from their base at Creil to participate in the operation.
15 Ramsey, W.G. (ed), op.cit. p167.
16 Norman, Bill, op.cit. pp147-148.
17 *Fw.* J. Ackermann (pilot), *Obgfr.* R. Weingand (observer), *Uffz.* H. Wandt(wireless op) and *Uffz.* R. Eysoldt(mechanic).

4

DESPERATE TIMES
(1943 - 1945)

The combined effect of operational losses and over stretched resources that had characterized the efforts of *Luftflotte 3* in the closing months of 1942 were not alleviated to any significant extent in 1943. In January of that year, the Luftwaffe had only about one hundred bombers and fighter-bombers for operations in the West and even that figure was reduced by the unserviceability of some machines, and this lack of operational strength ensured that the effort against Britain would continue to wane. In March 1943, the post of *Angriffsführer England* (Attack Leader England) was created to strengthen that bomber force and develop an effective operational strategy against Britain. However, by September the force charged with that task stood at only 135 aircraft (mainly Do217s and Ju88s) and replacements were barely keeping up with losses.

By the opening months of the new year, attempts to reduce losses had forced the Luftwaffe to modify its offensive tactics when approaching targets. Because of the numbers of night fighters waiting in those areas where incoming bombers climbed to attack height, low-flying approaches were abandoned and the climb was spread over the length of the entire flight across the North Sea. It was hoped that such a change would reduce the risk of interceptions while obviating the need for the precautionary evasive tactics that had previously made bombing accuracy so difficult.

Although the power of the German bomber force was decidedly failing by 1943, the two northern counties were subjected to a number of attacks during the year, with Sunderland being a particular point of focus. However, by May the bomber war against northern England was virtually over, although there would be two isolated incidents, in December 1944 and March 1945, to remind northerners that the skies were not totally free from danger.

The first raid of the year took place on the night of 13-14 January, when twelve aircraft sought to attack Sunderland's Doxford Works. Eight bombs fell around South Dock, the rest were distributed over other parts of the region. Ten nights later, a number of high explosives were sprinkled over south Durham, generally without effect, and nine nights after that another raid on Sunderland mirrored the first attack of the year, in both scale and result.

On two nights in mid-March, it was Newcastle's turn, though scattered locations south of the Tyne appear to have borne the brunt with Stockton and Thornaby suffering more than most, in spite of the fact that not many bombs dropped in either place.

The assault on Sunderland by thirty-three aircraft on the night of 14-15 March was more serious. A lethal combination of bombs and explosive incendiaries caused extensive damage, including the partial destruction of the town's Empress Hotel, in Union Street. Further south, the fifty-five explosive incendiaries that dropped around the Hartlepools fell largely in open country and resulted in minimal damage. Eight nights later, the Hartlepools experienced their final bombing attack when a number of incendiaries dropped harmlessly on Seaton Snooks.

In the last week of March the Tyne and the Wear areas were hit twice more and Tynemouth, North Shields, Sunderland and parts of eastern County Durham were on the receiving end of high explosives and incendiaries. The final bombing raids on the area occurred in May. On the night of 15-16 of the month, an estimated sixty-seven bombers unloaded 127 tons of bombs and 1,300 incendiaries over Sunderland, causing extensive damage and killing sixty-nine people. On the night of 23-24 May, sixty-two bombers made the final major raid and Sunderland was again the principal objective. Ten parachute mines, ninety-two high explosives and thousands of incendiaries caused widespread destruction of lives and property. Eighty-four people died in the attack. In the same raid, four 500kg bombs fell on South Shields, destroying much property and killing twenty-six people.

By then, the bomber war against Britain was, to all intents and purposes, finished, although an isolated incident that took place on 24 December 1944 is worthy of mention. On that Christmas Eve, forty-five Heinkel 111 bombers of KG53 launched V-1 'Flying Bombs' from a point some fifty miles off Skegness. The weapons were aimed at Manchester but a number of them went astray, including the one that dived to earth at Tudhoe, County Durham.

The last visit to the north of England by the Luftwaffe in strength occurred on the night of 3-4 March 1945, when Ju88 night fighters infiltrated streams of RAF bombers returning to Yorkshire after an attack on Kamen, in the Ruhr. A number of the raiders also carried out strafing attacks on towns and Darlington, Easington and South Shields were among the last towns in Britain to be attacked by the Luftwaffe during the Second World War.

Losses
January 1943 – August 1943

22 January 1943 (off Hartlepool)

In the evening of 22 January 1943, *IX Fliegerkorps* sent eight Dornier 217s of I./KG2 and seven Junkers 88s of III./KG6 on nuisance raids to, what was classified by the Luftwaffe as, 'the Humber area'. However, a number of raiders travelled further north. Two Dorniers bombed Sunderland from an altitude of 7,000 feet between 20.42 hours-20.44 hours and it was claimed that bombs fell on the northern part of the town. Three other crews claimed to have dropped bombs on the southern part of Middlesbrough between 20.45 hours-21.05 hours and two other Dorniers claimed to have visited Whitby and Hartlepool and dropped bombs there. The eighth Dornier crew abandoned the operation after their rubber dinghy released itself and was lost. Examination of available air raid records for the Tees area revealed that one high-explosive bomb fell between the river and the railway at Yarm (OS. 898328), making a crater twenty feet deep and thirty-five feet across but seemingly causing little other damage and no casualties.

Three Mosquitos of B Flight, 410 Squadron, Acklington, were scrambled at 20.30 hours. Flight Sergeant B.M. Haight (with Sergeant T. Kipling,) in Mosquito HJ929, intercepted a Do217 at 9,000 feet, fired three bursts at 100 yards' range and saw strikes on the port engine. The enemy aircraft turned into a spiral dive and the Mosquito fired two more bursts. The Do217 was followed down to 3,000 feet, where it disappeared into cloud. At approximately 20.50 hours, the time of the combat, the Observer Corps reported an enemy aircraft crashing into the sea off Hartlepool. Both the time and the location coincided with Haight's claim and it was accepted as 'destroyed'.

Other details of the enemy aircraft are not known at the time of writing. Examination of the Luftwaffe Loss Returns reveals no loss for KG2 or KG6 for this date.

3 February 1943

KG2 contributed to a force of some twenty aircraft that attacked the port installations of Sunderland on the night of 3 February 1943. Three aircraft turned back because of technical problems; two others failed to find their objective and attacked Hartlepool instead. Thirteen Do217s reached Sunderland between 20.31 hours-20.45 hours and dropped thirteen tons of high explosives and two and a half tons of incendiaries in the town area. Returning crews reported two medium-sized fires. Dornier 217E-4 U5+GL (w/nr. 5462), flown by *Oberfeldwebel* Karl

Müller of 3./KG2, was shot down by Flight Lieutenant John Willson, in a Beaufighter of 219 Squadron, Scorton, and crashed at Muston, near Filey (see *Broken Eagles, Yorkshire*). [1]

Balke[2] states that one Do217 of II./KG40 collided with a British night fighter at an altitude of 600 feet and although the badly damaged bomber managed to make its way back to base, it is claimed that the fighter crashed in flames into the sea. However, scrutiny of the Luftwaffe Loss Returns reveals no operational losses by II./KG40 for this night and Franks[3] shows no night fighter losses for the night of 3 February 1943.

11 March 1943 (off Cullercoates)

Aircraft:	Junkers 88A-14	3E+CT	w/nr. 144378	9./KG6
Crew:	Fw. Arnold Wissel	pilot	missing	
	Fw. Ludwig Wendel	observer	missing	
	Fw. Ludwig Walther	wireless op	+	
	Uffz. Wolfgang Gabow	mechanic	missing	

11 March 1943 (Great Stainton)

Aircraft:	Dornier 217E-4	U5+BL	w/nr. 5441	3./KG2
Crew:	Oblt. Ernst Schneiderbauer	pilot	pow	
	Uffz. Martin Hoffmann	observer	pow	
	Uffz. Hans Weber	wireless op	pow	
	Obfw. Gregor Eilbrecht	gunner	pow	

11 March 1943 (four miles north-west of Hartlepool?)

Aircraft:	Junkers 88A-14	3E+HL	w/nr. 4361	3./KG6
Crew:	Uffz. Herbert Braun	pilot	missing	
	Uffz. Albert Knittel	observer	missing	
	Uffz. Karl Panzer	wireless op	missing	
	Gefr. Hubert Grote	gunner	missing	

On the night of 11-12 March 1943, fifty-one aircraft of *IX Fliegerkorps* took off in two waves to bomb Newcastle-on-Tyne. The first wave consisted of twenty-one aircraft, fifteen of which bombed Newcastle between 21.49 hours-22.10 hours. One crew attacked the alternative target at Tynemouth, the remaining four crews abandoned their allotted tasks because of various technical problems and night-fighter attacks. Crews reported that visibilty over the target area was good, bombs were dropped according to orders and several fires were started in the target area. The second wave consisted of thirty aircraft, twenty-two of which bombed Newcastle between 23.18 hours-23.45 hours. By then there was a heavy haze over the town and the bombing was widely scattered. Returning crews reported several small and large fires in the target area. As in the first raid, one Do217 attacked the Tynemouth alternative.

Aircraft from at least three Luftwaffe units – KG2, KG6 and KG40 – took part in the raid and each lost at least one aircraft. The Luftwaffe lost

Ernst Schneiderbauer of 3./KG2 at the controls of a Do217K.
[Ernst Schneiderbauer via North East Air Museum]

Ernst Schneiderbauer in front of the aircraft that crashed at Great Stainton, Co. Durham, on the night of 11-12 March 1943. [via Chris Goss]

four aircraft in total and Beaufighter crews of 219 Squadron, Scorton, submitted claims for three enemy aircraft 'destroyed' and two 'probably destroyed' . However, the writer can attribute success with any certainty in only one instance – the shooting down of the Do217 U5+BL at Great Stainton by Flight Lieutenant John Willson, of 219 Squadron, although it seems highly likely that Willson accounted for three raiders that night.

John Willson (with Flying Officer Bunch) took off from Scorton in Beaufighter V8609 at 20.40 hours. They were on Ground Control Interception (GCI) practice when they were told that there were 'bogies' in the area. They were given vector 80 under GCI and told to climb to 12,000 feet, shortly after which they made contact with a Do217. Willson closed the range to 800 feet before the Dornier started to take evasive action, which consisted of violent dives to port and starboard. Then the raider levelled out for a very short while before dropping flares and bombs. Willson managed a two-second burst, apparently to no effect, before the Dornier dived away to starboard and eventually managed to escape.

Minutes later and still under GCI Control, Willson made another contact at 13,000 feet and at two and a half miles range. Under directions from Bunch, the pilot was able to follow the violently jinking target and gradually closed in. Visual confirmation that the raider was a Do217 came when Willson had closed to within 600 feet astern. Perhaps the Beaufighter was spotted at the same time as Willson made his identification for the enemy aircraft suddenly did a steep climbing turn to starboard, so steep, in fact, that it stalled and then fell away into what was to become an uncontrollable dive to port. As the Dornier began to drop, Willson opened up at 450 feet range with a two-second burst of gunfire, using two rings deflection. The Dornier flew straight into the cone of cannon shells and machine-gun bullets and exploded in mid-air, the remnants of the bomber, engulfed by a flaming ball of fire, diving straight into the sea some four miles east of Cullercoates at about 21.54 hours. Some of the wreckage remained burning on the surface for a short time after the impact. The crash was subsequently confirmed by both South Shields' Police and by the Observer Corps. There is a possibility that this aircraft was Do217 F8+LP of 6./KG40 but it is more likely that Willson misidentified his victim and that the aircraft was a Junkers 88 of 9./KG6.

Apparently, the only enemy aircraft shot down in the Cullercoates area that night was a Junkers 88A-14 (3E+CT) of 9./KG6. The proof of location is provided by the fact that the body of its wireless operator, *Feldwebel* Ludwig Walther, was recovered from the sea eight miles east-north-east of Blyth on 12 March 1943 by a Royal Navy vessel. Examination of the corpse revealed Walther to be the holder of the Iron

Cross First Class and the War Flights Badge in Gold (110 flights)[4]. Perhaps of more relevance to the cause of his demise was the fact that the flier's watch had stopped at 21.58 hours.[5] At the time of the incident, British Summer Time (used by the RAF) coincided with Central European Time (used by the Luftwaffe). Of the three 219 Squadron crews who submitted claims that night, only Willson gave one of his conquests as being in the Blyth-Cullercoates area. Willson gave the time of the crash as 21.54 hours – surely too close to the time that Walther's watch had stopped to be merely coincidental?

During the next hour, Willson and Bunch made three other contacts while they were 'freelancing'. Two of these were identified as hostile Do217s, but the evasive tactics of the aircraft intercepted were so violent that only one combat resulted. The target was another Dornier, which appeared from below the Beaufighter and passed from starboard to port in a climbing turn dead ahead of the night fighter. Like its predecessor near Cullercoates, the raider stalled at the top of its turn. As the bomber started to fall, Willson opened fire at a range of 500 feet and the enemy aircraft appeared to pass through the stream of gunfire from above to below. A moment later, the bomber seemed to climb practically out of control. Then it stalled again, hovered on top of the climb and then fell away almost on its back. The aircraft was so obviously out of control that Willson thought that the pilot had been killed or had, at least, been severely wounded. The Dornier began its dive at 6,000 feet. Willson tried to follow it, but although the Beaufighter dived steeply in pursuit and maintained radar contact with its quarry, Willson never re-established visual contact with it. As Willson's combat report states: 'Before the pilot re-obtained visual contact, the trace seemed to drop right off the tube and the Nav/Rad (Flying Officer Bunch) warned the pilot to pull out before they themselves dived into the sea.' This combat took place some four miles north-west of Hartlepool, between 22.30 hours–23.00 hours. Although Willson was of the opinion that the Dornier was obviously out of control, he claimed it only as 'damaged' because neither he nor Bunch had seen their victim going down in flames or crash into the sea. Although the Observer Corps stated that one enemy aircraft had crashed off the coast at Hartlepool at 22.55 hours, the night fighter crew were awarded only a 'probably destroyed'. No details of this aircraft are known at the time of writing. Minutes after this engagement, Willson intercepted Dornier 217E-4 U5+BL of 3./KG2 over Teesside after it had been caught by searchlights over Middlesbrough. He shot it down in flames over Darlington and sent it crashing to earth at Great Stainton. All members of the crew baled out and were made prisoners of war. The details of that particular engagement are recounted in *Luftwaffe over the North*.[6]

Sergeant Hollingworth (with Sergeant Alcock) in Beaufighter V8553 of

Above: *12 March 1943. The wreck of Oblt. Ernst Schneiderbauer's Do217E-4 U5+BL (w/nr. 5441) of 3./KG2. The Dornier was shot down the previous night by F/Lt. John Willson, 219 (Beaufighter) Squadron, Scorton.*
[Courtesy of the Northern Echo]

Right: *Fragments of Ernst Schneiderbauer's Dornier on display at the North East Air Museum, Sunderland.* [Author]

Below: *Part of the engine of Ernst Schneiderbauer's Do217 U5+BL on display at Derek Walton's Aviation Artefacts Museum at Bamburgh Castle.* [Author]

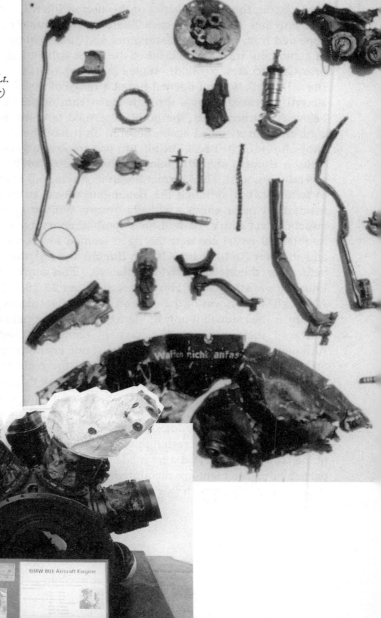

219 Squadron, Scorton, also claimed one Do217 destroyed, which was seen to crash into the sea at about 23.45 hours some fifty miles off the Yorkshire coast, the claim being confirmed by Flight Lieutenant Hooper who witnessed the contest. The writer hazards a guess that this was Dornier 217E-4 F8+LP (w/nr. 5313) of 6./KG40. [see *Broken Eagles* (*Yorkshire*)][7]

Apparently, 219 Squadron was also successful earlier in the evening when Flying Officer Wallace (with Sergeant Jollands) was awarded one 'probable' Do217 off Hartlepool. Wallace had taken off from Scorton at 19.30 hours. At 21.55 hours, when the night fighter was at 12,000 feet and under Sneaton Snook Control, Jollands got an AI contact at two and a half miles range. A three-minute chase followed, during which the enemy aircraft took no evasive action but merely flew straight and level. Wallace got a visual on his quarry, a Do217, when he closed to 1,000 feet. He reduced his range a further 600 feet before opening fire from below and to port of the bomber. Wallace saw strikes on the bomber's fuselage and port engine and pieces were seen to fly off before the enemy machine dived away vertically with its port engine stopped. There was no return fire from the German machine, which was eventually lost by the night fighter crew. They did not see it crash and so they submitted, and were granted, a claim for one enemy aircraft 'probably destroyed' fifteen miles east of Hartlepool. The Beaufighter crew landed back at Scorton at 23.10 hours.

Tantalizingly, Wallace gives no indication of where this particular interception took place, but the circumstances do fit with much of *Unteroffizier* Willi Brombach's account of his own brush with night fighters that night. Brombach was flying Do217E-4 U5+CP of 6./KG2 when gunfire from a night fighter stopped the bomber's left engine. Brombach recounts the tale in Balke's *Der Luftkrieg in Europa*[8]:

We crossed the North Sea at approximately twenty metres (sixty-five feet) altitude, climbing to 3,500 metres (11,300 feet) before the English coast. We then attacked a ball-bearing factory in Newcastle. On my approach to Newcastle I evaded two attacks by night fighters, and over the city I successfully got away from three more. In my attempts to escape, I flew in a wide circle over Gateshead to try to reach the open sea. Then a sixth night fighter finally got my left engine, and probably also the fuel tank. Then, to my horror, I found myself in a balloon barrage with the balloons at my altitude but I managed to miss them at the last minute. Now it was clear to me why the last night fighter had suddenly broken off the attack.

When I finally reached the coast, I went down to fifty metres (162 feet) altitude. I pumped the fuel from the left to the right tank. Without bombs and with half the fuel remaining, I could keep the aircraft good on one engine. Over Holland, I climbed to eighty metres (260 feet) and as I approached Hertogenbosch the fuel indicator showed enough fuel for half an hour. Eindhoven (his airfield) was only six minutes flying time away. Suddenly, the right engine stopped. I lowered the aircraft to thirty feet above the ground and it ripped through an avenue of poplar trees. Then it struck the ground and slid for two hundred metres (650 feet), scattering itself over the surrounding area in the process.

The crew of U5+CP were recovered from the wreckage by local Dutch people and were, in Brombach's words, '...very well looked after...' Three members of the crew were injured in the crash but the observer, *Obergefreiter* Heinz Jendges, was killed.

Now for a little speculation. If U5+CP was the Dornier engaged by Wallace, and it must be remembered that this is pure speculation, then that would leave only one lost enemy aircraft unaccounted for – Junkers 88A-14 3E+HL (w/nr. 4361) of 3./KG6. Assuming the correctness of the earlier speculations, only one claim remains outstanding – that of Willson's encounter four miles north-west of Hartlepool. As mentioned earlier, land-based witnesses claim to have seen an aircraft crash off the coast of Hartlepool at the time Willson claimed to have caused material damage to a raider. Is it possible that Willson did get a third victim but mistook a Ju88 3E+HL for a Dornier?

The Luftwaffe suffered further losses in addition to those mentioned above. Do217E-4 (w/nr. 5332) force-landed at Evreux (France) having sustained damage in an attack by fighters and two Ju88s of I./KG6 got home only with difficulty. One of these, Ju88A-14 (w/nr. 4319), experienced engine problems and suffered twenty per cent damage when it crash-landed at Deelen (Holland); the other, Ju88A-14 (w/nr. 4355), sustained eighty per cent damage when it crashed east of Hoorn (Holland) after losing its bearings and running short of fuel.

12 March 1943 (off Blyth)

Aircraft:	Dornier 217E-4	U5+BD	w/nr. 4737	7./KG2
Crew:	Lt. Bernhard Gerlach	pilot	missing	
	Obfw. Erich Überscär	observer	missing	
	Uffz. Otto Freidl	wireless op	missing	
	Obfw. Hermann Osburg	gunner	missing	

Flying Officer Hooper (with Pilot Officer Reid) of 219 Squadron took off from Scorton in Beaufighter V8560 at 20.50 hours to intercept hostile aircraft approaching from the north-east and aiming for Newcastle. Reid subsequently obtained a contact at a range of four miles while they were freelancing at an altitude of 8,000 feet. The ensuing chase lasted nine minutes before Hooper reduced the range to 1,000 feet and got a visual on a Do217. Hooper closed to 500 feet range and then opened fire with a two-second burst on his target from below and astern. He saw his shells striking home on the port engine of the Dornier and there was a large flash before pieces started to fly off and the engine seemed to stop. The Dornier's gunners replied instantly with very accurate gunfire, which hit the fighter's windscreen and instrument panel (rendering all of the instruments useless) and injured Hooper in the leg.

Hooper intially continued to follow the Dornier but then decided to come home and asked Control for an emergency landing. As a precaution, he increased his height and warned Reid that they might have to bale out. However, they eventually made base but found that the hydraulic system and the emergency pumps were useless. A crash-landing was thus inevitable and another aircraft took off from Scorton to act as a speed guide for Hooper on his approach. Hooper managed a belly-landing (at 120mph) on his second attempt and although their aircraft caught fire, both he and Reid got out immediately. The Dornier crashed into the sea off Blyth at about 21.45 hours, confirmation being provided by Blyth Observer Post.

14-15 March 1943 (off Hartlepool?)

Aircraft:	Junkers 88A-14	3E+BK	w/nr. 4345	2./KG6
Crew:	Uffz. Wilhelm Remer	pilot	missing	
	Obgfr. Alois Buster	observer	missing	
	Uffz. Werner Strange	wireless op	missing	
	Obgfr. Heinrich Koch	gunner	missing	

On the night of 14-15 March 1943, thirty-three bombers of *IX Fliegerkorps* were ordered to attack the shipyards and docks at Sunderland. The aircraft that took part were drawn from KG2, KG6 and II./KG40 and were armed with a total of ten parachute mines, 320 50kg explosive incendiary bombs and 6,720 other incendiaries. They bombed the town from altitudes ranging from 4,000 feet to 16,000 feet during the half hour before midnight, shortly after Pathfinders had marked the targets. According to returning crews, the bombs fell in their designated areas and a number of large fires developed, especially on the south side of the river Wear. However, contemporary British sources refuted these claims and countered that the raid was widely scattered and did minimal damage.

Returning crews also reported that night fighters had been particularly active in the target area. Sixteen of the crews who returned safely to base reported encounters with airborne defenders. Four of those crews had been forced to abort their missions because of such attacks. The operation cost I./KG6 one Ju88A-14 3E+BK, piloted by *Unteroffizier* Wilhelm Remer, and Do217E-4 U5+RN (w/nr.4258) of 5./KG2, flown by *Unteroffizier* Herbert Gahl. The latter aircraft turned back because of engine trouble and, after suffering the trauma of a single-engined return flight over the North Sea, ran short of petrol before reaching land. Gahl and his crew were forced to bale out over water thirty miles west of the Frisian island of Terschelling. The observer, *Unteroffizier* Kurt Friese, was subsequently found dead in a rubber dinghy; there was no trace of the rest of his crew. Nor were there any survivors from Remer's aircraft.

The crew of Do217E-4 U5+EL (w/nr. 5534) of 3./KG2, had better luck. On their approach to Sunderland, their pilot had performed a variety of furious diving and climbing defensive manoeuvres in order not to offer lurking night fighters an easy target. The strategy worked for they cleared the danger area without interference but a surprise awaited them in the blackness over the North Sea. An unnamed member of that crew recounted in *Der Luftkrieg in Europa*[9] what happened next:

> After successfully dropping the bombs, the Do217 went into low-level flight. The red-glowing fires and pincer-shaped piers flitted past. The blackness of the North Sea was reassuring after the excitement and strain of coming through the bombing: the ears could hear again the sound of the engines; the skin was cold with sweat.
>
> Earlier, when the night fighter defences were still in their infancy, one could go confidently on the homeward course. But now, night fighters were everywhere. Over 500kms (312 miles) of water lay between Sunderland and the Continental coast – and each kilometre could hold a fair amount of danger. We had already been flying over the sea for a while when my wireless operator reported that there was a twin-engine machine to our right: we were flying on an almost parallel course with a Beaufighter. Suddenly he became aware of our presence and turned to come astern of us to make his attack from a position where he could better exploit the moonlight.
>
> Immediately, I dived lower and then began a wild, but always considered, evasion according to all of the rules of blind flying. We were already fifty miles from the English coast and the uncanny silhouette was still there. Slowly, during this cat and mouse game, I began to break into a sweat. Many times our defensive movements took us so close to the water that the slipstream from the engines left a wake on the surface of the sea. Then the Beaufighter started his decisive attack. He could not attack from below and so he cut out to the left and then curved to the right. I saw the malicious glimmer of tracer, but the burst of fire did not hit us. Then he curved away at the last moment, but the turn was so steep that his wing touched the water (Balke gives the time as 23.46 hours). The crash and the explosion were as one and an enormous fist of burning fuel spilled across the water. As we flew away, the mechanic and the wireless operator watched the fire that the night fighter had intended for us still rocking on the waves.

U5+EL completed its flight over the North Sea, but it crash-landed at Schiphol. The aircraft suffered twenty-five per cent damage but, seemingly, its occupants survived their ordeal unscathed.

Among the Beaufighter crews scrambled to meet the raiders on the night of 14-15 March 1943 was Squadron Leader Morton (with Flight Lieutenant Strange) of 219 Squadron. They took off from Scorton at 22.40 hours and just over an hour later, Strange got a contact which was flying south-west at an altitude of 8,000 feet and at a range of three miles. Under Strange's guidance, Morton closed to 3,000 feet, when a visual was obtained on exhaust flames. When he had closed to 1,500 feet, Morton identified his would-be target as a Do217.

The enemy aircraft was doing violent evasive tactics, turning ninety degrees to port and then ninety degrees to starboard, as well as climbing and diving 100 feet to 300 feet from the horizontal; its speed was also being varied considerably. Morton closed in to 500 feet from below and astern and had just got the bomber in his sights when the enemy gunners opened fire with red tracer, which appeared to fall below the fighter and, seemingly, registered no hits. By that time, Morton had closed the gap to 300-400 feet and delivered a three-second burst of gunfire from dead astern as the bomber turned gently to port. Many strikes were seen on the starboard side and the top of the enemy's fuselage, as well as on the starboard engine. A large and very white flash came out of the raider's starboard motor and that was accompanied by what appeared to be 'liquid fire'. Whatever it was, according to Morton, it was too bright and too white for petrol, and it poured out of the middle underside of the bomber's fuselage and passed clear of the Beaufighter's port wing. The German pilot then put his machine into a steep dive.

Morton followed and was about to give his victim another burst when the Beaufighter was caught in the bomber's slipstream. At the same time, the fighter's starboard engine started 'running away' and the acceleration of the motor and the consequent vibration made it impossible for Morton to aim at the target. Then more 'liquid fire' came between the fighter and the raider before the enemy aircraft disappeared and was not seen again. However, even if the bomber had not been lost it is most unlikely that Morton could have continued the chase for, shortly after his engine started racing away, it also began to smoke and was soon threatening to burst into flames. Morton shut down the motor and broadcast a call for an emergency homing signal. Two minutes into his homeward run, and with his aircraft at 5,000 feet above the sea, Morton's situation worsened considerably when his starboard propeller fell off, tearing away most of the right-hand side of the cockpit with its compass and its trimming controls. Almost immediately, the port engine cut out and, in spite of trying everything, the pilot was unable to restart it. With ditching seemingly imminent, Morton ordered Strange to bale out while he himself began transmitting for an emergency fix to aid would-be rescuers but during the transmission the radio faded and the electrical system went dead.

Morton managed to keep his Beaufighter straight as it glided downwards but without any motive power whatsoever it was fast losing height. However, he hesitated about jumping because he wanted to be certain that Strange was safely out. A backward glance towards the navigator's position revealed a light near Strange's seat and the pilot thought that his navigator was having difficulty escaping, perhaps because the escape hatch had been damaged when the propeller had been lost. Shortly afterwards, as the fighter continued downwards, a second glance showed the light to be on the floor and Morton speculated that it must have been dropped as Strange made his exit.

That night, fate was to play a cruel trick on Flight Lieutenant Strange. Such is the nature of luck that shortly after he had taken to his parachute and just before Morton would have to take to his, the Beaufighter's descent took it below 3,000 feet and the port engine burst into life again. It ran very roughly and gave only part of its power but that was enough to reduce the rate of descent and to convince the pilot that he had a reasonable chance of reaching land. He did finally make it and, with his machine down to 1,500 feet above the countryside of County Durham, he abandoned his aircraft shortly before the Beaufighter crashed at Castle Eden. It impacted at 23.55 hours.

Squadron Leader Morton landed safely close by and lived to fight again but, sadly, Flight Lieutenant Strange did not. His body was found the next day by an air-sea rescue launch fifteen miles off Hartlepool. He had been in the water all night and it is believed that he had died from exposure. The would-be rescuers found a wheel and undercarriage of a Do217 close by. On the strength of this, and following a confirmatory statement from Hartlepool police that an aircraft had crashed into the sea off the town at about 23.51 hours, Morton submitted a claim for one Do217 destroyed. His claim was accepted.

Morton was not the only Scorton crew to submit a claim that night. Flying Officer Sloman (with Sergeant Cliffe) was freelancing at 23.33 hours on vector 150 under Sector Control when Sergeant Cliffe got an AI contact passing from starboard to port at a height of 7,500 feet and at four miles range. The Beaufighter was then some forty miles east of Hartlepool. The ensuing chase lasted for about fifteen minutes, during which Sloman closed the gap to 1,000 feet, having followed his quarry down to 1,000 feet above sea level. He visually identified it as a Do217 just seconds before the enemy aircraft started a series of violent evasive manoeuvres, consisting of hard turns to port and starboard and diving down to sea level. Sloman managed to fire two deflection shots at range 700 feet but did not see any strikes before chasing the bomber visually in a number of hard turns and easing to within 300 feet before opening fire with a three-second deflection shot, from below and astern to the port side. The enemy machine's port engine burst into flames and the fire spread instantly all over the aircraft before it plummeted into the sea, where it was seen burning on the surface for some seven minutes. The bomber offered no return fire during the whole engagement. Control took a fix on the Beaufighter's position at 23.50 hours and Sloman later

A Do217 of KG2 in its camouflaged hangar. The person in the middle is Fw. Gerhard Dörr, the mechanic/gunner of Oblt. Hartmut Holzapfel's Do217 U5+LP (6./KG2), which crashed near North Thoresby(Lincs.) on the night of 15-16 March 1943.
[Hartmut Holzapfel]

submitted a claim for one Do217 destroyed. Confirmation of the claim was provided by Hartlepool Police, who saw an aircraft go into the sea in the same area (as that 'fixed' by Control) at about 23.45 hours-23.50 hours. Sloman landed back at Scorton at 00.30 hours.

The Luftwaffe Loss Reports for 14-15 March 1943 show that one Ju88A-14 3E+BK (w/nr. 4345) was lost on operations, one Do217E-4 U5+RN (w/nr.4258) ditched off Terschelling after making an early return from operations, and that one Do217E-4 (w/nr. 5534) crash-landed at Schiphol on return from operations. These aircraft have been dealt with above.

It will be noticed that the Luftwaffe claimed that only one aircraft was unaccounted for but two crews of 219 Squadron each claimed one Dornier destroyed. Morton's combat report does not mention that he saw his victim crash but ground-based observers in Hartlepool claim to have seen the crash east of the town at 23.51 hours and the discovery of wreckage near to Flight Lieutenant Strange adds further credence. Sloman, on the other hand, clearly states that he shot his victim down in flames some forty miles off shore, the wreckage burning on the surface for some time. In this regard, Sloman's report bears similarities to the crew of Do217 U5+EL who were intercepted some fifty miles off the coast and who claim that their Beaufighter attacker accidentally touched the water during a maneouvre and crashed in flames, 'the debris burning on the surface for some time'. Balke[10] gives the demise of U5+EL's attacker as 23.46 hours. Ground-based observers in Hartlepool claimed to have seen that crash also and gave the time at between 23.45-23.50 hours. However, with the distance of Sloman's victim being some forty miles off shore, one tends to believe that witnesses on land might well have confused this incident with the one off Hartlepool.

But there is still an intriguing similarity in the Sloman and German accounts and certainly enough to suggest that Sloman and Dornier U5+EL were in the same area and witnessed the same incident but were apparently not involved with each other. Reference to Franks[11] reveals that Morton's aircraft was the only Beaufighter lost that night, but not in the circumstances described by the crew of U5+EL.

The evidence seems to suggest that the aircraft attacked by Morton some fifteen miles off Hartlepool was the one seen to crash by observers on the land but that it was a Ju88, not a Dornier as claimed. In the writer's view, the aircraft claimed by Sloman would have been too far out to sea to be observed from Hartlepool. Exactly what Sloman did get, and what the Dornier crew actually saw, currently remains a mystery.

22-23 March 1943 (off Hartlepool or Cullercoates?)

Aircraft:	Dornier 217E-4	U5+IN	w/nr. 1144	5./KG2
Crew:	Fw. Rudolf Wenkel	pilot	missing	
	Ogfr. Erich Hitziger	observer	missing	
	Uffz. Walter Böck	wireless op	missing	
	Ogfr. Otto Wilke	gunner	missing	

Aircraft:	Dornier 217E-4	U5+CR	w/nr. 4393	7./KG2
Crew:	Fw. Fritz Flohr	pilot	missing	
	Ogfr. Erich Tomuschat	observer	missing	
	Ogfr. Johannes Knecht	wireless op	missing	
	Gefr. Johannes Menzenbach	gunner	missing	

The Luftwaffe's *IX Fliegerkorps* mustered fifty aircraft for an attack on the shipbuilding and repair centre of Hartlepool on the night of 22-23 March 1943. The forty-four bombers that actually reached their target were over the South Durham area at various times between 22.58 hours and 23.22 hours, with a further aircraft attacking an alternative objective at Scarborough at 22.45 hours. Hartlepool was blanketed by nine-tenths cloud with the ceiling at 1,200 feet and so the attackers dropped their bombs by using dead-reckoning navigation and by observing the positions of anti-aircraft gun bursts. Their total bomb load included ten parachute mines and eleven 1,000kg high explosives, as well as numerous other bombs and incendiaries. However, the presence of the cloud unsighted the bomb aimers and the bombing, which was widely scattered, did little damage.

Berlin Radio subsequently announced that three of their aircraft failed to return from an attack which had 'Hartlepool as its target'. Two of those are shown above; the third was Ju88A-14 (w/nr. 144558) of I./KG6, which suffered seventy per cent damage when it force-landed at Heteren bei Arnhem while returning from operations. Balke[12] reports that participating crews witnessed the shooting down of one aircraft near Hartlepool at about 23.00 hours and fifteen minutes later saw another descending in flames before crashing into the sea. Precisely where the latter came down is not known to the writer.

Fritz Flohr, (shown here as a Gefreiter), pilot of Do217 J5+CR, which was lost over the north-east of England on the night of 22-23 March 1943. [via Melvin Brown & Steven Hall]

Fw. Rudolf Wenkel, pilot of Do217 U5+IN, which was lost over the north-east of England on the night of 22-23 March 1943. [via Melvin Brown & Steven Hall]

It may have fallen into the sea out of sight of land for the Middlesbrough *Evening Gazette* reported on 23 March 1943 that: 'So far, only one enemy aircraft is officially reported destroyed in the raid on the north-east coast last night.' According to the Hartlepool *Northern Daily Mail* on 23 March 1943, the raid on the town had been in progress only a few minutes when the aircraft was seen to come down in flames and to crash close inshore. However, it is not known which of the two Dorniers came to grief there.

At the time of the raid, Rudolf Dawson, now of Throston Grange, Hartlepool, was a thirteen year-old schoolboy living in the town's Harbour Terrace. He claims to have seen one of the bombers crash into Hartlepool dock. In an interview with the writer he said that:

Hartlepool was a busy place in the war years; in the coal dock there was always two or three destroyers because Gray's yard was an important ship repair base. And convoys used to sail from here – north to Russia and south to London. I remember that there was a raid on and that I was standing outside our communal shelter with a number of neighbours. We had an unobstructed view over the bay, where a number of merchant ships were at anchor, waiting to sail in convoy. There were barrage balloons up over the ships and the escort of destroyers and corvettes were firing at the planes. This made me think that the bombers were after the ships but there were also fires in the Middlesbrough area.[13]

The plane that crashed in the dock came over twice, somewhere between 10.30pm-11.00pm. The first time it passed over, folks outside the shelter said that it looked as if it was looking for somewhere to land. It seemed to be in difficulty: the engines sounded as if they were 'missing'. It came over very low and then disappeared over the bay towards Middlesbrough. It was flying in a loop. The next thing we knew, it was coming over the top of the embankment from the direction of the old town. We saw the fire first; it was trailing sparks, like a child's rocket. Then we saw the plane coming down very gently – almost as if gliding – into the dock. Maybe the reflecting light on the water made him think it was a safe landing area? It crashed in a tricky place between the piers, almost on the ledge of the shipping channel out of the dock.

The next morning, I went with a couple of friends to have a look. It had pancaked and the nose had stuck in the mud; the front was caved in and the windscreen smashed. There were no bodies there; apparently they had been washed out. We were after souvenirs. It was low tide and there were no guards around and so we waded out to it. I got a clock and a piece of the tail.

It disappeared within two or three days. I don't know whether the sea washed it out, or it was smashed up by storms or it just sank into the mud.

The writer does not know what caused the loss of the two Dorniers nor the cause of the Ju88's difficulties in Holland, although an engine fire was cited as the principal problem prior to the crash-landing. Night fighters were active over Durham and Northumberland that night but they appear to have achieved little. 409 Squadron scrambled two Beaufighters from Acklington at about 22.40 hours-22.50 hours, but no interceptions

Fritz Flohr (left) and friends in conversation with an Oberfeldwebel pilot.
[via Melvin Brown & Steven Hall]

were made. The Squadron Operations Record Book, which makes the interesting observation that the, 'enemy is very wary when he comes over and flies low and jinks violently', also states that, 'One enemy aircraft crashed in this area and is believed to be the result of a chase. No claim is made'. It does not, however, make any reference to the chaser nor to the location (but see below). The Scorton-based 219 Squadron scrambled five Beaufighters that night. However, only Flying Officer R.B.E. Sargeant (with Flying Officer Fowler) managed an interception, but the result was inconclusive.

Sargeant and Fowler took off at 22.55 hours to intercept a hostile aircraft coming over Middlesbrough from the north-east. Their GCI Controller gave them several vectors and at 23.20 hours, when the Beaufighter was on a northerly course, Fowler obtained an AI contact on an aircraft going west and passing from starboard to port. The 'bogey' was below the night fighter and to starboard at an altitude of 13,000 feet and a range of one and a half miles. Sargeant managed to get within 500 yards of his quarry and identified it as a Do217 just moments before the raider must have seen the Beaufighter. A chase ensued with the enemy aircraft taking violent evasive action consisting of turns, dives and climbs as well as speed variations of 240mph to 300mph. When it became clear that the bomber was increasing the distance from its pursuer, Sargeant fired a two-second burst at 500 yards. A few strikes were seen on the Dornier's mainplane before the bomber escaped, heading east and diving for cloud cover. The combat ended at 1,500 feet, eleven miles east of

Usworth, County Durham.

Currently there is no concrete evidence to suggest that Sargeant was responsible for any of the losses over the county that night. He was certainly too late for the first aircraft to be shot down but his interception at 23.20 hours is quite close in time to the reported loss of the second Dornier. Tantalizingly, there is additional evidence to suggest a possible connection. Tyne & Wear Archives at Newcastle have a map (File T383/345) of the Borough of Tynemouth which shows the locations of all bombs that fell in the area during the last war. The map also marks the spot where a Dornier 217 crashed just off the north pier at Cullercoates on 22 March 1943.

According to Sargeant's combat report, he believed that he was eleven miles east of Usworth when the raider escaped from him. If he was right, that location would have placed the enemy aircraft some four miles east of Sunderland and some twelve miles south-east of Cullercoates. Near enough to be a candidate, perhaps?

Of course, there were also other defences operating that night; balloon barrages were up and ships' guns were in action, as Rudolf Dawson pointed out. The Operations Record Book of 938 Balloon Barrage Squadron, which was located on Teesside, also records that area's anti-aircraft gunfire was heavy. Thus there were a number of gauntlets to be run by attacking bombers. Any one of them had the potential to bring down raiders but to date there is no conclusive indication which of these accounted for the Luftwaffe's losses over the north of England on the night of 23-23 March 1943.

EYEWITNESS

Plane crash
22-23 March 1943

Former merchant seaman George Mather, of Whitley Bay, believes that he witnessed an act of bravery by a German Air Force pilot on the night of 22-23 March 1943, when he saw a Dornier 217 crash half a mile offshore near his home town after narrowly missing houses there. He recalled the incident in a letter to the current writer:

> The night it happened I was alone in the house listening to the radio; the Alert had been sounded and that was followed by some gunfire. I went to the front door and guessed that the activity was to the north, in the Blyth area, which in those days was a base for submarines that operated in the coastal waters of Norway and Europe... I went back into the house and had just sat down when I heard the roar of a plane's engines. I dashed outside and was just in

time to see (what he thought then was) a Heinkel 111 roaring across the top of Rockcliffe School at a height of one hundred feet and heading in the direction of Windsor Crescent. His starboard engine and his tail were on fire. He appeared to be in level flight but with his nose slightly down. Fearing that the plane would hit the roofs of the higher houses on the sea front, where one of my friends lived, I ran as fast as I could down the street. If the plane crashed on to the houses, people were going to need help.

I turned round the corner of our street (Grafton Road) and crossed over Margaret Road into Windsor Avenue. By then the plane had cleared the roofs of the houses I had been concerned about and was now over the sea. Still running, I crossed over the sea front road. The plane was still on fire and I was thinking that, if the pilot could make a belly landing he might, with a bit of luck, put out the fires and the crew would be able to make their escape: they were not all that far from the shore.

I clambered over the first set of low railings, crossed over the grass verge and reached the high railings. In that short time, the plane had touched down and within seconds had erupted, setting the sea on fire. To my right, I heard a woman cry out and it was only then I became aware that there were people around me, a dozen or so. Inwardly, I was saying to myself: 'Get out! Get out!' I was willing them to get out. I stood there with the others under, what must have been, a full moon; it was so light. It was a mild night: no hint of breeze; no clouds; just a silver sea with a line of fire on it. I turned away and returned home. I felt sad, leaving someone I could not help: it was just like before when, powerless to help, we had left behind us a blazing ship in mid-Atlantic...

The next morning I joined a crowd of people on the bank top above Cullercoates Bay. Down on the beach, propped up against the North Pier near to the lifeboat house, there was a large aircraft wheel. A few people and the local policeman were down there looking it over. Within a week of this incident, I was away off to sea again.

In my eyes, the pilot avoided the houses deliberately. I thought he was so brave and I have always wanted to tell his relatives.

George Mather, seventeen year-old Assistant Steward (Merchant Navy), 1943

24-25 March 1943

On the night of 24-25 March 1943, the attack that the Luftwaffe launched against Edinburgh resulted in almost complete failure. Of the fifty-two machines of KG2 and KG6 that took off from their Dutch bases, five returned early because of technical problems and a further ten were lost through crashes or 'enemy influences'. Of the remaining thirty-seven aircraft, only fourteen managed to reach Edinburgh, the rest scattered their bombs on various alternative targets in northern England and Scotland.

Weather reconnaissance flights over the target area in the late afternoon had indicated that there would be little cloud over the town that night. However, on arrival, crews found the district completely overcast, with a solid bank of cloud reaching from 600 feet to 3000 feet high. Unable to see the target, crews bombed on dead reckoning, apparently with only limited success.

Things went wrong even before the attacking force left the Continent. According to the Luftwaffe Loss Returns for 24-25 March 1943, the operation got off to a bad start when a Junkers 88 (w/nr.144027) of I./ KG6 (pilot Rudolf Kosanke) crashed just after taking off from Deelen. A further tragedy occurred when, shortly after taking off from Soesterberg, the Do217E-4 of *Unteroffizier* Christian Kiechler U5+IP (w/nr.1183) of 6./KG2 collided with the transmitter tower of the radio station at Katwijk and killed the entire crew of the aircraft. During the rest of the operation I./KG6 and II./KG6 together lost a further five Ju88s from unknown causes and KG2 lost three Do217s.

Five of those aircraft crashed in areas not covered by this volume. 8./KG6 lost Ju88A-14 3E+BS (w/nr.144400), piloted by *Feldwebel* Hans-Jürgen Reis; and 9./KG6 lost Ju88 3E+KT (w/nr.144416), piloted by *Oberleutnant* Josef Wessberger. It is not known where these two aircraft came to grief but it is most unlikely that they came down on British soil. The following three raiders were lost nearer to their intended objective. Ju88A-14 3E+MN (w/nr.144550), piloted by *Oberleutnant* Paul Rogge of 5./KG6, crashed four miles east of Earleston, near Galashiels and was later credited to Squadron Leader G. Elms, 409 (Beaufighter) Squadron, Acklington.[14] Ju88A-14 3E+HM (w/nr.4537), piloted by *Oberleutnant* Förster of 4./KG6, was caught by anti-aircraft fire and came down at Balerno, seven miles south of Edinburgh, killing all members of the crew, and Do217E-4 U5+FR (w/nr. 4365), piloted by *Oberleutnant* Martin Pischke of 7./KG2, suffered engine failure and crashed at Carsphairn, Kirkcudbrightshire. Pischke was killed but the three members of his crew managed to bale out and were made prisoners of war.

In addition to the three aircraft that crashed in Scotland, the following three bombers fell in Northumberland.

Madan Law, Cheviot Hills

Aircraft:	Dornier 217E-4	U5+DL	w/nr. 5432	3./KG2
Crew:	Obfw. Fritz Kalbfleisch	pilot	+	
	Obgfr. Karl Lahr	observer	+	
	Uffz. Walter Frank	wireless op	+	
	Obgfr. Friedrich Freyh	gunner	+	

The crew of Do217E-4 U5+DL (w/nr. 5432) of 3./KG2 which crashed at Madan Law on the night of 24-25 March 1943. L-R: Obgfr. Karl Lahr (observer), Obfw. Fritz Kalbfleisch (pilot), Uffz. Walter Frank (wireless operator), Obgfr. Friedrich Freyh (gunner). [via Melvin Brown & Steven Hall]

According to the Air Ministry Intelligence Branch [AI1(g)][15], U5+ DL was flying at 1,200 feet on a south-westerly course when it hit the side of a hill at a shallow angle near Trowupburn,[16] Madan Law, Cheviot Hills. It broke up on impact, at 00.05 hours on 25 March, scattering wreckage over a wide area and killing the four members of the crew. AI1(g) reported that there were no reports of interceptions or of gunfire in the area at or before the time of the crash, but *Blitz,then and now*[17] claims that anti-aircraft fire might have been a factor. The crew of this aircraft are buried in the German Military Cemetery, Cannock Chase, Staffordshire.

Twice Brewed, Northumberland

Aircraft:	Dornier 217E-4	U5+KP[18]	w/nr. 1182	7./KG2
Crew:	Uffz. Willi Schneider	pilot	+	
	Lt. Rudolf Frase	observer	+	
	Obgfr. Alois Ille	wireless op	+	
	Obgfr. Siegfried Harz	gunner	+	

This aircraft was flying low when it struck the ground on a down grade and at a shallow angle at Steele Rigg, half a mile north of the Twice Brewed Inn (military map ref. Z2489) near Haltwhistle. The Dornier struck the ground at about 00.20 hours on 25 March and disintegrated on impact, the wreckage being scattered right down the valley. Such was the extent of the destruction that Air Ministry Intelligence [AI1(g)] could gather little information from the wreckage, which was partially burnt. The four members of the crew were killed.

Local reports state that machine-gun fire was heard in the district shortly before the crash, but there was no claim of fighter interception in the area and no claim from anti-aircraft units and so the loss was attributed to 'other causes'.[19]

Although the loss of U5+KP has been attributed to 'other causes', it is interesting to speculate on the experience of the Beaufighter crew of Flying Officer Robinson and Sergeant Hartley of 219 Squadron, Scorton. They took off from Scorton at 23.50 hours under the control of Goldsborough GCI and Robinson was subsequently ordered to intercept a hostile aircraft twenty miles north-east of Hartlepool. At 00.16 hours on 25 March, Hartley got AI contact at 8,000 feet altitude but in a shallow dive at four and a half miles range. When Robinson had closed to two miles, he had to reduce speed to avoid approaching too fast; he lowered his undercarriage to achieve this and reduced speed to 180 IAS. During this time, the enemy aircraft was using slight evasive action – twenty-degree jinks and losing height – but when the Beaufighter had closed to 3,000 feet range, the enemy aircraft suddenly peeled off violently to the right and to the left but Robinson stayed with it. He followed his quarry down to 3,000 feet, momentarily lost it and then found it again. At 00.26 hours, when the Beaufighter was fifteen miles east of Tynemouth and at an altitude and range of 1,500 feet, Robinson got a visual on the raider's engine exhausts. At 1,000 feet range, with the target slightly above him, he saw the two fins and exhausts of a Do217.

A short chase ensued, the Beaufighter following astern and below the bomber, before Robinson opened up with a four-second burst from cannons and machine guns. There was an immediate reply from the enemy's upper gun position but the shells passed well above the night fighter. Robinson's cannon strikes, however, were seen to explode on the German's fuselage and mainplane and the bomber's starboard engine stopped before the machine swung violently to starboard and began to lose height. Robinson then fired a deflection shot at his target as the Dornier tried to climb. As the bomber hung momentarily, Robinson fired a third burst. Strikes were seen all over the fuselage and large pieces flew off the tail of the Dornier and passed close to the Beaufighter's port wing. The raider then appeared to dive out of control and through thick haze to the sea.

It is interesting to note that Robinson did not claim to have seen his victim crash into the sea. It is conceivable, though not proven, that the damaged Dornier flew towards the north-east coast (perhaps seeking a place to land) before touching down at Steele Rigg, some thirty miles

Obfw. Karl Kleih (left) was the wireless operator of Ju88A-14 3E+BH that crashed near Linhope, Northumberland, on the night of 24-25 March 1943.
[via Melvin Brown & Steven Hall]

west of Tynemouth. Certainly Robinson engaged and damaged a raider (he identified it as a Do217) in reasonably close proximity to where U5+KP came down and the time of his engagement (00.26 hours) is a reasonable match to the time ('about 00.20 hours.') the Dornier was reported to have crashed at Steele Rigg. This is, however, pure speculation on the writer's part.

With the exception of Siegfried Harz, the crew of U5+KP are buried in Darlston Road Cemetery, Carlisle. It is not known where Harz is buried.

Linhope, Northumberland

Aircraft:	Junkers 88A-14	3E+BH	w/nr. 4354	1./KG6
Crew:	Obfw. Friedrich Lang	pilot	+	
	Uffz. Walter Schulz	observer	+	
	Obfw. Karl Kleih	wireless op	+	
	Gefr. Werner Fiedler	gunner	+	

This aircraft struck the hillside at Linhope Rigg[20] shortly after midnight. According to *Where the Hills Meet the Sky*,[21] it was seen circling Powburn before heading off to the west, its engines apparently running roughly. Shortly afterwards, it struck the ground about one mile west of Linhope village. The wreckage was found later that day by a local shepherd. AI1(g) investigators reported that the Junkers had hit the ground at a shallow angle, striking uphill and disintegrating. There was no fire. From the angle at which the bomber impacted, it seemed that the aircraft was either flying level or climbing. The investigators reported that the lower surfaces of bomber's wings were lamp-blacked over pale blue but that the underside of the fuselage had not been blacked. The propellers were wooden and the spinners were dark green with two white rings.

There was no claim of fighter interception in that area and no reports of gunfire so the loss was put down to 'other causes'. All of the crew were killed in the crash and were later buried at Chevington Cemetery, near Broomhill, Northumberland.

15-16 May 1943 (east of Sunderland)

Aircraft:	Dornier 217K-1	U5+DP	w/nr. 4584	6./KG2
Crew:	Uffz. Karl Roos	pilot	+	
	Obgfr. Günther Kaeber	observer	missing	
	Uffz. Bruno Mittlestädt	wireless op	+	
	Uffz. Alfred Richter	gunner	missing	

A combined force of Dornier 217s from KG2 and II./KG40 joined with Junkers 88s from KG6 to attack the dock and port installations at Sunderland on the night of 14-15 May 1943. The weather was clear with

Do217K-1 U5+AA (w/nr. 4415) of Stab./KG2 at Soesterberg in early 1943. The personnel include Major Gottfried Bucholz, Geschwader Technical Officer (first from left) and Major Walter Bradel, Kommandeur of II./KG2 (third from left). Bradel was the observer in this aircraft. He was killed on the night of 4-5 May 1943 when it crash-landed near Amsterdam, following an attack by a night fighter. [Alfred Schliebner]

Burial at the Acklam Road Cemetery, Thornaby-on-Tees, with full military honours. It is believed that this picture shows the funeral of Uffz. Karl Roos of 6./KG2, whose Do217 was shot down off Sunderland on the night of 15-16 May 1943.
[Author's collection]

good visibility and sixty-seven crews claimed to have been over the town between 01.52 hours-02.25 hours. It is believed that they dropped eighty-four tons of high explosives and six tons of incendiaries from heights of 4,000 feet – 9,000 feet. The raiders claimed that thirty tons of bombs struck the town, where some fifty fires were seen to break out. The Luftwaffe subsequently also claimed that heavy hits had been registered on eight important war industry installations, including the shipyards of T.W. Greenwell & Co., Sir James Laing & Sons, S.P. Austin & Sons and J.L. Thompson. Other industrial units believed to have been damaged included British Ropes Ltd., Richardson, Westgarth and Sunderland Power Station.

Balke[22] maintains that KG40, KG6 and KG2 each lost one aircraft on the raid. Examination of the Luftwaffe Loss Returns shows that II./KG40 lost one Do217E-4 (w/nr.4208), piloted by *Oberfeldwebel* Johannes Golland, which was returning to base when it collided with an obstacle near Bergen an Zee (Holland), killing the crew of four. The Returns contain no reference to a Ju88 of KG6 being lost on this date, although one Ju88 (w/nr.144554) of I./KG6 suffered twenty per cent damage. Both of these casualties occurred on operational sorties but in both instances the area of operations is not stated and thus it can only be guessed that these aircraft are those referred to by Balke. The third loss was the 6./KG2 Do217 of *Unteroffizier* Karl Roos, which was shot down over the sea thirty-five miles east of Sunderland at 02.12 hours by Flying Officer B.R. Keele of 604 Squadron, Scorton.

604 Squadron sent up three Beaufighters at 00.20 hours on 16 May. Sergeant J. Jeffreys (with Sergeant E. Hall) in Beaufighter V8610 obtained a visual on an enemy aircraft but was not able to engage it. Flying Officer W. Hamilton (with Flying Officer J.R. Coates) in Beaufighter V8554 did manage a combat but failed to return to Scorton and is believed to have been shot down. Flying Officer B.R. Keele (with Flying Officer G. Cowles) in Beaufighter V8617 claimed Roos.

Keele was freelancing some thirty miles off the Durham coast when Cowles got a contact on a west bound 'bogey' flying at altitude 7,000 feet to starboard and below the fighter at a range of two and a half miles. Keele reduced height and closed to 2,500 feet before getting a visual of an unidentifiable silhouette dead ahead. His would-be prey was weaving slowly from side to side and slowly losing altitude as it neared the target area. Keele had to ease his machine to within 400 feet range before he recognized that his quarry was a Do217. After dropping back a further 100 feet, Keele opened fire with a two and a half second burst of cannon and machine-gun fire. Strikes were observed on the bomber's fuselage and port wing seconds before the aircraft caught fire, turned to port and plunged straight into the sea.

Two of the crew were never found but the body of Karl Roos was washed ashore at Blackhall Rocks on 30 June 1943. He was buried at Acklam Road Cemetery, Thornaby-on-Tees, under that date. Mittlestädt's body was also recovered but the author has no details of its ultimate fate.

24 May 1943 (East of the Tyne)

Aircraft:	Dornier 217E-4	U5+HH	w/nr.4268	1./KG2
Crew:	Obfw. Herbert Mitzscherling	pilot	missing	
	Uffz. Rudolf Hanke	observer	missing	
	Uffz. Josef Haberl	wireless/op	missing	
	Uffz. Konrad Eduard Sikorski	gunner	missing	

Angriffsführer England ordered a combined attack on the dock installations at Sunderland for the night of 23-24 May 1943. Thirty-six Junkers 88s of KG6 and thirty-five Dornier 217s drawn from KG2 and II./KG40 were designated for the raid, with Do217s of the newly-formed KG66 acting as route markers (dropping flares at designated points just north of the English Channel and off Great Yarmouth) and as target markers at Sunderland.

Sixty-two raiders were over the target area between 03.00 hours-03.20 hours, the remaining eleven having broken off the operation for a variety of reasons, the principal one being technical problems. With good visibility and well-placed target markers, returning crews seemed satisfied that most bombs had fallen in the designated areas, with most impacting on dock installations on both sides of the river Wear, and on the port area. Thirty-six parachute mines, ten 1,000kg high explosives, sixty-four 500kg high explosives, forty-eight 50kg high explosives and numerous incendiaries were dropped. They caused extensive damage to industrial, dock and port installations but some also fell on adjoining residential areas.

The Germans lost three aircraft: one Ju88 3E+DR (w/nr.144545) from 7./KG6,[23] one Do217 F8+PN (w/nr.4293) from 3./KG40, piloted by *Leutnant* Friedrich Weiss and Do217 U5+HH of 1./ KG2. It is not known where the first two aircraft came to grief, but U5+HH is thought to have crashed some six to ten miles off the Tyne after being shot down by Squadron Leader G. Bower (with Sergeant W. Beynon) in a Beaufighter of 409 Squadron, Acklington,

Bower had been scrambled from Acklington at 02.40 hours to intercept raiders approaching the Tyne area. He was soon ordered up to altitude 10,000 feet by the Sector Controller and told to steer a course of 120 degrees. After some ten minutes, when the Beaufighter was at 9,000 feet, Bower glimpsed a twin-engine aircraft flying westwards 1,000 feet above him. He turned hard to port but saw nothing further and asked his GCI Controller for help. GCI then gave him a north-westerly vector on to a different target and Sergeant Beynon almost immediately got an AI contact on a 'bogey' going west slightly below, hard to starboard and at maximum range. Bower turned to follow and stalked the 'bogey', which by then was heading south-west towards the Tyne area. After a very short AI chase, and when both aircraft were 8,000 feet above north Tyneside, Bower saw an aircraft dead ahead, slightly above and at 700 yards range.

He eased closer, identified his quarry as a Do217, and opened fire from 250 yards. Bower ultimately fired eight bursts of combined cannon and machine-gun fire. No results were observed during the first assault other than the enemy aircraft began to take evasive action and its dorsal gunner offered ineffectual return fire. That response continued as Bower fired his second burst, which registered hits on the bomber's starboard wing. A more sustained third attack caught the raider's starboard wing again and set fire to the engine there. At that point the return fire ceased and the bomber released what Bower thought were flares. Evasive action by the Dornier stopped at the same time and the enemy aircraft started a gentle dive as fire increasingly consumed the wing. Bower followed his victim down to 4,000 feet, firing occasional bursts at the flaming target from about 200 yards. At 3,000 feet altitude, the crippled Dornier rolled over to starboard before diving vertically into the sea, its point of entry marked by a large burning patch that remained on the surface of the water for some time afterwards. After orbiting the position for a few moments, the Beaufighter returned to Acklington and touched down at 03.25 hours.

In pursuit of 'Weather Willies'

As Luftwaffe activities over the north of England started to decline, northern-based night fighter squadrons began looking farther afield for 'custom'. For some time they had been aware that the German Air Force sent daily weather reconnaissance aircraft out over the North Sea to gather information vital to the planning of air operations. It had also been noted that these 'Weather Willies', as some RAF crews called them, followed regular routes and usually flew a course parallel to the English coast but they stayed well to seaward and rarely came within 80-100 miles of land. However, land-based British radar and the RAF's interception of Luftwaffe radio transmissions could give a good indication of when and where such reconnaissance aircraft would be operating – and this knowledge provided a challenge to some twin-engined fighter crews.

Aircrews of 604 (Beaufighter) Squadron, Scorton, occasionally planned their own little 'hunting parties' and flew far out over the North Sea in search of 'Weather Willies', often with success. One such expedition took place on 23 August 1943.

23 August 1943 (130 miles north east of Teesside)

Aircraft:	Junkers 88D-1	D7+FH	w/nr. 430804	Wekusta 1
Crew:	Oblt. Karl Rapp	pilot	missing	
	Reg. Rat Otto Krug	observer	missing	
	Uffz. Alfred Schulz	wireless op	missing	
	Fw. Otto Kühle	mechanic	missing	

At 05.20 hours, Wing Commander Michael Constable-Maxwell, DFC (with Flight Lieutenant J. Quinton) and Flight Lieutenant J. Surman (with Flight Sergeant C. Weston) took off from Scorton in two Beaufighters of 604 Squadron to lie in wait for the daily German weather reconnaissance aircraft. They took off in radio silence under Goldsborough Chain Home Low radar station on a track of fifty-eight degrees and at 05.48 hours they arrived at the location where the enemy machine was expected.

They orbited there for thirty minutes at altitude 18,000 feet, waiting for an enemy that did not show up. Their Controller, by means of a prearranged code, then ordered the section to go eighteen miles further east. Once in position, the two Beaufighters orbited until they were given vector 250 and were told that an enemy machine was six miles ahead of them. The section closed on the position indicated but they did not gain visual or AI contact until they were instructed to turn to starboard, fly on a heading of sixty degrees and reduce height to 16,000 feet. At 06.35 hours and after flying for two minutes on the new heading, Maxwell saw an enemy machine two miles ahead, slightly to starboard and just above cloud some 5,000 feet below. He led Surman in an 'S' turn to the south in order to approach their target, a Ju88 with a perfectly white fin and rudder, to starboard and from out of the sun.

When the fighters were 500 yards behind the Junkers, black smoke came from the engines of the enemy machine as the pilot engaged boost. Maxwell, having gained speed from the dive, closed in at full throttle without difficulty until the German was at 300 yards range and thirty degrees above the Beaufighter. Then Maxwell pulled back the stick, raised the nose of his aircraft, and opened fire with cannon and machine gun at 250 yards range from dead astern. His shells found the port engine of the Junkers, the motor caught fire and the top port centre section came off, forcing Maxwell to break away to starboard in

1945. Michael Constable-Maxwell (on wing) and John Quinton with a Mosquito Mk VI of 84 Squadron. [via Alex Revell]

order to avoid collision with a large piece of engine cowling. As Maxwell veered off to the right the enemy machine, momentarily out of control, peeled left and dived towards cloud, its port engine enveloped in flames.

At that point, Surman, who was following from above, closed in quickly and fired a two-second burst from dead astern, seemingly without effect, before the German entered the cloud and his pursuer overshot. Following his starboard break, Maxwell turned hard to port and saw his No.2 making his attack. When Surman lost sight of his quarry, Maxwell followed the enemy machine through cloud on his AI and managed to get within 1,200 feet of the Junkers before both machines emerged below the cloud. By then, the flames that had enveloped the German's engine had also ignited his inner port fuel tank. Realizing that his victim was done for, Maxwell immediately broke off his attack to watch developments from a safer distance. As the fighter crews looked on, the crippled machine, its port motor and centre section blazing furiously and both engines issuing clouds of white smoke, gradually lost height as it staggered in its final orbit. The pilot made an attempt to ditch and managed to hold his aircraft a few feet above the North Sea for half a minute before it touched the water. The Junkers bounced only once and then exploded. It sank in ten seconds, leaving nothing but a large patch of oil on the water and an inflated dinghy without occupants.

The Luftwaffe Loss Returns show that Ju88D-1 D7+FH (w/nr. 430804) of *Wekusta 1* was lost over the North Sea on 23 August 1943 and that the cause was probably due to enemy action. It is highly likely that this aircraft was the one that Maxwell shot down 130 miles north-east of the river Tees.

The Wing Commander was a staunch Roman Catholic and at Scorton there was (and still is) a St John of God priory near the airfield. When Constable-Maxwell returned from his 'hunting trip', he went straight to the chapel in his flying clothes and arrived just as the priest was going up to the altar to say Mass. The Wing Commander went up to the priest and told him that he (Constable-Maxwell) had just killed four or five men and then he asked the priest to say his Mass for them.

Funny old thing, war – don't you think?

The German Military Cemetery (Deutschen Soldatenfriedhof), Cannock Chase, Staffordshire. [Author]

The North Sea off the coast of Northumberland occasionally gives up its secrets. Exhibits at Derek Walton's Aviation Artefacts Museum at Bamburgh Castle include (L-R): a propeller believed to be from a Ju88 or Me110, trawled up off Eyemouth in 1981, an Me110 mainwheel tyre washed up on the beach at Seahouses in June 1998 and a He111 engine (Junkers Jumo 211F), which was trawled up off Blyth in 1983.
[Author]

NOTES

1 Norman, Bill, *Broken Eagles, (Luftwaffe Losses Over Yorkshire, 1939-1945)*. Pen & Sword Books Ltd. 2001 pp169-170.
2 Balke, Ulf, *Der Luftkrieg in Europa Vol.2* Bernard & Graf Verlag, Koblenz 1990 p196.
3 Franks, Norman L.R., *Royal Air Force Fighter Command Losses of the Second World War Vol.2,* Midland Publishing Ltd. 1998.
4 AI(k) Report 125/1943 at the PRO.
5 Mortuary card for Walther Ludwig. Ref.*T15/1475. Civilian deaths due to war operations,* Tyne & Wear Archives.
6 Norman, Bill, *Luftwaffe over the North,* Pen & Sword Books 1993 pp166-172.
7 Norman, Bill, op.cit. pp170-171.
8 Balke, Ulf, op.cit. pp206-207.
9 Balke, Ulf, op.cit. p209.
10 Balke, Ulf, ibid.
11 Franks, Norman L.R., op.cit. p86.
12 Balke, Ulf, op.cit. p213
13 A number of incendiaries fell around Upleatham, Redcar and Warrenby and four high explosives fell into the sea just south of the South Gare. All of these locations are visible from Hartlepool.
14 Clark, Peter, *A Border Too High (a guide to wartime crashes in the Border hills),* Glen Graphics 1999 p74.
15 *In Crashed Enemy Aircraft.* Report Serial No.188 dated 28 March 1943. Report No.7/68 at the PRO.
16 Aviation enthusiast Jim Corbett, of Fenham, Newcastle-on-Tyne, has informed the writer that this aircraft crashed at map reference OS.74/869266.
17 Ramsey, W.G. (ed), op.cit. p238.
18 Luftwaffe Loss Returns give the code as U5+KP. Balke op. cit. p454 gives U5+KR.
19 Clark, Peter, op.cit. p75.
20 Derek Walton, of Seahouses, Northumberland, gives the map reference O.S. 906225.
21 Clark, Peter, *Where The Hills Meet the Sky (a guide to wartime crashes in the Cheviot Hills),* Glen Graphics 1997 p38.
22 Balke, Ulf, op. cit. p229.
23 The Luftwaffe Loss Return for this date is of poor quality but the pilot of 3E+DR appears to have been *Leutnant* Manfred Brünglemann.

Appendix 1

Known Luftwaffe losses in the Northumberland & Durham area, 1939 – 1943
(by cause and location)

Date	Aircraft	Unit	Code	w/nr	Cause	Location
17.10.39	Do18	Ku.Fl.Gr. 2./606	8L+DK	809	Gladiator	north-east of Berwick?
30.01.40	He111H-2	4./KG26	1H+KM	?	Hurricane	east of Coquet Island
03.02.40	He111H-3	3./KG26	1H+HL	?	Hurricane	Druridge Bay
03.02.40	He111	2./KG26	1H+GK	?	Hurricane	fifteen miles off the Tyne
27.02.40	He111H-3	3./KG26	1H+L	?	Spitfire	east of Coquet Island
29.03.40	Ju88	6./KG30	4D+AP	?	Naval gunfire	Druridge Bay
26-27.06.40	He111H-4	2./KG4	5J+EK	?	Fighter	off Blyth – or the Tees?
01.07.40	He59	SeenotflugKdo.3	D-ASAM	?	Spitfire	off Hartlepool
19-20.07.40	Fw200c	1./KG40	F8+EH	?	AA fire	off Crimdon
09.08.40	He111H-3	7./KG26	1H+ER	?	Hurricane	off Whitburn
15.08.40	He111H-4	1./KG26	1H+GH	?	Hurricane	Druridge Bay
15.08.40	He111H-4	8./KG26	1H+S	?	Fighter	off Northumberland/Durham coast
15.08.40	He111H-4	8./KG26	1H+S	?	Fighter	off Northumberland/Durham coast
15.08.40	He111H-4	8./KG26	1H+S	?	Fighter	off Northumberland/Durham coast
15.08.40	He111H-4	8./KG26	1H+S	?	Fighter	off Northumberland/Durham coast
15.08.40	Me110D	Stab.I/ZG76	M8+?B	?	Fighter	off Northumberland/Durham coast
15.08.40	Me110D	Stab.I/ZG76	M8+?B	?	Fighter	off Northumberland/Durham coast
15.08.40	Me110D	1./ ZG76	M8+CH	3155	Spitfire	Streatlam, Barnard Castle
15.08.40	Me110D	2./ ZG76	M8+?K	?	Fighter	off Northumberland/Durham coast
05.09.40	He111P	6./KG45	J+JP	3065	AA fire	Sunderland
15-16.09.40	He115c	Ku.Fl.Gr. 3./.506	S4+CL	32610	Naval gunfire	north-east of Eyemouth
17.11.40	Ju88A-5	3(F)/122	F6+HL	0426	Naval gunfire	off Whitburn
15-16.02.41	He111P-4	6./KG4	5J+GP	3085	AA fire	South Shields
13.03.41	Ju88A-5	Ku.Fl.Gr. 3./106	M2+JL	2234	Spitfire	east of Coquet Island
10.04.41	Ju88A-5	3(F)/122	F6+NL	0529	Spitfire	off Boulmer
27.04.41	He111H-5	1./KG26	1H+MH	3677	Naval gunfire	off Beadnell
30.04.41	Ju88	Ku.Fl.Gr. 1/506	S4+JH	715	Spitfire	off Farne Islands
05-06.05.41	He111H-5	1./KG4	5J+IH	3520	Defiant	Newcastle-on-Tyne
05-06.05.41	He111H-5	3./KG4	5J+KL	3794	Defiant	off Cresswell
06.07.05.41	He111H-5	2./KG53	A1+CK	3550	Defiant	Morpeth
06-07.05.41	Ju88A-5	5./KG30	4D+EN	7177	Defiant	Holy Island

Date	Aircraft	Unit	Werk Nr	Code	Cause	Location
02.06.41	Ju88A-5	Ku.Fl.Gr. 3./106	3422	M2+DL	Hurricane	off the Tyne
02.06.41	Ju88A-5	Ku.Fl.Gr. 3./106	6180	M2+BL	Naval gunfire?	off the Tyne?
24-25.06.41	He111H-5	2./1	3749	H+MK	Naval gunfire	off Seaham Harbour?
24-25.06.41	He111H-5	2./KG26	3671	1H+AK	Naval gunfire	off Blyth
23.08.41	He111H-5	Stab./KG26	3691	1H+EA	Naval gunfire	north of Holy Island
01.09.41	Ju88A-4	Stab.III/KG30	1064	4D+BD	Beaufighter	Bedlington Station
07.09.41	Do217E-1	4./KG40	125	F8+FM	Beaufighter	Newcastle on Tyne area?
30.09.41	Ju88A-4	7./KG30	3502	4D+MR	Beaufighter	off the Tyne?
02.10.41	Do217E-2	5./KG2	5309	U5+GN	Beaufighter	off the Tyne
16.11.41	Ju88		694	S4+KH	Spitfire	off Hartlepool?
09.12.41	Ju88D-1	3(F)/122	1465	F6+CL	Hurricane	east of Seaham Harbour
29.12.41	Ju88D-1	KGr.1/506	1341	S4+LH	Beaufighter	off Cresswell
15.01.42	Ju88A-4	KGr.1/506	1612	S4+EH	AA fire?	off the Tyne
15-16.02.42	Do217E-4	9./KG2	1167	U5+BD	Beaufighter	east of Blyth
15-16.02.42	Do217E-4	9./KG2	5343	U5+NT	Unknown	off Northumberland/Durham coast
26-27.03.42	Do217E-3	6./KG40	0063	F8+KP	AA fire?	East of Tynemouth
06-07.07.42	Do217E-4	9./KG2	4270	U5+BT	Beaufighter	off Amble
07-08.07.42	Do217E-4	4./KG2	5465	U5+BM	Beaufighter?	off Tyne /off Scarborough?
28-29.08.42	Ju88A-4	Stab I./KG77	144146	3Z+CB	Beaufighter	off Seaham Harbour
19.09.42	Do217E-4	7./KG2	4262	U5+KR	Beaufighter	offTynemouth
11.03.43	Ju88A-14	9./KG6	144378	3E+CT	Beaufighter	off Cullercoates
11.03.43	Do217E-4	3./KG2	5441	U5+BL	Beaufighter	Great Stainton
11.03.43	Ju88A-14	3./KG6	4361	3E+HL	Beaufighter?	off Hartlepool?
12.03.43	Do217E-4	7./KG2	4737	U5+BD	Beaufighter	off Blyth
14-15.03.43	Ju88A-14	2./KG6	4345	3E+BK	Beaufighter?	north-west of Hartlepool?
22-23.03.43	Do217E-4	5./KG2	1144	U5+IN	Unknown	off Hartlepool or Cullercoates?
22-23.03.43	Do217E-4	7./KG2	4393	U5+CR	Unknown	off Hartlepool or Cullercoates?
24-25.03.43	Do217E-4	3./KG2	5432	U5+DL	AA fire?	Madan Law, Cheviot Hills
24-25.03.43	Do217E-4	7./KG2	1182	U5+KP	Unknown	Twice Brewed, Northumberland
24-25.03.43	Ju88A-14	1./KG6	4354	3E+BH	Unknown	Linhope, Northumberland
15-16.05.43	Do217K-1	6./KG2	4584	U5+DP	Beaufighter	east of Sunderland
24.05.43	Do217E-4	1./KG2	4268	U5+HH	Beaufighter	off the Tyne
23.08.43	Ju88D-1	Wekusta 1	430804	D7+FH	Beaufighter	130 miles north-east of Tees

Appendix 1a
Luftwaffe losses in the Northumberland & Durham area, 1939 - 1943
(by cause and by date)

Cause	1939	1940	1941	1942	1943	1944	1945	TOTAL	
Day Fighter	1	16	6	-	-	-	-	23	(36%)
Night Fighter	-	-	9	5	8	-	-	22	(34.3%)
AA flak	-	2	1	2	1	-	-	6	(9.3%)
Naval flak	-	3	5	-	-	-	-	8	(12.5%)
Unknown	-	-	-	1	4	-	-	5	(7.9%)
TOTAL	1	21	21	8	13	-	-	64	(100%)

Appendix 1b
Luftwaffe losses in the Nothumberland & Durham area, 1939 - 1943
(by aircraft type and date)

Aircraft type	1939	1940	1941	1942	1943	1944	1945	TOTAL	
Do18	1	-	-	-	-	-	-	1	(1.5%)
Do217	-	-	2	6	8	-	-	16	(25%)
Ju88	-	2	11	2	5	-	-	20	(31.2%)
He111	-	12	8	-	-	-	-	20	(31.2%)
He59	-	1	-	-	-	-	-	1	(1.5%)
He115	-	1	-	-	-	-	-	1	(1.5%)
Me110	-	4	-	-	-	-	-	4	(6.6%)
FW200	-	1	-	-	-	-	-	1	(1.5%)
TOTAL	1	21	21	8	13	-	-	64	(100%)

Appendix 1c
Luftwaffe losses in the Northumberland & Durham area, 1939 - 1943
(by location and date)

Location	1939	1940	1941	1942	1943	1944	1945	TOTAL	
Northumberland:									
over land	-	-	4	-	3	-	-	7	(10.9%)
over sea	1	8	13	5	4	-	-	31	(48.4%)
County Durham:									
over land	-	2	1	-	1	-	-	4	(6.3%)
over sea	-	5	3	1	1	-	-	10	(15.7%)
Unknown	-	6	-	2	4	-	-	12	(18.7%)
TOTAL	1	21	21	8	13	-	-	64	(100%)

Appendix 2

Luftwaffe crew losses in the Northumberland and Durham area, 1939 - 1943 (by unit)

Unit	Killed	Missing	Pow	TOTAL
3(F)/122	6	6	-	12
1./KG2	-	4	-	4
3./KG2	4	-	4	8
4./KG2	2	2	-	4
5./KG2	1	4	3	8
6./KG2	2	2	-	4
7./KG2	4	8	-	12
9./KG2	-	12	-	12
2./KG4	-	-	4	4
3./KG4	1	3	-	4
6./KG4	9	-	-	9
1./KG6	4	-	-	4
2./KG6	1	4	-	5
3./KG6	-	4	-	4
9./KG6	1	3	-	4
Stab./KG26	-	-	4	4
1./KG26	1	-	8	9
2./KG26	1	-	11	12
3./KG26	5	4	-	9
4./KG26	1	3	-	4
7./KG26	2	1	4	7
8./KG26	2	12	5	19
StabIII./KG30	4	-	-	4
5./KG30	-	-	4	4
6./KG30	4	-	-	4
7./KG30	-	4	-	4
1./KG40	2	2	5	9
4./KG40	-	4	-	4
6./KG40	1	3	-	4
2./KG53	-	-	5	5
StabI./KG77	2	-	2	4
Ku.Fl.Gr. 3./106	3	7	2	12
Ku.Fl.Gr. 1./506	4	-	-	4
Ku.Fl.Gr. 3./506	-	-	4	4
Ku.Fl.Gr. 2./606	1	-	3	4
KGr.1./506	2	10	-	12
SeenotKdo.3	-	-	4	4
StabI./ZG76	4	-	-	4
1./ZG76	-	-	2	2
2./ZG76	-	1	1	2
Wekusta 1	-	4	-	4
TOTAL	**74**	**107**	**75**	**256**
	28.9%	**41.8%**	**29.3%**	**100%**

Appendix 3

Luftwaffe crew losses in the Northumberland and Durham area, 1939 - 1943
(by aircraft and crews)

Date	Aircraft	Unit	Pilot	Observer	Wireless op	Mech/Gun	A.N.O
17.10.39	Do18	Ku.Fl.Gr. 2./606?	Grabbert	S. Seloga	H. Grimm	? Seydel	
30.01.40	He111H-2	4./KG26	H. Höfer	R. Feist	A. Hain	W.Korsinsky	
03.02.40	He111H-3	3./KG26	W. Remischke	L. von Brüning	H. Panzlaff	H. Peterson	
03.02.40	He111H-3	2./KG26	F. Wiemer	F. Schnee	A. Dittrich	W. Wolff	
						K-E. Thiede	H-J. Helm *
27.02.40	He111H-3	3./KG26	H. Buckisch *	K. Lassnig *	A. Thiele *	W.Rixen *	
29.03.40	Ju88	6/KG30	R. Quadt *	G. Hartung *	E. Hesse *	A. Wunderling *	
26-27.06.40	He111H-4	2./KG4	S. Gessert	K-H. Beck	W. Dieter	H. Filihowski	
01.07.40	He59	Seenotflug.Kdo.3	E.O. Ielsen	H-J. Fehske	E. Philipp	? Stuckmann	S. Zraunig
19-20.07 40	FW200c	1./KG40	H. Külken	R. Stessy	K. Nicolai	W. Meyer	
09.08.40	He111H-3	7./KG26	O. Denner	W.Haertel	F. Feinekat	G. Karkos	E. Henrichsen
15.08.40	He111H-4	1./KG26	W. Zimmerman	R. Roch	E. Kulick	A. Machalett	
15.08.40	He111H-4	8./KG26	H. von Lüpke	K. Hennicke	M. Knauer	K. Schlick	F. Reichelt
15.08.40	He111H-4	8./KG26	H. von Besser	F. Brehm	A. Rehm	E. Hofmann	K. Lotz
15.08.40	He111H-4	8./KG26	H. Puchstein	W. Burck	H-K. Klug	H. Hofmann	C. Schumann
15.08.40	He111H-4	8./KG26	F. Baldauf	A. Renner	W. Rössinger	W. Lorenz	
15.08.40	Me110D	Stab.I/ZG76	W. Restemeyer		W. Eichert	—	
15.08.40	Me110D	Stab.I/ZG76	G. Loobes		X. Brock	—	
15.08.40	Me110D	1./ZG76	H-U. Kettling		F. Volk	—	
15.08.40	Me110D	2./ZG76	K. Ladwein		K. Lenk	J.Wich	
05.09.40	He111P	6./KG4	K.H-W. Schröder	F. Reitz	R. Marten	—	H. Kriependorf
15-16.09.40	He115c	Ku.Fl.Gr. 3./506	C. Lucas	E-W. Bergmann	E. Kalinowski	P.Hippenstiel	
17.11.40	Ju88A-5	3(F)/122	P. Thallmaier	H. Maisbaum	A. Leise	F. Janechitz	H. Jeckstadt
15-16.02.41	He111P-4	6./KG4	W. Beetz	H. Styra	K-G. Brützam	H. Vandanne	
13.03.41	Ju88A-5	Ku.Fl.Gr. 3./106	H.Voigtländer-Tetzner	Rudolf Dietze	W. Wesserer	O. Gröbke	
10.04.41	Ju88A-5	3(F)/122	R. Bröse	E.E. Helmer	K. Düx	J. Schügerl	
27.04.41	He111H-5	1./KG26	E. Fenchal	R. Klamand	S. Warko	J. Schumacher	
30.04.41	Ju88	Ku.Fl.Gr. 1/506	K. Pahnke	H. Jark	J. Schaare	H. Schiedlinski	
05-06.05.41	He111H-5	1./KG4	F. Olsson	E. Eichler	W. Koch	W. Willeke	
05-06.05.41	He111H-5	3./KG4	K. Arnold	W. Weisslener	H. Böhen	W. Schmidt	
06-07.05.41	He111H-5	2./KG53	K. Raflloff	E. Lembass	K. Simon	W. Arndt	H. Quittenbaum
06-07.05.41	Ju88A-5	5./KG30	H. Schaber	H. Nöske	P. Graupner		

Date	Aircraft	Unit	Pilot	Observer	Wireless op	Mech/Gun	A.N.O
02.06.41	Ju88A-5	Ku.Fl.Gr. 3./106	B. Winse	H. Berger	K. Schummers	H. Forstbach	
02.06.41	Ju88A-5	Ku.Fl.Gr. 3./106	H. Vieck	W. Maschmann	G. Emmerich	W. Börge	
24-25.06.41	He111H-5	2./KG26	H. Oswald	H. Dahnke	O. Meyer	W. Ölgarth	
24-25.06.41	He111H-5	2./KG26	W. Kerney	H. Ackermann	H. Wolf	R. Oed	
23.08.41	He111H-5	Stab./KG26	G. Wilhelm	H. Hilpert	O. Siedel	F. Schmidt	
01.09.41	Ju88A-4	Stab.III/KG30	H. Riede	R. Elle	H. Dorn	W. Müller	
07.09.41	Do217E-1	4./KG40	W. Nemming	J. Jujowa	E. Etterlien	H. Alexander	
30.09.41	Ju88A-4	7./KG30	W. Kühnle	R. Callier	H. Bartelt	G. Petzka	
02.10.41	Do217E-2	5./KG2	F. Menzel	J. Rüth	H. Schleussner	A. Herold	
16.11.41	Ju88	KGr.1./506	B. Schlau	D. Kutz	K. Wilhelm	F. Hölzgen	
09.12.41	Ju88D-1	3(F)/122	L. Volk	F. Böhme	F. Shackert	W. Lentfert	
29.12.41	Ju88D-1	KGr.1./506	W. Tschorn	H. Fleck	R. Hermann	A. Reckweg	
15.01.42	Ju88A-4	KGr.1./506	F. Pett	D. Andresen	J. Scholze	F. Gruschka	
15-16.02.42	Do217E-4	9./KG2	K. Pellar	G. Klostermann	J. Uhl	H. Göggerle	
15-16.02.42	Do217E-4	9./KG2	E. Aster	A. Neumann	H. Lehmann	K. Thomas	
26-27.03.42	Do217E-3	6./KG40	G. Westphal	R. Bonceck	H. Esslinger	I. Hartl	
06-07.07.42	Do217E-4	9./KG2	G. Lanz	E. Jörs	A. Engler	J. Klatt	
07-08.07.42	Ju88A-4	4./KG2	J. Grandl	J. Bredtmeyer	H. Müller	F. Meindl	
28-29.08.42	Do217E-4	Stab.I/KG77	A. Riedel	J. Pfeffer	P. Kolodzie	J. Sanden	
19.09.42	Do217E-4	7./KG2	H. Ahrendholz	E. Moll	P. Hartmann	H. Woelke	
11.03.43	Ju88A-14	9./KG6	A. Wissel	L.Wendel	L. Walther	W. Gabow	
11.03.43	Do217E-4	3./KG2	E. Schneiderbauer	M. Hoffmann	H. Weber	G. Eilbrecht	
11.03.43	Ju88A-14	3./KG6	H. Braun	A. Knittel	K. Panzer	H. Grote	
12.03.43	Do217E-4	7./KG2	B. Gerlach	E. Überscär	O. Freidl	H. Osburg	
14-15.03.43	Ju88A-14	2./KG6	W. Remer	A.Buster	W. Strange	H. Koch	
22-23.03.43	Do217E-4	5./KG2	R. Wenkel	E. Hitziger	W. Bück	O. Wilke	
22-23.03.43	Do217E-4	7./KG2	F. Flohr	E. Tomuschat	J. Knecht	J. Menzenbach	
24-25.03.43	Do217E-4	3./KG2	F. Kalbfleisch	K. Lahr	W. Frank	F. Freyh	
24-25.03.43	Do217E-4	7./KG2	W. Schneider	R. Frase	A. Ille	S. Harz	
24-25.03.43	Ju88A-14	1./KG6	F. Lang	W. Schulz	K. Klein	W. Fiedler	
15-16.05.43	Do217K-1	6./KG2	K. Roos	G. Kaeber	B. Mittlestädt	A. Richter	
24.05.43	Do217E-4	1./KG2	H. Mitzscherling	R. Hanke	J. Haberl	K.E. Sikorski	
23.08.43	Ju88D-1	Wekusta 1	K. Rapp	O. Krug	A. Schulz	O. Kühle	

[* Some doubt about these roles]

213

Appendix 4

Luftwaffe crew losses in the Northumberland and Durham area, 1939 – 1943 (by name and by fate)

Number	Name	Rank	Unit	Date of loss	Fate	Burial place
	Ackermann, Helmut	Gefr.	2./KG26	24-25.06.41	pow	German Military Cem. Cannock Chase
57358-129	Ahrendtholz, Helmut	Obfw.	7./KG26	19.09.42	killed	
	Alexander, Helmut	Uffz.	4./KG40	07.09.41	missing	
	Andresen, Dieter	Lt. z. See	KGr.1./506	15.01.42	killed	Hylton Cem. Castletown, nr Sunderland
62749/ 49	Arndt, Werner	Gefr.	5./KG30	06-07.05.41	pow	
	Arnold, Karl	Uffz.	3./KG4	05-06.05.41	missing	
	Aster, Emil	Uffz.	9./KG2	15-16.02.42	missing	
51 904/ 98	Baldauf, Fritz	Fw.	8./KG26	15.08.40	pow	
	Bartelt, Heinz	Uffz.	7./KG30	30.09.41	missing	
	Beck, Karl-Heinz	Uffz.	2./KG4	26-27.06.40	pow	
55538-96	Beetz, Wilhelm	Obfw.	6./KG4	15-16.02.41	killed	Hylton Cem. Castletown, nr Sunderland
	Berger, Hans	Oblt.z. See	Ku.Fl.Gr. 3./106	02.06.41	pow	
	Bergmann, E-Wilhelm	Hptm.	Ku.Fl.Gr. 3./506	15-16.09.40	pow	
	Böhme, Herbert	Uffz.	3./KG4	05-06.05.41	killed	
	Böhme, Fritz	Lt.	3(F)/122	09.12.41	killed	
	Bonceck, Rudolf	Obgfr.	6./KG40	26-27.03.42	missing	
	Börge, Walter	Uffz.	Ku.Fl.Gr. 3./106	02.06.41	missing	
	Braun, Herbert	Uffz.	3./KG6	11.03.43	missing	
58 213/ 22	Bredtmeyer, Johannes	Lt.	4./KG2	07-08.07.42	missing	
51 904/ 21	Brehm, Franz	Uffz.	8./KG26	15.08.40	missing	
53593/ 24	Brock, Xaver	Uffz.	Stab.I/ZG76	15.08.40	killed	
	Bröse, Rolf	Lt.	3(F)/122	10.04.41	missing	
	Brützam, Karl-G.	Uffz.	6./KG4	15-16.02.41	killed	Hylton Cem. Castletown, nr Sunderland
58 215/ 166	Bück, Walter	Uffz.	5./KG2	22-23.03.43	missing	
	Buckisch, Heinrich	Uffz.	3./KG26	27.02.40	missing	
	Burck, Wolfgang	Lt.	8./KG26	15.08.40	missing	
53557/ 4	Buster, Alois	Obgfr.	2./KG6	14-15.03.43	missing	
	Callier, Rudolf	Fw.	7./KG30	30.09.41	missing	
	Dahnke, Herbert	Fw.	2./KG26	24-25.06.41	pow	
	Denner, Otto	Uffz.	7./KG26	09.08.40	pow	
	Dieter, Wilhelm	Uffz.	2./KG4	26-27.06.40	pow	
59 73172	Dietze, Rudolf	Lt. z. See	Ku.Fl.Gr. 3./106	13.03.41	missing	
	Dittrich, Alfred	Uffz.	2./KG26	03.02.40	pow	
57302-8	Dorn, Helmut	Obfw.	Stab.III/KG30	01.09.41	killed	Chevington Cem. nr Broomhill, Northumberland
	Düx, Karl	Fw.	3(F)/122	10.04.41	missing	

Serial	Name	Rank	Unit	Date	Fate	Cemetery
53593/ 18	Eichert, Werner	Uffz.	Stab.I/ZG76	15.08.40	killed	
	Eichler, Eugen	Hptm.	1./KG40	05-06.05.41	pow	
53911/ 9	Eilbrecht, Gregor	Obfw.	3./KG2	11.03.43	pow	
57302-3	Elle, Rudolf	Oblt.	Stab.III/KG30	01.09.41	killed	Chevington Cem. nr Broomhill, Northumberland
	Elterlien, Ernst	Obfw.	4./KG40	07.09.41	missing	
	Emmerich, Gerhard	Uffz.	Ku.Fl.Gr. 3./106	02.06.41	missing	
53578/ 636	Engler, Alfred	Uffz.	9./KG2	06-07.07.42	missing	
	Esslinger, Hugo	Uffz.	6./KG40	26-27.03.42	missing	
	Fehske, Hans-Joachim	Lt.	Seenotflug.Kdo.3	01.07.40	pow	
	Feinekat, Fritz	Uffz.	7./KG26	09.08.40	pow	
	Feist, Richard	Uffz.	4./KG26	30.01.40	killed	
65124-121	Fenchal, Erich	Obfw.	1./KG26	27.04.41	pow	
	Fiedler, Werner	Gefr.	1./KG6	24-25.03.43	killed	
	Filihowski, Horst	Gefr.	2./KG4	26-27.06.40	pow	German Military Cem. Cannock Chase
58 207/ 149	Fleck, Heinrich	Lt. z. See	KGr.1./506	29.12.41	missing	Darlston Road Cem. Carlisle
	Flohr, Fritz	Fw.	7./KG2	22-23.03.43	missing	
	Forstbach, Heinrich	Obgfr.	Ku.Fl.Gr. 3./106	02.06.41	killed	
57358	Frank, Walter	Uffz.	3./KG2	24-25.03.43	killed	German Military Cem. Cannock Chase
57357-114	Frase, Rudolf	Lt.	7./KG2	24-25.03.43	killed	
	Freidl, Otto	Uffz.	7./KG2	12.03.43	missing	
57358-201	Freyh, Friedrich	Obgfr.	3./KG2	24-25.03.43	killed	
	Gabow, Wolfgang	Uffz.	9./KG6	11.03.43	missing	
	Gerlach, Bernhard	Lt.	7./KG2	12.03.43	missing	
	Gessert, Siegfried	Fw.	2./KG4	26-27.06.40	pow	
	Göggerle, Hans	Fw.	9./KG2	15-16.02.42	missing	
	Grabbet, ?	Fw.	Ku.Fl.Gr. 2./606	17.10.39	pow	
53 576/ 1269	Grandl, Johann	Fw.	4./KG2	07-08.07.42	killed	
62749/ 30	Graupner, Paul	Fw.	5./KG30	06-07.05.41	pow	
	Grimm, Hilmar	Unfw.	Ku.Fl.Gr. 2./606	17.10.39	pow	German Military Cem. Cannock Chase
62524-28	Gröbke, Otto	Fw.	3(F)/122	10.04.41	killed	
	Grote, Hubert	Gefr.	3./KG6	11.03.43	missing	
	Gruschka, Franz	Fw.	KGr.1./506	15.01.42	missing	
	Habert, Josef	Uffz.	1./KG2	24.05.43	missing	
	Haertel, Willi	Fw.	7./KG26	09.08.40	pow	
	Hain, Albert	Obgfr.	4./KG26	30.01.40	missing	
	Hanke, Rudolf	Uffz.	1./KG2	24.05.43	missing	
57 538/ 126	Hartl, Ignaz	Fw.	6./KG40	26-27.03.42	missing	
	Hartmann, Peter	Uffz.	7./KG26	19.09.42	killed	Chevington Cem. nr Broomhill, Northumberland
62750.9.	Hartung, Gustav	Fw.	6/KG30	29.03.40	killed	

No.	Name	Rank	Unit	Date	Fate	Burial location
	Harz, Siegfried	Obgfr.	7./KG2	24-25.03.43	killed	Chevington Cem. nr Broomhill, Northumberland
	Helm, Hans-Joachim	Hptm.	3./KG26	27.02.40	killed	
51 904/ 92	Helmer, E.Ernst	Uffz.	3(F)/122	10.04.41	missing	
62712/ 72	Hennicke, Karl	Obfw.	8./KG26	15.08.40	killed	
	Henrichsen, Ernst	Flgr.	1./KG26	15.08.40	pow	
	Hermann, Rudolf	Uffz.	KGr.1./506	29.12.41	missing	
58 214/ 76	Herold, Arno	Uffz.	5./KG2	02.10.41	pow	Chevington Cem. nr Broomhill, Northumberland
53000-111P	Hesse, Ernst	Uffz.	6./KG30	29.03.40	killed	
	Hilpert, Hans	Uffz.	Stab./KG26	23.08.41	pow	
	Hippenstiel, Paul	Uffz.	3(F)/122	17.11.40	missing	
58 215/ 187	Hitziger, Erich	Obgfr.	5./KG2	22-23.03.43	missing	
	Höfer, Helmut	Fw.	4./KG26	30.01.40	missing	
51 904/ 27	Hofmann, Eberhard	Uffz.	8./KG26	15.08.40	missing	
53557/ 34	Hofmann, Hans	Uffz.	8./KG26	15.08.40	missing	
57359/ 12	Hoffmann, Martin	Uffz.	3./KG2	11.03.43	pow	
	Hölzgen, Fritz	Obgfr.	KGr.1./506	16.11.41	missing	
	Ielsen, Ernst Otto	Uffz.	Seenotflug.Kdo.3	01.07.40	pow	
57358-259	Ille, Alois	Obgfr.	7./KG2	24-25.03.43	killed	Darlston Road Cem. Carlisle
	Janeschitz, Franz	Gefr.	6./KG4	15-16.02.41	killed	Hylton Cem. Castletown, nr Sunderland
	Jark, Hans	Lt.	Ku.Fl.Gr.1./506	30.04.41	killed	
55538-81	Jeckstadt, Helmut	Uffz.	6./KG4	15-16.02.41	missing	Hylton Cem. Castletown, nr Sunderland
53577/743	Jörs, Ewald	Fw.	9./KG2	06-07.07.42	missing	
	Jujowa, Johann	Lt.	4./KG40	07.09.41	missing	
58 215/ 157	Kaeber, Günther	Obgfr.	6./KG2	15-16.05.43	missing	
	Kalbfleisch, Fritz	Obfw.	3./KG2	24-25.03.43	killed	
	Kalinowski, Ernst	Fw.	Ku.Fl.Gr. 3./506	15-16.09.40	pow	
	Karkos, Gustav	Uffz.	7./KG26	09.08.40	pow	
	Kerney, Willi	Uffz.	2./KG26	24-25.06.41	pow	
53591/ 4	Kettling, Hans-Ulrich	Oblt.	1./ZG76	15.08.40	pow	Chevington Cem. nr Broomhill, Northumberland
	Klamand, Rudolf	Gefr.	1./KG26	27.04.41	pow	
57359/ 147	Klatt, Johannes	Fw.	9./KG2	06-07.07.42	missing	
65102-10	Kleih, Karl	Obfw.	1./KG6	24-25.03.43	killed	
	Klostermann, Gerhard	Maj.	9./KG2	15-16.02.42	missing	
53557/ 40	Klug, Hans-Karl	Uffz.	8./KG26	15.08.40	missing	
51 904/ 93	Knauer, Max	Uffz.	8./KG26	15.08.40	missing	
58 207/ 155	Knecht, Johannes	Obgfr.	7./KG2	22-23.03.43	missing	
	Knittel, Albert	Uffz.	3./KG6	11.03.43	missing	
	Koch, Heinrich	Obgfr.	2./KG6	14-15.03.43	missing	
53585-81	Koch, Wilhelm	Obgfr.	1./KG40	05-06.05.41	killed	German Military Cem. Cannock Chase

ID	Name	Rank	Unit	Date	Status	Location
65119-30	Kolodzie, Paul	Obfw.	Stab.I/KG77	28-29.08.42	killed	Acklam Road Cem. Thornaby-on-Tees
	Korsinsky, Werner	Gefr.	4./KG26	30.01.40	missing	
	Kriependorf, Hans	Hptm.	Ku.Fl.Gr. 3./506	15-16.09.40	pow	
	Krug, Otto	Reg. Rat.	Wekusta 1	23.08.43	missing	
	Kühle, Otto	Fw.	Wekusta 1	23.08.43	missing	
	Kühnle, Werner	Lt.	7./KG30	30.09.41	missing	
53557/ 65	Kulick, Erwin	Gefr.	1./KG26	15.08.40	pow	
	Külken, Herbert	Fw.	1./KG40	19-20.07 40	pow	
69011/ 6	Kutz, Diete	Ohfr. z. See	KGr.1./506	16.11.41	killed	German Military Cem. Cannock Chase
57358-172	Ladwein, Klaus	Fw.	2./ZG76	15.08.40	pow	Chevington Cem. nr Broomhill, Northumberland
65112-98	Lahr, Karl	Obgfr.	3./KG2	24-25.03.43	killed	
57356/ 2	Lang, Friedrich	Obfw.	1./KG6	24-25.03.43	killed	Chevington Cem. nr Broomhill, Northumberland
	Lanz, Günther	Oblt.	9./KG2	06-07.07.42	missing	
	Lassnig, Karl	Uffz.	3./KG26	27.02.40	killed	
	Lehmann, Hans	Gefr.	9./KG2	15-16.02.42	missing	
53592/ 18	Leise, Albert	Fw.	3(F)/122	17.11.40	missing	
	Lenk, Karl	Obgfr.	2./ZG76	15.08.40	missing	
	Lentfert, Walter	Fw.	3(F)/122	09.12.41	killed	
53578/ 532	Lernbass, Emmerich	Gefr.	2./KG53	06.07.05.41	pow	Hylton Cem. Castletown, nr Sunderland
53593/ 5	Loobes, Gustav	Oblt.	Stab.I/ZG76	15.08.40	killed	
51 904/99	Lorenz, Walter	Gefr.	8./KG26	15.08.40	pow	
51 904/62	Lotz, Karl	Uffz.	8./KG26	15.08.40	missing	
62712/ 64	Lucas, Clement	Oblt.	Ku.Fl.Gr. 3./506	15-16.09.40	pow	Buried at sea
	Machalett, Alwin	Gefr.	1./KG26	15.08.40	pow	
	Maisbaum, Henry	Uffz.	3(F)/122	17.11.40	killed	
55538-77	Marten, Rudolf	Obgfr.	6./KG4	05.09.40	killed	German Military Cem. Cannock Chase
	Maschmann, Wilhelm	Oblt. z. See	Ku.Fl.Gr. 3./106	02.06.41	missing	
57 359/ 36	Meindl, Franz	Uffz.	4./KG2	07-08.07.42	missing	
53 578/ 556	Menzel, Fritz	Fw.	5./KG2	02.10.41	killed	
58 214/ 241	Menzenbach, Johannes	Gefr.	7./KG2	22-23.03.43	missing	
	Meyer, Otto	Uffz.	2./KG26	24-25.06.41	pow	
62751-62	Meyer, Willi	Fw.	1./KG40	19-20.07 40	pow	Chevington Cem. nr Broomhill, Northumberland
58 215/ 159	Mittlestädt, Bruno	Uffz.	6./KG2	15-16.05.43	killed	
	Mitzscherling, Herbert	Obfw.	1./KG2	24.05.43	missing	
57 358/ 134	Moll, Edgar	Uffz.	7./KG26	19.09.42	killed	
58 213/ 44	Müller, Horst	Uffz.	4./KG2	07-08.07.42	killed	
57302-13	Müller, Walter	Fw.	Stab.III/KG30	01.09.41	killed	
	Nemming, Walter	Fw.	4./KG40	07.09.41	missing	
	Neumann, Arnold	Uffz.	9./KG2	15-16.02.42	missing	

Casualty No.	Name	Rank	Unit	Date	Fate	Burial
62749/84	Nicolai, Karl	Fw.	1./KG40	19-20.07 40	pow	
	Nöske, Heinz	Gefr.	5./KG30	06-07.05.41	pow	
	Oed, Rudolf	Obgfr.	2./KG26	24-25.06.41	pow	
	Ölgarth, Werner	Gefr.	2./KG26	24-25.06.41	pow	
	Olsson, Franz	Fw.	1./KG40	05-06.05.41	pow	
	Osburg, Hermann	Uffz.	7./KG2	12.03.43	missing	
	Oswald, Heinrich	Oblt.	2./KG26	24-25.06.41	pow	
	Pahnke, Kurt	Fw.	Ku.Fl.Gr. 1./506	30.04.41	killed	Chevington Cem. nr Broomhill, Northumberland
	Panzer, Karl	Uffz.	3./KG6	11.03.43	missing	
	Panzlaff, Herbert	Fw.	3./KG26	03.02.40	killed	
	Pellar, Konrad	Lt.	9./KG2	15-16.02.42	missing	
	Peterson, Herbert	Fw.	3./KG26	03.02.40	missing	
	Pett, Friedrich	Uffz.	KGr.1./506	15.01.42	missing	
	Petzka, Gustav	Obgfr.	7./KG30	30.09.41	missing	
53557/64	Pfeffer, Josef	Fw.	Stab.I/KG77	28-29.08.42	pow	
	Philipp, Erich	Obgfr.	Seenotflug.Kdo.3	01.07.40	pow	
53557/67	Puchstein, Heinz	Uffz.	8./KG26	15.08.40	missing	
62750 1.	Quadt, Rudolf	Oblt.	6/KG30	29.03.40	killed	Chevington Cem. nr Broomhill, Northumberland
53578/544	Quittenbaum, Heinz	Gefr.	2./KG53	06-07.05.41	missing	
	Rapp, Karl	Oblt.	Wekusta 1	23.08.43	pow	
53578/513	Rafloff, Karl	Uffz.	2./KG53	06.07.05.41	missing	
	Reckweg, Axel	Uffz.	KGr.1./506	29.12.41	missing	
51 904/24	Rehm, Alfons	Uffz.	8./KG26	15.08.40	missing	
51 904/44	Reichelt, Franz	Uffz.	8./KG26	15.08.40	missing	
55538-59	Reitz, Fritz	Uffz.	6./KG4	05.09.40	killed	Hylton Cem. Castletown, nr Sunderland
	Remer, Wilhelm	Uffz.	2./KG6	14-15.03.43	missing	
	Remischke, Walter	Uffz.	3./KG26	03.02.40	killed	Chevington Cem. nr Broomhill, Northumberland
51 904/97	Renner, Adolf	Hptm.	8./KG26	15.08.40	missing	
53590/9	Restemeyer, Werner	Uffz.	Stab.I/ZG76	15.08.40	killed	
58 215/162	Richter, Alfred	Uffz.	6./KG2	15-16.05.43	missing	
57302-10	Riede, Helmut	Obfw.	Stab.III/KG30	01.09.41	killed	Chevington Cem. nr Broomhill, Northumberland
B 65121/10	Riedel, Alfred	Obfw.	Stab.I/KG77	28-29.08.42	pow	
	Rixen, Walter	Gefr.	3./KG26	27.02.40	missing	
62712/76	Roch, Rudolf	Oblt.	1./KG26	15.08.40	pow	
58215-161	Roos, Karl	Uffz.	6./KG2	15-16.05.43	killed	Acklam Road Cem, Thornaby-on-Tees
51 904/94	Rössiger, Wilhelm	Obgfr.	8./KG26	15.08.40	pow	
58 214/116	Rüth, Josef	Fw.	5./KG2	02.10.41	killed	Acklam Road Cem, Thornaby-on-Tees
55512-125	Sanden, Josef	Gefr.	Stab.I/KG77	28-29.08.42	killed	
	Schaare, Johann	Uffz.	Ku.Fl.Gr. 1./506	30.04.41	killed	

	Name	Rank	Unit	Date	Fate	Location
62749/ 25	Schaber, Hans	Uffz.	5./KG30	06-07.05.41	pow	
	Schiedlinski, Han	Gefr.	1./KG40	05-06.05.41	pow	
	Schlau, Bruno	Fw.	KGr.1./506	16.11.41	missing	
58 215/ 121	Schleussner, Horst	Fw.	5./KG2	02.10.41	pow	
51 904/ 89	Schlick, Karl	Uffz.	8./KG26	15.08.40	missing	
	Schmidt, Franz	Obgfr.	Stab./KG26	23.08.41	pow	
5357876/ 431	Schmidt, Walter	Gefr.	2./KG53	06.07.05.41	pow	
	Schnee, Franz	Fw.	2./KG26	03.02.40	pow	Darlston Road Cem. Carlisle
57358-269	Schneider, Willi	Uffz.	7./KG2	24-25.03.43	killed	
53578/ 230	Schneiderbauer, Ernst	Oblt.	3./KG2	11.03.43	pow	
	Scholze, Josef	Uffz.	KGr.1./506	15.01.42	missing	Hylton Cem. Castletown, nr Sunderland
55538-83	Schröder, Hans-Werner	Oblt.	6./KG4	05.09.40	killed	
	Schügerl, Johann	Gefr.	1./KG26	27.04.41	killed	
	Schulz, Alfred	Uffz.	Wekusta 1	23.08.43	missing	
65124-2	Schulz, Walter	Uffz.	1./KG6	24-25.03.43	killed	Chevington Cem. nr Broomhill, Northumberland
73038-208	Schumacher, J	Hptgfr.	Ku.Fl.Gr. 1./506	30.04.41	killed	Churchyard, Brandsburton, nr Hornsea
51904/ 26	Schumann, Christoph	Uffz.	8./KG26	15.08.40	pow	
	Schummers, Karl	Obgfr.	Ku.Fl.Gr. 3./106	02.06.41	pow	
	Seloga, Siegfried	Oblt. z. See	Ku.Fl.Gr. 2./606	17.10.39	killed	
	Seydel, ?	Uffz.	Ku.Fl.Gr. 2./606	17.10.39	killed	
	Shackert, Fritz	Obfw.	3(F)/122	09.12.41	killed	
	Siedel, Otto	Uffz.	Stab./KG26	23.08.41	pow	
	Sikorski, Konrad E.	Uffz.	1./KG2	24.05.43	missing	
53578/ 527	Simon, Karl	Uffz.	2./KG53	06.07.05.41	pow	Hylton Cem. Castletown, nr Sunderland
	Stessyn, Roman	Hptm.	1./KG40	19-20.07 40	missing	
	Strange, Werner	Uffz.	2./KG6	14-15.03.43	missing	
	Stuckmann, ?	Uffz.	Seenotflug.Kdo.3	01.07.40	missing	
	Styra, Heinz	Hptm.	6./KG4	15-16.02.41	pow	
	Thallmaier, Paul	Lt.	3(F)/122	17.11.40	killed	Scarthro Road Cem. Grimsby
2/KG26	Thiede, Karl-Ernst	Uffz.	2./KG6	03.02.40	missing	
	Thiele, Artur	Obfw.	3./KG26	27.02.40	killed	
	Thomas, Karl	Uffz.	9./KG2	15-16.02.42	missing	
57 359/ 156	Tomuschat, Erich	Obgfr.	7./KG2	22-23.03.43	missing	
	Tschorn, Walter	Fw.	KGr.1./506	29.12.41	missing	
	Überscär, Erich	Obfw.	7./KG2	12.03.43	missing	
	Uhl, Josef	Uffz.	9./KG2	15-16.02.42	missing	
RA 2/506 160	Vandanne, Hans	Obgfr.	Ku.Fl.Gr. 3./106	13.03.41	missing	
	Vieck, Hans	Obfw.	Ku.Fl.Gr. 3./106	02.06.41	missing	
	Voigtländer-Tetzner, H.	Oblt.	Ku.Fl.Gr. 3./106	13.03.41	killed	Acklam Road Cem, Thornaby-on-Tees

	Name	Rank	Unit	Date	Status	Burial
53591/ 21	Volk, Fritz	Obgfr.	1./ZG76	15.08.40	pow	
	Volk, Ludwig	Obfw.	3(F)/122	09.12.41	killed	
51 904/ 3	von Besser, Horst	Oblt.	8./KG26	15.08.40	missing	
	von Brüning, Luther	Lt.	3./KG26	03.02.40	killed	Chevington Cem. nr Broomhill, Northumberland
51 904/ 86	von Lüpke, Hans	Oblt.	8./KG26	15.08.40	killed	
53563-161	Walther, Ludwig	Fw.	9./KG6	11.03.43	killed	German Military Cem. Cannock Chase
	Warko, Siegfried	Uffz.	1./KG26	27.04.41	pow	
62688/ 14	Weber, Hans	Uffz.	3./KG2	11.03.43	pow	
	Weisslener, Walter	Lt.	3./KG4	05–06.05.41	missing	
	Wendel, Ludwig	Fw.	9./KG6	11.03.43	missing	
58 215/ 164	Wenkel, Rudolf	Fw.	5./KG2	22–23.03.43	missing	
	Wesserer, Walter	Obgfr.	Ku.Fl.Gr. 3./106	13.03.41	missing	German Military Cem. Cannock Chase
4.FL.AUSB.RGT 7	Westphal, Gerhard	Lt.	6./KG40	26–27.03.42	killed	
55538–77	Wich, Josef	Gefr.	6./KG4	05.09.40	killed	Hylton Cem. Castletown, nr Sunderland
	Wiemer, Fritz	Obfw.	2./KG26	03.02.40	pow	
	Wilhelm, Georg	Hptm.	Stab./KG26	23.08.41	pow	
	Wilhelm, Karl	Uffz.	KGr.1./506	16.11.41	missing	
58 215/ 193	Wilke, Otto	Obgfr.	5./KG2	22–23.03.43	missing	
	Willeke, Werner	Gefr.	3./KG4	05–06.05.41	killed	
	Winse, Bernhard	Obfw.	Ku.Fl.Gr. 3./106	02.06.41	killed	
	Wissel, Arnold	Fw.	9./KG6	11.03.43	missing	
57 359/ 208	Woelke, Hans	Uffz.	7./KG26	19.09.42	missing	
	Wolf, Herbert	Gefr.	2./KG26	24–25.06.41	pow	
	Wolff, Willi	Uffz.	2./KG26	03.02.40	killed	Chevington Cem. nr Broomhill, Northumberland
62750.25	Wunderling, Andreas	Uffz.	6./KG30	29.03.40	killed	
53557/ 68	Zimmerman, Willi	Uffz.	1./KG26	15.08.40	pow	
	Zraunig, Silverius	Gefr.	1./KG40	19–20.07.40	missing	

BIBLIOGRAPHY

Bundesarchiv-Militärarchiv, Freiburg
Luftwaffe Quartermeistergeneral's Flugzeugverluste (Luftwaffe aircraft losses).

Commonwealth War Graves Commission
German Foreign Nationals in the Care of CWGC (WW2) Commemorated in the United Kingdom. (from the data base of the CWGC).

Deutsche-Dienststelle, Berlin
Luftwaffe Angehörigeverluste, (Losses of personnel).

Imperial War Museum
Air warfare against England, August 1940 - December 1941. (Luftwaffe 8th Abteilung) Document 2402 (Tin 38).
Hauptmann Otto Bechtle: Luftwaffe Operation against England; their tactics and deductions, 1940-43. Document 2390 (Tin 38).

National Archives of Canada
406 Squadron RCAF Operations Record Book 1939-45.
409 Squadron RCAF Operations Record Book 1939-45.
410 Squadron RCAF Operations Record Book 1939-45.

Northumberland County Council Records Centre, Morpeth
Northumberland Constabulary War Dept Records, NC/6/10.

Public Records Office, Kew
41 Squadron AIR27/425, AIR50/18.
43 Squadron AIR27/441, AIR50/19.
72 Squadron AIR27/624, AIR50/30.
111 Squadron AIR27/865, AIR50/43.
141 Squadron AIR27/969, AIR50/61.
145 Squadron AIR50/62.
151 Squadron AIR27/1019.
152 Squadron AIR27/1025, AIR50/64.
249 Squadron AIR50/96.
255 Squadron AIR27/1518; AIR50/98.
302 Polish) Squadron AIR27/1661, AIR50/97.
406 Squadron AIR27/1791, AIR50/139.
604 Squadron AIR27/2084, AIR50/168.
607 Squadron AIR50/170.
609 Squadron AIR27/2102, AIR50/171.
611 Squadron AIR27/2109, AIR50/173.
616 Squadron AIR27/2126, AIR50/176.
936 Barrage Balloon(Tyne)Squadron AIR27.
938 Balloon Barrage Squadron AIR27/2281.
RAF Usworth Operations Record Book AIR28/870.
63rd Heavy Anti-Aircraft Regiment, Royal Artillery War Diary WO166/2465.
Crashed Enemy Aircraft. Reports 7/62, 7/64, 7/68. AIR22/267.
Enemy Attacks on Coastal Convoys, 1941 ADM199/102, ADM199/1181.
Interrogation of Prisoners of War AIR40/2394, 2395, 2397, 2398, 2406, 2407.
Locations of Enemy Aircraft Brought Down AIR22/266-267.

Tyne & Wear Archives, Newcastle
Deaths due to War Operations. File T15/1475.
Map of county borough of Tynemouth. File T383/345.
Reports on Wartime Air Raids. Files 209/110-113.

Journals and Newspapers
Amateur Radio April 1987. Article *The Secret War* by Bryan Johnson.
Consett Chronicle, 12 September 1940.
Northern Daily Mail, 3 October 1941, 8 July 1942, 23 March 1943.
North Eastern Evening Gazette, 2 November 1940, 3 October 1941, 23 March 1943,
    15 December 1994, 29 April 1995.
QRV: Journal of the RAF Amateur Radio Society Autumn 1993. Article *Radio
Counter Measures - Meaconing* by Vic Flowers.
Sunderland Echo, 28 September 1971, 26 March 1972.
The Times Saturday Review, 14 July 1990.

Books
Anon., *Front Line, 1940-41 (the official story of the Civil Defence of Britain)* HMSO,
    1942
Anon., *The Rise and Fall of the German Air Force*. HMSO, Arms & Armour edition,
    1983
Anon., *British Vessels Lost at Sea, 1914-18 and 1939-45*. HMSO, Patrick Stephens
    edition, 1988
Balke, Ulf, *Der Luftkrieg in Europa: die operativen Ensätze des Kampgeschwaders 2 im
    zweiten Weltkrieg*. vol.2, Bernard & Graefe Verlag, 1990 Koblenz
Baumbach, Werner, *Broken Swastika: the defeat of the Luftwaffe*, 1992 ed. Dorset Press,
    USA
Beedle, J., *43 Squadron*, Beaumont Aviation, 1966
Bolitho, Hector, *Combat Report, the story of a fighter pilot*, Batsford, 1942
Bowyer, Chaz, *Fighter Pilots of the RAF*, William Kimber, 1984
Brandon, Lewis, *Night Flyer*, William Kimber, 1969
Brady, Kevin, *Sunderland's Blitz*, The People's History Ltd., 1999
Brettingham, Laurie, *Beam Benders; No.80 [Signals] Wing, 1940-1945* Midland
Publishing Ltd., 1997
Clark, Peter; *Where the Hills meet the Sky (a guide to wartime air crashes in the
    Cheviot Hills)*, Glen Graphics, 1997
    A Border too High (a guide to wartime crashes in the Border Hills), Glen
    Graphics, 1999
Collings, Peter, *The Divers Guide to the North-East Coast*, Collings & Brodie, 1986
Flagg, Amy, *History of Bomb Damage (South Shields)*, Unpublished MSS (undated),
    South Shields Library
Franks, Norman L.R., *Royal Air Force Fighter Command Losses of the Second
    World War, Vol.2 1942-1943*, Midland Publishing Ltd., 1998
Goss, Chris, *The Luftwaffe Bombers' Battle of Britain*, Crecy Publishing Ltd., 2002
Gundelach, Karl, *Kampfgeschwader 'General Wever' 4*, Motorbuch Verlag, Stuttgart,
    1978
Hague, Arnold, *The Allied Convoy System, 1939-1945*, Vanwell Publishing (Canada),
    2000
Hough, Richard and Richards, Dennis, *The Battle of Britain, a jubilee history*, Hodder
    & Stoughton, 1989
Jefford, Wing Commander C.G., *RAF Squadrons; a comprehensive record of the
    movement and equipment of all RAF squadrons and their antecedents since 1912*,
    Airlife, 1988
Jones, R.V., *Most Secret War*, Hamish Hamilton, 1978

Kiehl, Heinz, *Kampfgeschwader 'Legion Condor' 53*, Motorbuch Verlag, 1996

Kurowski, Franz, *Seekrieg aus der Luft*, ES Mittler Verlag, Germany, 1979

Lee, Asher, *Goering: Air Leader*, Duckworth, 1972

Lenton, H.T., *British and Empire Warships of the Second World War*, Greenhill Books, 1998

Liskutin, M.A., *Challenge in the Air*, Kimber, 1988

MacMillan, Captain Norman, MC AFC, *The Royal Air Force in the World War Vol.iv 1940-1945*, Harrap, 1950

Mason, Francis K., *Battle over Britain*, Aston Publications, 1990

McKee, Alexander, *The Coal Scuttle Brigade*, Hamlyn, 1981

Nelson-Edwards, Wing Commander George, DFC, *Spit and Sawdust*, Newton, 1995

Norman, Bill, *Luftwaffe over the North*, Leo Cooper, 1993

    Broken Eagles (Luftwaffe Losses over Yorkshire, 1939-1945), Leo Cooper, 2001

Price, Alfred, *The Luftwaffe Data Book*, Greenhill Books, 1997

Ramsey, Winston G. ed., *The Blitz, then and now. vols 1-3*, Battle of Britain Prints International, 1987-1990

    The Battle of Britain, then and now, Battle of Britain Prints International, 1980

Revell, Alex, *The Vivid Air*, Kimber, 1978

Ripley, Roy and Pears, Bryan, *North East Diary, 1939-1945*, Unpublished MSS (undated), Darlington Central Library

Schmidt, Rudi, *Achtung - Torpedos Los!: der stratigische und operative Einsätze des Kampfgeschwader 26*, Bernard & Graefe Verlag, Koblenz, 1991

Townsend, Peter, *Duel of Eagles*, Weidenfeld & Nicholson, 1970

Wakefield, Ken, *Pfadfinder; Luftwaffe Pathfinder Operations over Britain, 1940-1944*, Tempus, 1999

Walmesley, Leo, *Fisherman at War*, Collins, 1941.

Wynn, Kenneth G., *Men of the Battle of Britain*, Gliddon Books, 1989

Ziegler, H. Frank, *The Story of 609 Squadron (under the White Rose)*, Crecy ed. (updated by Chris Goss), 1993